Prakaraṇa Series: 1

Tattvabodhaḥ

Swami Dayananda Saraswati
Arsha Vidya

Arsha Vidya
Research and Publication Trust
Chennai

Published by :
Arsha Vidya Research and Publication Trust
4 ' Srinidhi ' Apts 3rd Floor
Sir Desika Road Mylapore
Chennai 600 004 INDIA
Tel : 044 2499 7023
Telefax : 2499 7131
Email : avrandpt@gmail.com
Website : www.avrpt.com

ISBN : 978-93-80049-43-4

First Edition : April 2012 Copies : 1000
1st Reprint : January 2013 Copies : 1000

Design & Layout :
Graaphic Design

Printed at :
Sudarsan Graphics
27, Neelakanta Mehta Street
T. Nagar, Chennai 600 017
Email : info@sudarsan.com

PREFACE

I teach *Tattvabodha* as an introductory text in a long-term study program of Vedanta. With pithy definitions, the text completely covers the various terms and topics. As a book of Vedanta also *Tattvabodha* is an eye-opener in terms of human problems and their solutions.

Swami Dayananda Saraswati
Arsha Vidya

Key to Transliteration and Pronunciation of Sanskrit Letters

Sanskrit is a highly phonetic language and hence accuracy in articulation of the letters is important. For those unfamiliar with the *Devanāgari* script, the international transliteration is a guide to the proper pronunciation of Sanskrit letters.

अ	*a*	*(but)*
आ	*ā*	*(father)*
इ	*i*	*(it)*
ई	*ī*	*(beat)*
उ	*u*	*(full)*
ऊ	*ū*	*(pool)*
ऋ	*ṛ*	*(rhythm)*
ॠ	*ṝ*	*(marine)*
ऌ	*ḷ*	*(revelry)*
ए	*e*	*(play)*
ऐ	*ai*	*(aisle)*
ओ	*o*	*(go)*
औ	*au*	*(loud)*
क	*ka*	*(seek)* 1
ख	*kha*	*(blockhead)**1
ग	*ga*	*(get)* 1
घ	*gha*	*(log hut)**1
ङ	*ṅa*	*(sing)* 1
च	*ca*	*(chunk)* 2
छ	*cha*	*(catch him)**2
ज	*ja*	*(jump)* 2
झ	*jha*	*(hedgehog)**2
ञ	*ña*	*(bunch)* 2
ट	*ṭa*	*(true)**3
ठ	*ṭha*	*(anthill)**3
ड	*ḍa*	*(drum)**3
ढ	*ḍha*	*(godhead)**3
ण	*ṇa*	*(under)**3
त	*ta*	*(path)**4
थ	*tha*	*(thunder)**4
द	*da*	*(that)**4
ध	*dha*	*(breathe)**4
न	*na*	*(nut)**4
प	*pa*	*(put)* 5
फ	*pha*	*(loophole)**5
ब	*ba*	*(bin)* 5
भ	*bha*	*(abhor)**5
म	*ma*	*(much)* 5
य	*ya*	*(loyal)*
र	*ra*	*(red)*
ल	*la*	*(luck)*
व	*va*	*(vase)*
श	*śa*	*(sure)*
ष	*ṣa*	*(shun)*
स	*sa*	*(so)*
ह	*ha*	*(hum)*

ं	*ṁ*	*anusvāra*	(nasalisation of preceding vowel)
:	*ḥ*	*visarga*	(aspiration of preceding vowel)
*			No exact English equivalents for these letters

1.	Guttural	–	Pronounced from throat
2.	Palatal	–	Pronounced from palate
3.	Lingual	–	Pronounced from cerebrum
4.	Dental	–	Pronounced from teeth
5.	Labial	–	Pronounced from lips

The 5th letter of each of the above class – called nasals – are also pronounced nasally.

Contents

Introduction	1
Prayer	4
Sādhanacatuṣṭayam	14
Nityānitya-vastu-vivekaḥ	27
Vairāgya	45
Śamādi-ṣaṭka-sampattiḥ	50
Śama	51
Dama	59
Uparama	63
Titikṣā	66
Śraddhā	71
Samādhāna	85
Mokṣa	89
Understanding realities: satya and mithyā	93
Defining ātmā	105
Confusion about ātman is universal	109
Methods of analysis to resolve the confusion about ātman	111
Ātman is other than sthūla-sūkṣma-kāraṇa śarīra	112
Ātman is pañca-kośātīta	115
Ātman is avasthā-traya-sākṣin	117

Negation of not-I	119
Extending the knower-known boundary	122
The invariable consciousness 'I' is ātma-svarūpa	132
Consciousness is not an object and cannot be displaced	134
Discerning what is real	142
Ātman is not mortal but the truth of time	145
Ātman is free from unhappiness	149
Unhappiness is against one's nature	156
Ātman has no spatial limitation	158
Nothing is away from ātman	163
Ignorance denies recognition of being limitless	165
Wholeness is never lost	167
Ānanda is ananta – limitlessness	171
Svarūpa-ānanda and Experiential-ānanda	173
Sthūla-śarīra	177
sūkṣma-śarīra	184
Pañca-jñānendriyas, their function and presiding deities	195
Pañca- karmendriyas – their function and their presiding deities	204
Kāraṇa-śarīra	210
Avidyā is anādi – beginningless	212
Avidyā is anirvācya	213

Avasthā-trayam 218

Five basic levels of error about ātman 232

Annamaya-kośa 236

Prāṇamaya-kośa 239

Manomaya-kośa 243

Vijñānamaya-kośa 244

Ānandamaya-kośa 247

Ātman is not any of these 249

Ātman is saccidānanda svarūpaḥ 254

Sat 255

Cit 260

Ānanda 262

Understanding 'tat' in tattvamasi 264

Creation 267

Brahman along with māyā is the cause of the jagat 269

Creation of the five elements 285

From the sāttvika aspect of the five elements comes the subtle sense organs 287

Creation and nature of the mind – antaḥ-karaṇa 291

Presiding deities of the mental functions 296

From the rajas aspect of the five elements comes the subtle organs of action 298

Grossification of the elements 302

From the tamas aspect of the five elements
comes the tangible world 303

The process of grossification 305

Identity of Individual and Cosmos 308

The jīva 311

Īśvara 317

Saṁsāra is due to bheda-dṛṣṭi 319

An objection 324

Equation of oneness is by implied
meaning – lakṣyārtha 326

Jīvanmukti 339

Necessity for a Sadguru 342

More about the jīvan-mukta 343

Three types of karma 353

Sañcita-karma 358

Prārabdha-karma 359

Āgāmi-karma 360

Three-fold karma for a jīvan-mukta 360

The one who knows ātman crosses sorrow 370

Introduction

The source book of self-knowledge is Vedanta, which is the *upaniṣad*. But before we take up any given *upaniṣad*, we look into the subject matter of the *upaniṣad* presented in a separate book called as '*prakaraṇa*' by a given qualified author. '*Tattvabodha*' is one such *prakaraṇa*.

'*Tattvabodha*' means knowledge, *bodha*, of reality, *tattva*. '*Tattva*' means generally the 'ness,' the essential nature of anything, the truth of it. Here, it is used in the sense of the ultimate truth. When we say that *tattva* is the ultimate truth, there is a definite meaning for it.

There is a truth, *tattva*, for everything. The pot has pot-ness as its truth because without the pot-ness there is no pot. And the pot-ness itself does not exist without a substantive, which, for a clay pot, is clay. So, does the clay have pot-ness? Clay cannot have pot-ness as its truth; it can have only clay-ness. Therefore, pot-ness is an incidental attribute to clay, while clay-ness appears to be non-incidental attribute of clay. Clay-ness itself is an incidental attribute because clay cannot exist without being atoms. It being so, clay-ness is an incidental attribute to atoms, and those atoms themselves have atom-ness, which are incidental attribute to particles.

As we analyse the truth of something, we keep finding that it is not the truth of that thing. And if we arrive at a truth that is not an incidental attribute, which itself is the truth, then it would be the ultimate truth. We need to use the word 'ultimate' because of this situation. We will analyse this later. Let us understand that *tattva* means the truth of everything. So, knowledge, *bodha*, of that truth, *tattva*, is unfolded in this book. It is a small book of definitions unfolding Vedanta. Therefore, *Tattvabodha* is the first book that we choose to study.

This is not a work that is traditionally enjoined. I picked up this book in order to teach somebody, so there is a story about how I came upon this book. I did not know that *Tattvabodha* existed in Vedanta literature. One Swami from the Fiji Islands came to me when I was in Rishikesh, and asked me to give ten talks on the *Bhagavadgītā*. He was curious. Later, I came to know that he had received *sannyāsa* by post from a respected Swami in Rishikesh. Now, he wanted me to give him ten talks on the *Gītā*. I asked him, "Why ten talks? Why don't you study the whole *Gītā*? I am here and we can have regular classes."

He said, "No Swamiji, I am going to the States, and there I want to give some talks on the *Gītā*."

"Without knowledge of the *Gītā* how are you going to give talks on the *Gītā*?" "Just give me ten talks; it is good enough."

The Swami also said that he could sing some *bhajans* and play the harmonium, so ten talks were enough. I said, "I will not do it. If you want to study, you have to study properly." He replied, "Swamiji, I have no time, I have to go." I thought I should give him something which has some truth, and looked for a book which I could teach him in ten days. One Swami had passed away and all his books were sent to me. I looked into those books to see if there was anything that I could teach him, when I came upon this book *Tattvabodha*. I thought it was a simple book and I could teach it to him. So, I began to teach him. He did not complete this book, and at some point he felt satisfied he had enough for his *satsaṅga* talks. He went abroad.

This is how I came upon the book, *Tattvabodha*. Since then, I have been teaching it as the first book in every course that I have conducted. It seems to work, so let us look into it.

Prayer

वासुदेवेन्द्रयोगीन्द्रं नत्वा ज्ञानप्रदं गुरुम् ।
मुमुक्षूणां हितार्थाय तत्त्वबोधोऽभिधीयते ॥

vāsudevendrayogīndraṁ natvā jñānapradaṁ gurum
mumukṣūṇāṁ hitārthāya tattvabodho'bhidhīyate.

natvā – having saluted; *vāsudevendra-yogīndram* – Vāsudevendra, the foremost of the *yogins*; *gurum* – the *guru*; *jñāna-pradam* – one who gives knowledge; *tattvabodhaḥ* – knowledge of truth; *mumukṣūṇām* – of those desirous of liberation; *hitārthāya* – for the benefit; *abhidhīyate* – is presented.

Having saluted Vāsudevendra, the foremost of the *yogins*, the *guru* who gives knowledge, *Tattvabodha*, the knowledge of the truth is presented for the benefit of those desirous of liberation.

As every book opens with a prayer, *Tattvabodha* also has a prayer. The prayer is for the completion of the book, and also for the book to serve the purpose for which it is written. This person's prayer, I think, was good because so many people have been reading it. It is written for those who are being initiated into the *vedānta-śāstra*, and for them, let this book be useful.

So, for the successful completion of the book, and also to reach the hands of the right people, the author makes this prayer when he writes this book. Prayer can also be mental. One need not write it. One can just pray and start. But then, one generally writes the prayer as a verse, making it a part of the book itself in order to reveal the tradition.

The tradition is that one does not undertake something without a prayer, because there are many obstacles, *vighna*s. The human being has limited knowledge, limited power, limited skill, and therefore, there are many slips between the cup and the lip. One may start something, but may not survive to complete it. One may complete it, but the book may be *aja-bhakṣita*, eaten by goats, and a book like this was written on palm leaves. Or it may get burnt. Numerous manuscripts got burnt, some deliberately by people who did not have a value for them. Like the library of Alexandria was burnt, in this country also, a lot of manuscripts were burnt. One good thing about the Britisher was that he came and took away all the manuscripts. Whether[1] he understood them, he knew

---

[1] Whether or not is a common expression but the correct usage is only 'whether' without being followed by 'or not'. Whether one likes this, grammatically this is right.
(Swami Dayananda Saraswati)

that one day they would be valuable, and so housed them in a library in London. Even today people go there to copy manuscripts. Others burnt them all, but in spite of them, some of the manuscripts survived, and *Tattvabodha* definitely survived. So, the author made this prayer and it worked, which is why one is able to read it today. With limited knowledge and limited power, one does not know whether this work is going to serve its purpose. Therefore, there is a prayer before one undertakes this, or anything. In this way, one's whole life becomes prayerful. Without a prayer one does not undertake anything. One also takes the result of the undertaking with a prayer. Here, the first verse is a prayer. Even when we start the class we say, '*Oṁ sahanāvavatu…*' which is a Vedic prayer. The prayer in this book is a verse composed by the author, not a Vedic prayer.

He prays here, offering his salutations to his own *guru*, teacher, and through the *guru* to Īśvara. The *guru* tells, 'You are the whole, *tat tvam asi*.' When he says, 'You are the cause of everything, you are the whole,' then the *guru* also must certainly be the whole. Otherwise, he cannot say that you are the whole. The *guru* is the same as Parameśvara. This is how we look upon it; there is a truth in it but we need to understand it properly. We have verses that express this – *gururbrahmaḥ gururviṣṇuḥ gururdevo maheśvaraḥ,* the *guru* is Brahmāji, the *guru* is Viṣṇu, the *guru* is Maheśvara. Here, the author looks upon his *guru* as Īśvara. And through his worship to the *guru* he worships the Lord.

The verb in this verse is *abhidhīyate,* undertaken, presented.[2] What is *abhidhīyate*? In this book, the knowledge of the *tattva,* is presented.

To whom it is presented he is going to tell now. When he says, '*natvā*' it means saluting, surrendering, offering prostrations. To whom? *Gurum,* his own *guru*. What kind of *guru*? You know, there are *guru*s and *guru*s; even the one from whom you learn music is called *guru*. The teachers of martial arts are also called *guru*s. When I was a young boy, I went to a person who knew martial art and asked him to teach me one martial art, stick play. He said, "Well, bring *guru-dakṣiṇā*." You have to give him *guru-dakṣiṇā,* only then will he start teaching because that is the tradition. So, from martial arts onwards everybody is a *guru*. The one who initiates you into a *mantra* is also a *guru*. Then, what kind of *guru* is pointed out here?

---

[2] Alternative reading is *vidhīyate* but the meaning is the same.

Jñāna-pradaṁ gurum. The one who gives, *dadāti*, is called *daḥ*. And one who gives properly, adequately, is called *pradaḥ*. What does he give adequately? *Jñāna*. Here, *jñāna* is real knowledge – knowledge that is neither subject to negation, nor improvement. It is knowledge of the whole; it cannot be improved upon. It cannot be negated either, because it is *tattva*. Knowledge of any particular object in this world can be improved upon or even negated because in the wake of new discoveries, you can know something more about it. But here, it is knowledge of that which cannot be enhanced, which cannot be improved upon, and therefore, cannot be negated at all. That kind of *jñāna* is only of the whole. And *jñāna-pradaṁ gurum* is the one who gives that knowledge. In other words, the one who gives *ātma-jñāna, brahma-jñāna*.

And again, who is that *guru* here? His own *guru*. Every *guru* needs to be a *jñāna-prada*, giver of knowledge. The author's *guru* is no exception. Who is he?

Vāsudevendrayogīndra – His name is Vāsudevendra Saraswati – Vāsudeva Indra Saraswati. It is clear that he belonged to the Kāñci-maṭh, where all the Swamis are called Indra Saraswati, like Jayendra Saraswati, Vijayendra Saraswati. He need not be the pontiff of Kāñci, but *sannyāsin*s connected to Kāñci-maṭh are called Indra Saraswati.

Vāsu means the one in whom everything dwells, and *deva* means the one who is effulgent, the Lord. He is *vāsu* and he is *deva*. Lord Kṛṣṇa is called Vāsudeva; he is the son of Vasudeva. So, we have *vāsudeva*, a word, and Vāsudeva, Lord Kṛṣṇa's name. The name of this author's *guru* is Vāsudevendra. And he is *yogīndra*, *yogināṃ indraḥ*. *Indra* means *rājā*, so he is the one who is the king of the *yogi*s, a man of knowledge. Here, *yoga* is *jñāna*. The author praises his *guru*, Vāsudevendra, as the one who is the *rājā* of all *jñāna-yogi*s. *Natvā*, having saluted him, remembering him, this book, *Tattvabodha*, is undertaken by me, *abhidhīyate mayā*.

There are already so many books of Vedanta, so why is he writing another one? If the author is repeating what somebody else has written, it is an unnecessary effort. In the tradition there is a responsibility on the part of the author to prove the necessity to write a book. Even Śaṅkara had to defend Vyāsa's writing of the *Brahma-sūtra*s, a work analysing the subject matter of the *upaniṣad*s. Śaṅkara wrote a commentary on it. And the one who comments upon Śaṅkara's commentary has to defend Śaṅkara; each one has to defend the previous one. In fact, there was a panel of judges who had to approve it. In the Kāśi-pīṭha and the Majura-pīṭha there was a panel to decide that. Just as a research paper is accepted by a panel, similarly, any terse work, a manuscript, which had some value, had to be accepted by a panel. And the author himself has to be convinced that he has got to write a book. It is purely self-discipline. Why is he writing it?

He says, *mumukṣūṇāṁ hitārthāya. Mumukṣu* is a desiderative word. In Sanskrit we have a single word derived directly from the verbal root, which reveals the type of desire you want to accomplish. If you want *mokṣa,* you are called a *mumukṣu, moktum icchuḥ,* the one who has a desire to be free. The one who wants to do something is called *cikīrṣu, kartum icchuḥ.* The one who wants to enjoy is *bhubhukṣu, bhoktum icchuḥ;* the one who wants to know is *jijñāsu, jñātum icchuḥ* – these are very beautiful words. So, a *mumukṣu* is one who wants to be free from *saṁsāra,* a life of becoming.

We study Vedanta for *mokṣa.* Vedanta is not merely for the study of Sanskrit, even though Sanskrit is part of the programme. We are not studying Vedanta to study Sanskrit; we are studying Sanskrit to understand Vedanta. It is not for intellectual knowledge – getting the theory first and later practicing; there is no such thing. The study of Vedanta is study of the *mokṣa-śāstra.* Hence, this work is begun for the benefit, *hitārthāya,* of those people who have this great desire for *mokṣa, mumukṣūṇām. Artha* means purpose, *arthāya* means for the purpose. *Hita* means good – so, for the purpose of something good for the *mumukṣus*.

What is *hita*? Very simply, when it is really cold in the morning and you have a hot water bath, it is *hita*. If it is very cold and you pour cold water on your head, it is not *hita*, it is *ahita*. If the food that you eat is good for your health, good for digestion, and also tasty, it is *hita*. Now, you can understand what is *hita*. Kind words, consoling words, which make you recognise your goodness and strength, are *hita*. Words that are damaging are not *hita*, they are *ahita*.

There is an order in the study of the *upaniṣads*. And the first *upaniṣad* we take is *Īśa*, in which the opening verse is – *pūrṇamadaḥ pūrṇamidaṁ purṇāt pūrṇamudacayate pūrṇasya pūrṇamādāya pūrṇameva avaśiṣyate*. What is the meaning? If you do not know Sanskrit, you have to rely on a translation such as this – 'That is whole, this is whole, from that whole, this whole came, and when you remove that whole from this whole, what remains is a whole.' Definitely this is not *hita*. It is like pouring cold water on the person who is shivering.

You require what is *hita*, something that does not intimidate you but gives you the sense that you are understanding. It is important you get that sense – 'at this level of my understanding, I get only as much as will give me the sense that I am with the subject matter, that I am not left out, not lagging behind.' This is proper teaching.

Before entering into the portals of the *upaniṣads*, the source books of this knowledge, or other analytical books, let us just present something that allows the *mumukṣus* to get a sense of the subject matter without being intimidated by language, by logic, analysis, and so on. So, *hita* here is for the purpose of easy understanding on the part of the seekers of *mokṣa*. 'It is for that purpose this book called *Tattvabodha* is undertaken by me.' That is the prayer.

In this, the author reveals not only his salutation but also the subject matter by saying, '*Tattvabodhaḥ*.' The very first verse tells you the subject matter. Being a palm leaf manuscript, you do not know what it is until you open it. There are all kinds of palm leaves available that deal with different topics from astronomy onwards. When you open the palm leaf and see that the first verse says, '*tattvabodhaḥ abhidhīyate*,' then you know the subject matter is *tattvabodha*. You can understand it means *ātma-vidyā*.

The author also tells who is the *adhikārin* for this. By saying to whom it is addressed, he makes it clear that the subject matter is self-knowledge. *Tattvabodha* can be taken to be knowledge of any *tattva,* including the *sāṅkhya-tattva*. Then, what *tattva* is this book talking about? Here, because *tattvabodha* is together with *mumukṣūṇām,* the *adhikārin* is clear, and, by implication, the subject matter is introduced. This subject matter is for the one who is committed to *mokṣa*. The *adhikārin* is the one who wants *mokṣa,* and for that person, *tattvabodhaḥ abhidhīyate*. So, the subject matter as well as the *adhikārin,* the *mumukṣu,* are introduced.

You can ask, "If I am interested in *mokṣa,* why should I study *tattvabodha*?" *Tattvabodha,* knowledge of the *tattva,* which is yourself, is *mokṣa*. By the study of *tattvabodha* you get the result, *mokṣa*. "That is the *tattvabodha* I am interested in, but then, why should I study a book?" Because the book is meant for *tattvabodha,* it is called *Tattvabodha*. Like a book titled '*Indian History*' has Indian history between its covers, similarly here, between the book and the subject matter, which will give you *mokṣa,* there is a connection, *sambandha*. One is the revealer, the other is revealed. It is exactly what you have in the *upaniṣad*. When you study the *upaniṣad,* these are the four things you need to know – the eligible student, *adhikārin;* the result, *phala;* topic, *viṣaya;* and the connection, *sambandha*.

They are the same here, this book being a simple, uncomplicated presentation of the subject matter of the *upaniṣad*. The eligible student is the same, yet, the author is going to explain here who is the *adhikārin*, the *mumukṣu*. So, all that is said in the *upaniṣad* is presented well here.

Sādhanacatuṣṭayam

साधनचतुष्टयसम्पन्नाधिकारिणां मोक्षसाधनभूतं
तत्त्वविवेकप्रकारं वक्ष्यामः ।

sādhana-catuṣṭaya-sampannādhikāriṇāṁ mokṣa-sādhana-bhūtaṁ tattva-viveka-prakāraṁ vakṣyāmaḥ.

vakṣyāmaḥ – we shall describe; *tattva-viveka-prakāram* – the method of discriminative enquiry of truth; *mokṣa-sādhana-bhūtam* – which is the (direct) means for liberation; *sādhana-catuṣṭaya-sampanna-adhikāriṇām* – for the qualified ones who are endowed with the four-fold *sādhana*s (qualifications).

> We shall describe the method of discriminative enquiry of truth which is the (direct) means for liberation for the qualified ones who are endowed with the four-fold *sādhana*s (qualifications).

Vakṣyāmaḥ, we will say now. When he uses the plural, the author not only identifies with his *guru,* but also the lineage of teachers, *paramparā,* who came before. Therefore, *vakṣyāmaḥ,* we will explain here the *prakāra* of *tattva-viveka. Prakāra* means a method. Here, it is the method of *viveka,* discriminative enquiry. Of what? Of *tattva,* truth, ultimate truth. What does it mean?

The subject matter, the self, is not totally unknown to you. Suppose someone says, "We will now describe the black hole." They say that there is a black hole, and they will talk about the black hole. It is totally an unknown topic to you, and you have no confusion about it. When they talk about the possibility of a black hole, its nature and so on, it is simple enquiry. It is not discriminative enquiry. However, the subject matter of this enquiry is understood and not understood; in fact, it is misunderstood. So, we need to examine it in order to understand it properly, because things are mixed up. Here, the self, *ātman,* is the subject matter, which is going to be revealed as the *tattva,* as we will discover. The *ātman* is taken to be certain things which it is not. It is taken to be that which is subject to limitations, even though the limitations do not belong to *ātman* at all. Therefore, *ātman* is known to you, because it is you, 'I am,' but the conclusion is, 'I am a *saṁsārin*, a becoming person, someone who is subject to various forms of limitations.

This is not true. If it is true, then there is no necessity to study this book. If it is not true, we need to enquire into the *ātman,* which is not totally unknown like the black hole, quantum objects and so on. *Ātman* is something known and unknown. 'I' *ātman* is taken to be a *saṁsārin;* that is the confusion. Wherever there is confusion, there is reason for the confusion. It is like a cluster of threads. Sometimes, these threads get all knotted into a bundle, and in trying to unravel it, you do not get the hang of it. You pull one thread, because it is hanging out, and the bundle becomes tighter. This is the problem of confusion. You have to really find out what will resolve the knot and what will make it more knotted. To resolve the confusion, you need to understand what belongs to what. There is a logic in all this. We can even show why this very confusion came about. It is something like thinking that the sun really rises in the eastern sky. It is real because you see it. Not only do you see it, I also see it. We see that the sun does rise in the eastern sky and travels to disappear in the western sky, and again comes back to the eastern sky. Therefore, we conclude that the sun is travelling and we are stationary. There is a perception and a perception-based conclusion.

We know that this conclusion is wrong because the sun really does not travel. The planet earth is travelling, spinning on its own axis, and going around the sun in its own orbit. When we explain it like this, we are explaining how there is a sunrise and a sunset without the sun rising and setting. On the basis of perception there is a conclusion that the sun rises and travels to the west, which is established without enquiry, *vicāra*. On enquiry, we find that it is not true but just an appearance. And why there is this appearance is also explained.

Similarly, that people uniformly commit the mistake about *ātman* is explainable. Resolving the confusion is called *tattva-viveka-prakāra*. *Viveka* is discriminative analysis. Because things are mixed up, a discriminative enquiry will help you discriminate the *tattva*. There is a method, *prakāra*, and this method is important because it helps you resolve the problem, like a mathematical problem is solved by following certain method. The method has to be meticulously followed at every step, then you find that the problem is solved. Here, we have a method that is appropriate for solving this problem of confusion.

That appropriate method, *tattva-viveka-prakāra,* we will explain, *vakṣyāmaḥ.*

The author tells why *tattva-viveka* is necessary. Someone may argue, "When I come to you for *mokṣa,* why are you asking me to study all these? I want *mokṣa.*" All this is for *mokṣa,* and there is nothing else that gives you *mokṣa* either. This method of discriminative enquiry, *tattva-viveka-prakāra,* is *mokṣa-sādhana-bhūta,* a means for *mokṣa,* whose subject matter is *tattva,* the ultimate truth. There is a confusion, and we need to resolve the confusion by enquiry into what is what. And there is a method for that.

For whom is this *mokṣa-sādhana* ? For the *mumukṣu*s who want freedom, who see it as 'the end' to be accomplished in life; they are the *adhikārin*s for this knowledge. And these *adhikārin*s are those who have the *sādhana-catuṣṭaya,* the four-fold qualifications that serve as a means for *mokṣa.* The author will mention what this *sādhana-catuṣṭaya* is by posing a question and then answering it.

At this stage, we need to know that Vedanta is a *pramāṇa,* a means of knowledge, and the *prameya,* what is to be known, is *ātman,* which is evident as oneself, but not known as it is. In a confused form it is known. As it is, *ātman* is free from all problems, and has to be known as such. So, *ātman* becomes *jñeya*, to be known as it is. We now require a means of knowledge.

The means of knowledge such as perception and inference are not meant for knowing the *ātman*, since through them we can only know objects. We require another means of knowledge. That is *śabda*, the words of the teaching of the *śruti*.

If the teaching is there and *ātman* is there, then knowledge should take place. If knowledge does not take place, one can assume that either the teaching is not a *pramāṇa* or *ātman* is not free of all problems. "Swamiji, my *ātman* is different. I do not see it as free, whole and so on, which are simply words. *Ātman* may be okay but the *śruti pramāṇa* is not either adequate or appropriate. I need to do something else in order to know *ātman*." One person told me, "I have listened to *śruti-vedānta*, yet I have not realised *ātman*, so I am doing something else." It is like saying, "I have used my eyes, and still, I haven't seen the colour, so I am using my nose." If one does not see the colour, one should go to an opthalmologist and find out whether one has colour-blindness. Just because one does not see, a *pramāṇa* does not cease to be one because it works for someone else. And, according to the *pramāṇa*, there is only one *ātman* which is the whole, the limitless.

Therefore, one's *ātman* is not any different from that of anyone else.

It is obvious that there is a third factor which denies one this knowledge. The knowledge has to take place in the *antaḥ-karaṇa*, the mind, and the mind has got to be ready for it. Preparedness for *ātma-jñāna* is necessary. That preparedness is to be a fully grown individual, an adult – an adult who has certain objectivity, dispassion that he or she has come to discover in life by going through experiences. Life's experiences have given rise to certain maturity in a person who is prepared for this knowledge. One may be young in age but can be an adult in thinking. One may be aged but still very childish in thinking, immature emotionally. So, one needs to have an understanding, certain composure and self-possession. This is pointed out so that one can equip oneself wherever necessary. Wherever there is a lack, it can be taken care of.

One thing that is common in all the people who come to study Vedanta is the love to know. It may be in the form of curiosity to know or it may be a spiritual commitment but not knowing very clearly what is that spiritual end. Yet, an answer, a solution, is sought. Or, really understanding everything, knowing what one is seeking, after analysing all other pursuits and seeing their limitations, one comes to *mokṣa*. That is a very rare case.

Whatever may be the reason, you have this book, *Tattvabodha,* in your hands. It is not for reading like a novel. There are no characters. You are the hero here. Anybody can take up this book, just by chance, but if that person keeps reading we must understand that the person has a love for gaining this knowledge. Otherwise, the person will not stay with it. If there is a love for knowing, and the *pramāṇa* is available, *ātman,* the reality, *tattva,* is available, then knowledge, *bodha,* should take place. If it does not take place, we understand that a few things are necessary. It is not to discourage the people who study this book that the qualifications are told, but to understand the *prāmāṇya,* the status of the words as a means of knowledge. If the teaching is not understood, you may dismiss it by questioning the validity of this *pramāṇa.*

So, we need to establish that Vedanta is an independent *pramāṇa.* Without any other help it is an independent means of knowledge. All you require is a prepared mind. If that mind is there, this knowledge takes place. Whether you like it, in the alignment of the *prameya,* the object of knowledge, *pramāṇa,* knowledge, takes place without taking permission from you. And this is proven all the time by your nose. Whether you like it, you pick up different fragrance and smells. That is the nature of a *pramāṇa* – it gives knowledge. And if knowledge does not take place, you must assume that there is a lack in prerequisites. That lack is pointed out for two reasons. One is, if you know what is required, you can equip yourself, and the other is, the status of Vedanta as a *pramāṇa* is preserved. When you understand or someone else understands, you know that it is a *pramāṇa*. In order to safeguard Vedanta as a *pramāṇa*, we need to point out the prescribed qualifications. Only with these in place does the *pramāṇa* work without any let or hindrance, and without any other aid. You need to be ready for it.

It is for these reasons that we have the *sādhana-catuṣṭaya* that are drawn from an analysis of the various things said in the *śruti, upaniṣad*.

There are certain phrases in the *upaniṣad* like, *parīkṣya lokān nirvedamāyāt...*, examining his experiences he would gain dispassion (*Muṇḍakopaniṣad* 1.2.12), from which are drawn the qualifications that characterise the preparedness of the individual. Here, the author himself lists them by asking the question and answering it.

साधनचतुष्टयं किम् ?

sādhana-catuṣṭayaṁ kim?

sādhana-catuṣṭayam – the four-fold qualifications (for gaining *mokṣa*) ; *kim* – what?

What are the four-fold qualifications (for gaining *mokṣa*)?

नित्यानित्यवस्तुविवेकः । इहामुत्रार्थफलभोगविरागः ।
शमादिषट्कसम्पत्तिः । मुमुक्षुत्वं चेति ।

nityānitya-vastuvivekaḥ, ihāmutrārtha-phalabhoga-virāgaḥ, śamādi-ṣaṭkasampattiḥ, mumukṣutvaṁ ceti.

nitya-anitya-vastu-vivekaḥ – discriminative understanding of the difference between the timeless and time-bound; *iha-amutra-artha-phala-bhoga-virāgaḥ* – dispassion for the results of experience here (in this world) and in the hereafter; *śamādi-ṣaṭka-sampattiḥ* – the six-fold accomplishments (wealth) beginning with *śama* (inner composure) etc.; *mumukṣutvam ca* – and a desire for freedom from becoming; *iti* (*sādhana-catuṣṭayam*) – thus (the four-fold qualifications).

(The four-fold qualifications are) Discriminative understanding of the difference

> between the timeless and time-bound, dispassion for the results of experience here (in this world) and in the hereafter, the six-fold accomplishments (wealth) beginning with *śama*, (inner composure) etc., and a desire for freedom from becoming.

What are the four-fold means, *sādhana*? First he says, *nitya-anitya-vastu-vivekaḥ*. *Viveka* is discriminative understanding of *anitya*, what is not *nitya*. What then can be *nitya*? *Nitya* is that which is always there, and *anitya* is that which is not always there. *Anitya* is temporary, empirical and finite. What is not finite is not known, really, as we will see. *Vastu* means an object. Any object can be called a *vastu*. Reality is also called *vastu*. Here, what is to be understood is what is *anitya-vastu*, that which is not *nitya*. Later he is going to explain all this, but here we just need to understand the words, *nityānitya-vastu-viveka*. This is one qualification.

The second qualification is *iha-amutra-artha-phalabhoga-virāga*. *Virāga* means dispassion, a disposition in which there is absence of *rāga*, longing. *Rāga* is *rañjanātmaka*, imbued with excessive value. When there is *rāga* for something, you have not just a value for it, but something more – the capacity to solve the basic problem; the problem of self-disapproval. If the thinking, 'This is going to solve the problem,' is not there, then it is called *vi-rāga*. When you do not look upon a situation as something that is going to solve your problem of self-disapproval, you have dispassion, objectivity, towards it.

Now, this *virāga*, freedom from *rāga*, is with reference to what? *Phala-bhoga*, that is, *karma-phala-bhoge virāgaḥ*. *Bhoga* is enjoyment and *phala-bhoga* is enjoyment of the fruits of your undertaking, *karma*. The *phala* is in the form of a desirable situation either *iha*, here, in this world, or, *amutra*, later, after death. He mentions this because the situation after death is also very attractive to some people. They are highly committed here, now, in order to enjoy there, later, after death in other *loka*s. Out of faith or belief, people live their entire life here, very carefully, in order to go to heaven; we have people who are interested in heaven. So, the *karma-phala* is a situation which is either here or in the hereafter. The qualification here is dispassion to the experience, *bhoga*, of all of them. He is going to explain each one of these later by asking a question such as, 'What is *viveka*?' and answering it.

The next qualification is *śamādi-ṣaṭka-sampatti*. *Śama-ādi* – *ādi* means etcetera, (literally 'beginning with') and here there are five in addition to *śama*. So, it is six-fold, *ṣaṭka,* virtue, accomplishment, *sampatti*. What are these six?

The first one in the group is *śama*. A mental resolution is called *śama* – an inner resolution, a resolved state of mind in which there is composure. Once you mention *śama*, the word '*ādi*' will naturally bring in anything that is connected to it. When *śamādi* is mentioned, it is generally known that it means *śama, dama, uparati, titikṣā, śraddhā, samādhānam*. Mention of one thing of a group followed by *ādi* will bring in the rest of its members. Suppose you mention, eyes, etc. Does it mean eyes, trees, leaves and so on? No. It means eyes, ears, sense of smell, taste, and sense of touch; the five senses go together. He is going to say one by one what is the six-fold accomplishment of *śama*, etc.

Lastly, the fourth qualification, *mumukṣutvaṁ ceti*. *Mumukṣu* means the one who wants *mokṣa* as the end in life. The one who has committed oneself to *mokṣa* is a *mumukṣu*, and the state of his or her mind is called *mumukṣutva*. The person's status is that of being a desirer of *mokṣa*. It is the person that is pointed out, not *mokṣa*. *Mumukṣutva* is separately mentioned because it is not mere curiosity but a value to which one is committed. This is the difference between someone who is interested in studying Vedanta in order to know what Vedanta says, and the one who wants *mokṣa*. It is different. Therefore, this knowledge is purely for the person who discerns in *mokṣa* a value. For that person Vedanta becomes highly meaningful. So, these are the four-fold qualifications.

Nityānitya-vastu-vivekaḥ

> नित्यानित्यवस्तुविवेकः कः ?
>
> *nityānitya-vastu-vivekaḥ kaḥ?*

nitya-anitya-vastu-vivekaḥ – the discriminative understanding between the timeless (*nitya*) and the time-bound (*anitya*); *kaḥ* – what?

> What is the discriminative understanding between the (*nitya*) and the time-bound (*anitya*)?

> नित्यवस्त्वेकं ब्रह्म तद्व्यतिरिक्तं सर्वमनित्यम्। अयमेव नित्यानित्यवस्तुविवेकः।
>
> *nitya vastvekaṁ brahma tadvyatiriktaṁ sarvam anityam, ayameva nityānitya-vastu-vivekaḥ.*

nitya-vastu – the timeless (infinite); *ekaṁ brahma* – one Brahman (limitless); *tad-vyatiriktam* – other than that;

sarvam – all else; *anityam* – (is) time-bound (finite); *ayam eva* – this alone; *nitya-anitya-vastu-vivekaḥ* – (is) the discriminative understanding between the timeless and the time-bound.

> The timeless (infinite) is one, Brahman (limitless). All else other than that is time-bound (finite). This alone is the discriminative understanding between the timeless and the time-bound.

Nityānitya-vastu-viveka is what we call *puruṣārtha-viveka*. *Puruṣārtha* is what is desired by a person. A person desires different things, and all these are reduced to a few in this enquiry. The pursuit of money, power and so on, is reduced to *artha*. The pursuit of pleasure, in various forms, is reduced to one – *kāma*. We now have *artha* and *kāma*. Then there is the pursuit of *dharma* that is for one's own growth; there *dharma* is a value in its own right. And *dharma* is also *puṇya,* gaining some grace by which one can attain something here, or in the hereafter, that is a more conducive situation in which one will be more happy than one is now. This is also *dharma*. All religious pursuits of different religions come under *dharma*. So, *dharma*, *artha* and *kāma* are called *puruṣārtha*s, human goals.

Now, I ask the question, "Are you really seeking security or are you seeking freedom from insecurity?" It is a very important question. Who wants crutches? Who is the person who wants crutches? The one who cannot stand on one's own legs. As long as you are insecure on your legs, you want crutches, you need crutches. The one who is secure does not need them. Crutches are not a part of your outfit. You do not dress up nicely and don some crutches also! No. People need crutches only when they feel insecure on their own legs. The more you need crutches, the more insecure you feel. Tell me now, do you want crutches or do you want freedom from insecurity?

Nobody wants crutches. The more crutches you have, the more insecure you are. And there are many crutches. Finances are crutches, name is a crutch, fame is a crutch, power is a crutch, community is a crutch. All these are crutches. You want to become a member of a community so that you will feel good, which is why all cults will tell you, "You are special." Somebody is there to keep you under their control, telling you that you are someone special, that it is you against many.

When we seek security, it means we feel insecure. There is nothing wrong or right here. We are only trying to undertstand what is going on. We are not making any judgement that this person is right and the other one is wrong. 'Right and wrong' is not the point. What we are trying to get at is, we feel insecure about ourselves. Being self-conscious, the human being is insecure. And there are definitely reasons for this sense of insecurity, but they seem valid according to the person.

We are going to analyse these reasons that seem to be very valid. We are going to question their validity by seeing thoroughly the fallacy of all those arguments that seem to support the sense of insecurity. If they do not have a standing, they fall apart; naturally, the insecurity also goes away along with them.

It is important to understand that you are not seeking security. You cannot stand being insecure. It means you are seeking freedom from insecurity. When you seek freedom from insecurity, should you seek security or should you question, "Why am I insecure?" When you seek security, you are taking youself for granted as someone who is insecure; you have already concluded that you are insecure.

Now, how real is this conclusion? What are the reasons for it? All these we analyse. That is the *viveka* here. "Am I really insecure, or is something else insecure which I take to be myself, and then feel insecure?"

If *ātman*, I, is the body, definitely *ātman* is insecure because the body is insecure. It is subject to every microbe that is passing by. It is subject to age, subject to time, and so it is going to join the majority, the dead, one day. You know this very well, and you are insecure. Any which way you look at this body, it is insecure. If *ātman* is as good as the body, then it is subject to time, ageing and illness; therefore, you are insecure. If you are not subject to all these, but think that you are, then there is confusion. When there is confusion, you require an enquiry that will resolve the confusion. Because there is confusion, the enquiry has to be called *viveka*, not just *vicāra*. *Vicāra* means enquiry. *Viveka* is also enquiry but enquiry wherein there is confusion, where two things are mixed up.

This security is what we mean by the *puruṣārtha* of *artha*, but security is not really the *puruṣārtha*. Freedom from insecurity is the *puruṣārtha*. What does it mean? *Mokṣa* from insecurity. Now you can understand what *mokṣa* is. It is not one of the *puruṣārtha*s. Generally they say, *caturvidānāṁ puruṣārthānāṁ madhye mokṣa eva parama-puruṣārthaḥ*, there are four *puruṣārtha*s, *dharma, artha, kāma, mokṣa*, and among them, *mokṣa* is the best.

This is childish. In fact, when they say *mokṣa* is the best, the idea is freedom from seeking security, *artha*, or anything else. That is called *puruṣārtha*. Now, between *artha* and *mokṣa*, how many *puruṣārtha*s do you have? You are seeking *artha* and another person is seeking *mokṣa*. Do you have two *puruṣārtha*s here? No, the two are reduced to one, *mokṣa*.

Let us look at the other *puruṣārtha, kāma*, seeking pleasure. Pleasure means all conducive situations wherein you can tap some happiness for yourself. What does it mean? You are unhappy, so naturally you are seeking happiness. But it is not happiness that you want, you want to be a happy person. Happiness is not an object. If there is an object called 'happiness' in the world, then we all can make a beeline towards that object, and all of us can get a little bit of happiness. Just as we go to the gas station and ask for so many gallons or litres of gas, we can go to this particular station called, 'happiness-station' and ask the attendant, "Give me two units of happiness." There is no such object in the world. Therefore, you cannot seek happiness. You seek the happy person. There is only one object, happiness, but in pursuit of it, one person goes to the beach and another leaves the beach. One person is going to the mountain top, another is coming down.

Does it mean he or she has had enough of happiness? The one going up is in a hurry and the one coming down is also in a hurry. If you watch the streets, you will find the traffic going both ways. One person is going that way to find happiness and someone else is coming away from there. All of them are going in different directions. What does it mean?

It is clear that nobody seeks happiness, because it is neither in the East nor in the West, North, South. It is neither up nor below. All that one wants is to be the happy self. And to be the happy self, does one have to go to the mountain top or come down, or go to the beach or leave the beach? Where is the happy self? 'I do not know, maybe on the mountain top or on the beach, I will come across the happy self.' So, all the time one is seeking the happy self.

When you are seeking the happy self, what kind of self do you have? I may not say it is an unhappy self but definitely not a happy self; that is better. You may not be positively unhappy now, but occasionally unhappy, and otherwise not happy. So, saying that you are not happy now will include being unhappy. What obtains is, "I am the 'not happy' self." Therefore, are you seeking the happy self or are you seeking freedom from the 'not happy' self? If you are seeking freedom from the 'not happy' self, how many *puruṣārtha*s do you have here? *Kāma* and *mokṣa*? Freedom is *mokṣa*. Freedom from the 'not happy' self, freedom from the 'insecure' self, is what you are seeking. There is no *artha* that you are seeking, no *kāma* that you are seeking. What is it? You start with *artha, kāma* and end up in *mokṣa*.

Then, there is someone who says, "I want to go to heaven, and therefore I want *puṇya*." Going to heaven is **the end** for a lot of people in the world, they are waiting to go to heaven. And if you say to such a person, "Do you want to go to heaven? Let us go today," he will say, "No, no, no, not today." Why? Because he is not sure about heaven, so he wants to live his life. Suppose such a heaven is available. What do you want in heaven? "Here I am imperfect and I have to be saved. I will be saved in heaven." Again he seeks freedom from the same thing – being insecure, unhappy; it is the same.

What one wants is freedom from this conclusion, 'I am imperfect, I am a sinner.' This is the pursuit of *dharma*. We now have *dharma, artha* and *kāma*. The pursuit of growth is also *dharma*. Even as a grown up person, you will have legitimate anger, legitimate problems; therefore you will be legitimately insecure, unhappy and so on. So, the grown up person is the limited person. Because you think that you are the body, all the limitations beginning with, 'I am a mortal' will not go away. Whatever you are seeking in the grown up person, you see the limitations there. And nobody wants to be a limited person. Whether you are seeking *puṇya* or growth or anything else, the seeking is because of a conclusion, and that conlusion we question here. It is the sense arising from the conclusion that you want to be free from. If you are imperfect and you want to be free from imperfection, what can you possibly do?

If I am imperfect, how will I become perfect? My nose is imperfect, so what do I do to make it perfect? What is it that will make me perfect, if I am imperfect? Nothing will make me perfect. Even if I go to heaven, it is the imperfect person going to heaven; I am bound to be disappointed. The point is, wherever the imperfect person goes, he or she will find imperfection. Therefore, I am not seeking perfection, which itself is silly. I am seeking freedom from imperfection.

Now, how many *puruṣārtha*s do we have? Only one. Except for *dharma*, as growth, which can be a *puruṣārtha*, everything else is not a *puruṣārtha*. In the pursuit of *artha* you discover your growth, in the pursuit of *kāma* you discover your growth. Only self-growth can be a *puruṣārtha*, a relative *puruṣārtha*, nothing else, really speaking. And that is also not going to be the *puruṣārtha* because, there again, you will see yourself as limited, wanting. Therefore, freedom from limitation, freedom from insecurity, and freedom from being unhappy is the *puruṣārtha*. There is only one *puruṣārtha* that is sought after by all. Who is not seeking it? But there is no *viveka*. Even though everybody is seeking *mokṣa*, they do not know they are seeking *mokṣa*. And so, there is confusion.

The fallacy in the conclusion that I am insecure is not discerned. That I am seeking freedom from insecurity is not discerned, and because of that, I seek security. That I am seeking freedom from being unhappy is not discerned, so I seek myself as the happy person by manipulating the world or manipulating the mind. Somebody manipulates the mind, somebody manipulates the world – both of them are *saṁsārins*. One tries to manipulate the mind, but in fact, the mind manipulates the person. That one wants to manipulate the mind is dictated by the very mind. The mind makes the person manipulate the mind, really.

What you need to understand is that the one who wants to manipulate the mind and the one who wants to manipulate the world, are both *saṁsārins*, because they are both trying to 'become'. 'I am unhappy' is the conclusion from which you want to become free. It is freedom that you are seeking. Therefore, it is very clear that there is a lack of discrimination.

If you think that in heaven you can solve the problem, as though there is a problem right now and it cannot be solved, that is also lack of discrimination. Even in heaven the problem is not going to be solved, because if you go to heaven, you are going to be there as an individual, different from everyone else, so it will be the same situation. Suppose, you think that you will lose your individuality in heaven; it only means individuality can be lost. Only what can be lost can be lost. And what can be lost is not real; it is what we call *anitya*. What can be lost is *anitya*. What is, is *nitya*. Therefore, *dharma-artha-kāma* are for only one *puruṣārtha* – *mokṣa*. This is called *viveka*.

What is, is not going to be produced. What you want is to be free from all crutches. By a process of change you are not going to become the happy person, the secure person, the limitless person. The limited person cannot become limitless by a process of change. What is limited will continue to be limited, no matter how many changes are brought in. You can embellish a broomstick with any amount of ornamentation, but still, it is a broomstick. Please understand this. The problem remains.

Why not solve the problem? To solve the problem is to understand that the process of becoming itself is *anitya*. Anything that 'becomes' is subject to becoming, and that new condition is also subject to become something else. The old status is gone, the new status is gained, only to go away and again be replaced by a new status, and again, a new status. This continues. And even if you get a new birth, let us extend it further, again you will find yourself with the same problem. This is the process of becoming which is *anitya*. So, no matter what you do, you are not going to accomplish what you want to be. If there is really a solution, it is not within the sphere of becoming. If you have to solve the problem without becoming, it means the solution should be you. That is called *nitya*. You can say that you do not know what *nitya* is, but this much you know – *nitya* cannot be produced. What is eternal cannot be produced, which is why an eternal heaven does not exist at all. If it exists, it should be you, right now. If it is you, and you cannot see that it is you, the problem is due to ignorance. This is *nitya-anitya-vastu viveka*.

We want the seeking to end, which means to accomplish something that is free from being finite.

In other words, we are seeking what is eternal. Even though we are not seeking what is non-eternal, what we are doing will only result in what is non-eternal. Any change is, again, only for the finite being, so even a heavenly abode is not going to really make a difference. And that is what is said here.

What is eternal is not going to be created by anything, *nāsti akṛtaḥ kṛtena*.[3] Only what is uncreated is eternal. If at all there is something eternal, it is not going to be created, it is not going to come in time. That means it should already be here.

Here, if one is a little more informed about the tradition, one can say, *nityaṁ vastu ekaṁ brahma*. This is the advantage of the Vedic background. The Veda tells us that there is one *vastu*, one reality, which is *ekam*, one, non-dual, and it is *brahma*. What is indicated by the word '*brahma*' is *nitya*, and that alone is *nitya*.

So, you seek Brahman which is *nityaṁ vastu*. And everything else other than that Brahman is *anitya, tad vyatiriktaṁ sarvam anityam. Tad vyatiriktam* here is other than that Brahman. Heaven is not *nitya* – it begins at a given time and it will be lost in time too. All that you seek locally is also non-eternal, not only in terms of

[3] *Muṇḍakopaniṣad* 1.2.12

time, but in degrees, in its quality, in its capacity to make you happy, secure and so on. Everything is found wanting. Therefore, anything that you seek, which is within time, is going to be non-eternal. What you are really seeking is freedom from this seeking itself. This is *mokṣa,* and if that is what you are seeking, then you need to seek Brahman, which is eternal.

Now, we have this statement that there is one *vastu,* Brahman, and that is *nityaṁ vastu.* This is the Vedic information we have, and with this Vedic information we know that what we are seeking is eternal, and it is Brahman, which is one. We also know that it is to be sought, gained, in terms of knowing. This much knowledge we need to have – *nityaṁ vastu ekaṁ brahma.* And everything other than that Brahman is not eternal, *tadvyatiriktaṁ sarvam anityam.* This is *nityānitya-vastu-viveka.* Brahman is still not known. We are only talking about qualifications here. Brahman is not known, but there is something to be known, which is Brahman. That level of understanding is what is called *viveka. Viveka* is achieved by assimilating the human experiences, and from there, extending our reasoning to also cover the experiences one may gain after death in another incarnation. Whether it is here or elsewhere, heaven or anything else, it is all going to be finite. The *saṁsārin*, the becoming person, will continue to become; there is no solution to this. What one is seeking is not available in the sphere of seeking. Such an understanding is again *viveka*.

Being born and brought up in the Vedic culture, you can even say, "What I want is Brahman." Only then can you go and ask the teacher, "Please teach me what is Brahman."[4] For that, you need to have knowledge of what you are seeking. You cannot desire a thing that is totally unknown to you. The person here who goes and asks the *guru*, the teacher, knows where to go and seek, and also knows what to seek, *adhīhi bhagavo brahmeti* – this is Bhṛgu, the son of Varuṇa, who was a great learned person, a wise man. Bhṛgu had never cared to ask of him this knowledge, but one day realised that he should ask. It means he had gone through the experiences of life, assimilated them, and said, "Okay, I have had enough; now let me understand Brahman." Then, he approached his father and asked, "Please teach me what is Brahman." Bhṛgu knew that he has to gain Brahman in terms of knowledge.

If you have to gain something that is eternal, then it cannot be a product of your action, *karma-phala*. Why?

---

[4] *adhīhi bhagavo brahmeti*... (*Taittirīyopaniṣad* 3.1)

Because *karma* is finite; it is done in time. An action, including prayer, is done in time, and therefore, prayer and its result are finite. This is very important to know. Prayer is an action, which is why it is available for choice; you can pray in different forms. We allow that, but the result is not going to be the end that we are really seeking. It is where people commit mistakes. All religions talk about prayers and say that prayers will produce results. In this we have no problem whatsoever. We validate every form of prayer. Whether it is a Hebrew prayer or it is in Latin or Sanskirt, it is all the same. Therefore, we can say that all prayers are efficacious. But it does not mean all religions lead to the same goal. We need to know this. The goal of prayer is only a finite result; prayer being finite, the result will also be finite. We want finite results too. Eating produces finite results, which is why in the morning we eat, again, at lunch time we eat, and in the evening we eat. When we say that eating produces only a finite result, it does not mean that we do not eat.

What you need to understand here is that prayers have their results and they are finite in nature. If it is so, then whatever be the *karma*, action, you do; even if it is a sophisticated prayer, the result of that *karma* is finite. If it is finite, then in that you cannot seek any freedom from this becoming.

The becoming process is *anitya,* And you cannot free yourself from this process of becoming, called *saṁsāra,* by gaining a particular result, because it will be lost. Again you have to 'become.' Therefore, what is *nitya,* eternal, cannot be a product of a change, *karma.* It should already be existent and it should not be separate from you either. It has got to be you, as we will see clearly.

If it is yourself, then it is a matter of knowing. This much *viveka* you need to have, which is why there is a big introduction. You cannot suddenly start Vedanta. The whole discriminative process, *viveka,* must be there – that it has got to be myself alone, and if it is myself, then I am separate from it purely by ignorance. Therefore, to dispel that ignorance, I need to know, I need *tattva-viveka.* That is why the author said, "I will explain the method for discerning the truth, which is the means for *mokṣa, mokṣa-sādhana-bhūtaṁ tattva-viveka-prakāraṁ vakṣyāmaḥ.*" So, I need this discrimination that what I am seeking is not elsewhere.

You have no choice in knowing. If you want to see a colour you have to use your eyes. What choice do you have? You cannot use your nose. It is not fanaticism, either. Where there are options, there can be fanaticism. If you hold on to some particular thing, excluding all others without valid reason, that is fanaticism. But here, what we are saying is that you are the solution for the problem you think you have. Nobody else, nothing else, no heaven, can be the solution. Even if you go to heaven you have to discover yourself. You have no option whatsoever. You have to know. It is not fanaticism; it is knowledge. Knowing what you are is freedom from seeking, and you can see that right now, here. Therefore, *mokṣa* is the end and it is in the form of self-knowledge. This is *viveka*.

Viveka also implies certain discipline in your thinking. It is the cognitive ability, the intellectual discipline. When Vedanta is taught, the student has to study Sanskrit grammar because that requires logic. Sanskrit language, presented through a meta-language in the *Pāṇinian* system, is logical. You have to open those grammar *sūtra*s, and it is only by logic that you can understand what is being said there; by the study of grammar you develop acumen. There is a special *śāstra* for that, the *nyāya-śāstra*, which is studied in order to become skilfull in reasoning. Intellectual discipline is what helps you discover fallacies in reasoning. Dispassionate reasoning is essential; otherwise, you will succumb to emotional logic. Therefore, dispassionate reasoning without being cantenkerous, but at the same time seeing the fallacies in thinking, is a must. So, intellectual discipline is also included in *viveka.* Discriminative enquiry implies cognitive skills. In modern times, we assume that the modern education must have given you the intellectual discipline you require for this. Otherwise, I would first have to teach you maths, then later we would start Vedanta. The assumption is that having gone through the study of exact disciplines like physics, mathematics, etc., you will have the required acumen. That is also included in *viveka.* When *viveka* is there you become more objective. This is called dispassion, *vairāgya.*

Vairāgya

> विरागः कः?
> इह-स्वर्गभोगेषु इच्छाराहित्यम्।
> *virāgaḥ kaḥ?*
> *iha-svargabhogeṣu icchārāhityam.*

virāgaḥ – dispassion; *kaḥ* – what is?

iha-svargabhogeṣu – in the enjoyments here (in this world) and in the enjoyments of heaven; *icchā-rāhityam* – absence of desire.

What is *virāga*?

(Dispassion is) Absence of desire in the enjoyments here (in this world) and in the enjoyments of heaven.

This is very important. What is said here is very cryptic; we need to see it properly. *Virāga* is absence of *rāga*, longing. The word '*rāga*' means a simple desire but it can become a longing. It implies that you see something that is not there. And what you see is something fascinating. In reality, there is nothing there to fascinate. For instance, desire for food is real. Hunger is empirically real, and so desire for eating is as real. You want food, and it is a real desire. This is one thing; there is objectivity here.

Then what is *vairāgya*? Let us consider money. Money is also real. Who says it is not? Money has buying power. As long as it is not de-monetised, currency is money. But if they withdraw the buying power, it is merely a coloured paper. This is money; it has buying power. It is real.

Now, if you say that money will solve the problem of your insecurity, then that is a value superimposed upon it. Superimposition is of two types. One is when you mistake an object for something else. The other is, if you do not mistake an object for something else but add a value to it, which is not there at all, that is also superimposition. If you take it to be more valuable than it is, there is lack of objectivity, lack of *vairāgya*. So, what does *vairāgya* mean? Objectivity, maximum objectivity. It means the least amount of subjective value is added to various things with which you are connected in your life. Understand, everything has its objective value, and if you give it more than that, leading to longing, it is lack of *vairāgya*.

Holding on to something also indicates lack of *vairāgya*. Whether you hold on to money, power, people, or some situation, you are adding a value to something which, unfortunately, it does not have. This is lack of objectivity, otherwise called lack of *vairāgya*.

If you think that heaven, *svarga*, is going to save you, it definitely is not. Even in heaven, if you have gone there as an individual, you are going to remain an individual and will have all the problems of the individual. This is emphasised here because unless the concept of heaven is understood as a limited end, you are not going to think properly. To think that heaven is beyond the clouds is clouded thinking. So he says here, *svarga bhogeṣu icchārāhityam*, absence of desire, *vairāgya*, with reference to all those promised enjoyments and pleasures in heaven. This can be total. With regard to what is here it may not be total, but definitely there, with respect to heaven, it can be total. You need to see this because *svarga*, heaven, may be there, or may not be there. Even if it is there it is just like having a holiday out; you will come back again. That kind of dispassion towards heaven – heavenly enjoyments and promises – is *vairāgya*. Now, we know that many religions will fall by the way side because of this understanding. They can get hold of you only if you are interested in heaven. Therefore, *svarga bhogeṣu icchārāhityam*, absence of desire for enjoyments promised in heaven, is required here.

Iha Bhoga. Suppose someone says, "Swamiji, I am not interested in heavenly enjoyments. If I were interested, why should I listen to your classes? I am here because I am interested in what is here, *iha-bhogeṣu icchā*."

There can be desires for enjoyments here, but again, these desires need to be understood. They can be binding or non-binding. If they are non-binding, you have dispassion, *vairāgya*. If they are binding, then you need to make them non-binding. A binding desire is one towards which you have the sense, "Without this, my life is empty." It is lack of objectivity.

When you have certain objectivity towards every pursuit, your mind is available for *mokṣa*. When *viveka* is there, *vairāgya* will also be there. Then, life itself becomes *yoga*. Marriage and other pursuits become *yoga* because there is objectivity. Greater the objectivity, greater is the commitment to *mokṣa*, because *viveka* and *vairāgya* go together.

Vairāgya is commonly understood as turning away from everything. But, when you turn away from everything, you carry it all in your head. Whatever you turn away from will always catch you; it travels with you. But when you are in the midst of things, and you discover certain objectivity, it is dispassion born of discriminate thinking. There is less subjectivity. It means you do not superimpose values, which are your own creation.

Even a relationship, like marriage, can help you only when you are objective. If you marry for the sake of marriage, as an end, then the marriage will end. Marriage cannot be an end; if it is, it is an ideal, and there is no ideal marriage at all. Marriage is a means where both partners help each other to gain the end. Then, it becomes *yoga*; it is a means for an end. In Indian marriages we have a seven-step ritual, *saptapadi*, in which the couple walk together towards a common goal as friends. Therefore, there is no bad marriage at all, if it is a means. If it is an end, there is no good marriage either. This is what we call objectivity. *Vairāgya* is not running away from everything. Marriage and other meaningful pursuits we have, are a means for an end, *mokṣa*. This is *virāga*, dispassion, in *ihāmutrārtha-phalabhoga-virāgaḥ*. We will discover all this more and more. As we proceed, these things will repeat themselves in all the texts, so everytime we will get something more, not totally different, but something further.

Śamādi-ṣaṭka-sampattiḥ

शमादि-साधन-सम्पत्तिः का ?
शमो दम उपरमस्तितिक्षा श्रद्धा समाधानं चेति ।

śamādi-sādhana-sampattiḥ kā?
śamo dama uparamastitikṣā śraddhā
samādhānaṁ ceti.

śamādi-sādhana-sampattiḥ – the (six-fold) accomplishment of *sādhana* of *śama*, etc. ; *kā* – what (is)?

śamaḥ – inner peace; *damaḥ* – control of the external organs; *uparamaḥ* – observance of one's own duties; *titikṣā* – endurance; *śraddhā* – faith (trust;) *samādhānam ca* – and single-pointedness; *iti* – thus.

What is the (six-fold) accomplishment of *sādhana* of *śama*, etc.?

(They are) inner peace, control of the external organs, observance of one's own duties, endurance, faith (trust) ; and single-pointedness.

In the four-fold qualification, the third is *śamādi-ṣaṭka-sampattiḥ*, which consists of six, *ṣaṭka*. He is going to tell the six-fold accomplishment that makes one equipped for *mokṣa*.

First, he tells us just the names – *śamaḥ, damaḥ, uparamaḥ, titikṣā, śraddhā, samādhānam ca iti. Iti* means thus. These six are called *ṣaṭka-sampattiḥ*. He explains them one by one.

Śama

शमः कः ?
मनोनिग्रहः ।

śamaḥ kaḥ?
mano nigrahaḥ

śamaḥ – *śama*; *kaḥ* – what (is)?
mano-nigrahaḥ – resolution of the mind (is *śama*).

What is *śama*?
Resolution of the mind (is *śama*).

What does *mano-nigrahaḥ* mean? They will generally translate this as mind control or mind destruction, as though the mind needs to be destroyed. Anyone who wants mind destruction is already destroyed, otherwise, why should one need that? One's whole thinking is destroyed, so one wants to get rid of the mind. Mind baiting is the biggest thing in the world; it is big business too.

If I say, "The mind is turbulent," people will nod their heads, "Ah! You said it."

"Nobody can easily control the mind."

"That is true."

"You have to work hard to control the mind."

"That is true, I have to work hard."

"Even if you have worked hard, and you think that you have controlled it, it just goes away."

"That is true."

Everything looks so true, which is why mind control is a billion dollar business.

The mind is the most beautiful instrument that every human being has. Even every animal has. A police man takes the help of a dog. That dog is the sleuth and not the police. Consider a bat. It can fly in the night. People think it is able to see in the dark, but it does not see anything. It just goes on squeaking and sending out sounds that rebound. It is able to interpret those sounds and detect an obstruction while in flight, and guide its way. It is all sonar. It can detect sounds that signal whether it is a leaf or a fruit. And it can also distinguish whether a piece of fruit is ripe, and go after what it chooses. Animals are better equipped than we are, in so many ways. The only thing that makes the human special is the mind that makes one self aware. It is a great endowment for a human being. It has to be used; it is meant for use. Therefore, you need to pay attention to your mind. It cannot be taken for granted, nor should it be looked upon as something that causes problems.

Mainly, the mind is meant for knowing, remembering and also to entertain emotions. It is the seat of emotion and knowledge as well. So, there is an emotional mind, a cognitive mind, and also a recollecting mind. Because it is instrumental in knowing, it is called *karaṇa*, an instrument, *antaḥ-karaṇa*, inner instrument. It is necessary for knowing; without the mind you cannot know. The eyes are also a *karaṇa*, a sense organ, which enable you to see colours and forms, and so too, the ears are a *karaṇa*. But the eyes, ears and other senses cannot function by themselves without being backed by the mind. Therefore, the mind is also looked upon as a *karaṇa,* a means. You are able recognise something only with the help of the mind.

Now, let us look into this mind. What is it that really bothers a person? Really speaking, it is the person that is bothered and not the mind. In this, the mind seems to play a role in creating certain emotions such as fear, anger and so on. But, fear is for the person, and not for the mind. It is the person who is afraid, who is anxious, who is angry. And there are also emotions like love, compassion, empathy, and so on. These emotions also manifest in the mind, and they only reveal the person. Compassion reveals the compassionate person. The emotion 'compassion' is for the person who is compassionate. Here, you always include the person, otherwise the mind will become the whipping boy for all your problems. It is the person viewed from the standpoint of the mind. Whenever the *śāstra* deals with the mind, it actually deals with the person with reference to the mind. Because you are compassionate, loving, there is compassion and love. It is not that because there is love you become loving or there is fear you are frightened. It is, rather, because you are frightened there is fear, because you are agitated, there is agitation, because you are anxious, there is anxiety, and because you are hateful, therefore there is hatred.

However, you tend to separate the mind from yourself and whip it unnecessarily. You are what you are, again, because of certain laws. When you talk about the mind you need to be responsible, otherwise you may create problems for others. It is very easy to conclude, "My mind is no good at all." There is no bad mind. The mind is always good; it does everything for you. If you are anxious, it presents anxiety for you, but that does not mean the mind is bad. It is not that your mind is something special that gives you anxiety. You are the person, the affected person, and the mind gives you an indication that you need to pay certain attention. This paying attention is called *śama*.

You need to learn to deal with the situations that the mind reveals, like anxiety, depression, anger, especially an anger that is not warranted at all. The situation does not deserve such an anger, so if it is there, you must understand that it is the person, the already angry person, who manifests in the form of anger. But it is the mind that tells you exactly what is going on, which is why the mind is pointed out in *mano nigraha*. The mind, and not the person, is pointed out, because through the mind alone you understand the person. You have varieties of emotions that are not liked by you, or by anyone. You do not like yourself being angry, anxious, frightened, and so on. But then, you are. So, how do you gain a resolution of this?

There are so many methods. People follow various means, but one thing that is common in all of them is that you have to accept the emotion. If you are frightened, you need to accept that you are frightened. The thinking, "I should not be frightened, or should not have been frightened," is not going to help you. They only confuse the whole situation. And such confusions are promoted in the spiritual world by people and books.

At the same time, you do need a mind that is more or less abiding, a mind that is available for your understanding, for your pursuits, for your contemplation. This availability is exactly what is said here. Otherwise, there is no necessity to specify all this. When you apply for admission to a school, they do not ask, "Do you have *śama*, do you have *dama*?" They just ask you, in effect, "Are you ready for this?" If you have done your B.Sc., then you can join the M.Sc. programme; that is all. This is *adhikṛtasya adhikāraḥ*. If you have completed your under-graduate studies, then you can do the post-graduate studies. It is so simple. They do not ask for anything else, like *śama, dama,* and so on.

Here, however, the subject matter is 'you'. Understand the difference. The subject matter of Vedanta is 'you,' and you have to deal with yourself. The emotional person is a very important person. You cannot bypass emotion. You cannot bypass anything – the world, your body, your mind. Even a bypass road does not bypass the reality of the traffic congestion in the other road. In heart surgery there is a bypass, because bypassing is dealing with a problem. You are not bypassing the problem; you are bypassing to solve the problem.

In listing the things that you cannot bypass, the author of *Tattvabodha* only points out the qualifications of *śama* and so on, but does not tell what are the things that will give you the qualifications. Those you have to discover in your study of the *Gītā*, etc. One thing I can say here is that *śama* is resolution of the mind. Resolution of the mind does not mean the mind becomes like a blank paper. Rather, the mind is just available for you. When you sit in contemplation it is available for you. When you study it is available for you. And when you are sitting and listening to me, it is available for you. When it is available for you like this, why do you bother about the mind? The mind is serving you. It is available for you, cognitively. Sometimes, the mind looks like it disturbs you, but, in fact, it is already a disturbed mind, and it wants to get rid of the disturbance – the old disturbance. So, it comes in the form of the disturbance that needs to be released. It comes in the form of fear that was locked up underneath, and that fear gets released. You need to understand such situations very clearly. You can now look at that as fear released, rather than fear gained. You can look at it as an anxiety released, rather than an anxiety gained. You can look at it either way, but if you look at anxiety as a new gain, then you are going to conclude that you are anxious, and nothing is happening. In fact, nothing needs to happen; let the old anxiety go, let the old pain go, old hatred, jealousy, whatever is there underneath, let it all go. They are more going than coming, especially when you are addressing the problem. Here, when you do not bypass, you are looking at yourself because you are the prime subject matter in the study of Vedanta. Naturally, whatever is there will come out.

The more you are able to look at all of it with a sense of surrender, the better. Surrender to what? Surrender to the order, which includes psychology. That order is Īśvara, as we will see later. So, through prayers, meditation, *japa*, duties, and anything that is necessary to nourish yourself, you take care of the mind.

Śama, then, is the availability of the mind for you to proceed, *śamaḥ mano nigrahaḥ*. It is mental time. Physical time may be available but not mental time. If mental time is available, then physical time will always accommodate that. Mental time is something that is not usually available for people, because the mind is too busy. And so, resolution of the mind, *śama*, is taken here as a qualification.

This is where the religious life comes in. Originally, in a structured religious life, this was easier. One who has a religious life finds a bonding with Īśvara, and that person can relax. Thereby, the person finds certain resolution. It is purely by devotion, by bonding with Īśvara, which will be analysed later. This is a very responsible topic, a topic that needs to be sensitively dealt with and understood properly.

Dama

दमः कः ?
चक्षुरादिबाह्येन्द्रियनिग्रहः ।

damaḥ kaḥ?
cakṣurādi-bāhyendriya-nigrahaḥ.

damaḥ – *dama; kaḥ* – what is?
cakṣurādi-bāhyendriya-nigrahaḥ – control of/mastery over the external organs such as eyes etc.

What is *dama*?
(It is) the control of/mastery over external organs such as eyes etc.

Cakṣu means eyes, and by adding *ādi,* he includes not only the eyes, but other sense organs as well. *Bāhyendriya* are external which are both organs of sense perception and of action. With reference to them, there is restraint, *nigraha*. This is *dama*.

Suppose *śama* is lacking; one is angry. The anger shows there is no *śama*, but 'I am angry' is a fact. This anger can express itself, and when it does, it is not going to be very pleasant, especially for the other person, the object of anger. That person is not going to be given a bouquet of flowers. In anger, even if one gives flowers, one throws them at the person, and it becomes another way of assaulting him or her. Anger is not going to be pleasant in its expression, and in anger one cannot be expected to be reasonable. This is so because the rational being is often overwhelmed by the emotional person, especially if the emotion is anger. So, what can one do?

This is something you can practice. When you feel angry you have the right to terminate a conversation. You need to know that you have a right to terminate a conversation. And if the other person is angry, you can point it out and say that you will talk later. You have the right to do that; it is called drawing boundaries. Drawing boundaries does not mean confining yourself to a living space, but placing limits on situations such as this – pointing out to the person, "You are angry now, so why don't we talk later?" If the person says, "No, I want to talk about it now," you just say, "No, let us talk later," and walk away, without hurting further. This is *dama*. Of course, this is the thing you have to develop. You need to discover in yourself certain space which gives you the freedom to stop a conversation that is getting worse because of your anger. You can say, "I am angry and I will talk about it later." If you can do this, you have already learnt how to manage anger. This is drawing a boundary for yourself and for others. "I will talk to you later" is *dama*. At that level, the physical manifestation, the level of talking, you pull down the shutters, *bāhyendriya-nigraha*. It is clean.

But then what about *śama*? How do you arrive at that now? The anger is already there, and has to be expressed appropriately. The inappropriate expression is avoided by saying, "We will talk later," but anger has already happened, and if it is not resolved, there is no *śama*. At every stage *śama* has to be gained. That resolution, *upaśama*, you have to arrive at. And how do you arrive at it? Anger has already happened and has to be resolved; the resolution of anger is only by expression, not by any other means. By saying that you should not have got angry, or that you should not get angry, nothing will be resolved. Now that the anger is there, how do you resolve it? You need to have *śama*.

Dama and *śama* are very significant words. *Dama* is an external expression in which anger is restrained, and *śama* is what you arrive at by the appropriate expression of that anger. What is appropriate expression? It means that nobody is hurt, except a towel! You take a wet towel, wet because it will make a sound, and then beat the floor. And tell your friend in the next room, "When you hear some abnormal sounds, do not be afraid. In fact, you are spared!" This is one form of appropriate expression. Or, just go to the wilderness somewhere, where nobody is around, and shout. Use your language and bring all the words that are inside, out. Who hears them? The wind, the sun, the trees; let them all hear. That is how you scream your anger out. Or write down all that you have to write – what you would have done, what you would have said, write all of it; tear the papers into pieces and throw them away. Or, if there is any sympathetic person, talk to that person. In fact, after doing all this, you had better talk. This is how you get *śama*. Here, you do not require advice but understanding. The more you understand, the easier it is for you to deal with all this. Let this not be taken as advice. I am not giving advice. Just understand how *dama* is important and how *śama* can be arrived at. If *śama* is there, you do not require *dama*. Only when *śama* is missing, is *dama* required, which is why *dama* is mentioned after *śama*. *Dama* is appropriate behavior and *śama* is whatever insight you have, and the resolution of your response to the situation that required *dama*. Prayer can also be made use of.

Uparama

> उपरमः कः ?
> स्वधर्मानुष्ठानमेव ।
>
> *uparamaḥ kaḥ?*
> *svadharmānuṣṭhānameva.*

uparamaḥ kaḥ – what is *uparama*?
svadharma-anuṣṭhānam eva – the very observance of one's own (*dharma*) duties.

What is *uparama*?
(It is) the very observance of one's own (*dharma*) duties.

Svadharma-anuṣṭhānam eva uparamaḥ. This is a very interesting meaning. *Uparama* is getting back to yourself. There is a tendency to omit what you have to do, and do what you need not do. This is the tendency that everybody has. A withdrawal from that, and doing what is to be done is *uparama, svadharma-anuṣṭhānam eva*. *Svadharma, sva* means one's own, and *dharma*, here, is what is to be done. What is to be done is to be done. You cannot say, "I do not feel like doing it," and not do it. It is abuse of freedom. Even though you do not feel like it, sometimes it has to be done. What is to be done, you do, even though you do not feel like doing it, and what is not to be done, even if you feel like doing it, you do not. This is *uparama*.

Uparama is also translated as *sannyāsa*, renunciation. Taking to a life of renunciation for a dedicated pursuit of this knowledge is *uparama*. In fact, this is a more suitable meaning for all of us. But here, he says it is *svadharma-anuṣṭhānam eva*, whatever is your *dharma*, to be done at a given place, in a given situation, that you do, whether you like it.

This is how you gain certain mastery over your likes and dislikes. Otherwise they dictate your behaviour all the time, and that is a meaningless life, really speaking. As long as they conform to *dharma*, they are fine. If what is to be done conforms to *dharma*, it is good for you, and you like it, you do it; in fact, you will be spontaneous. It is something like a doctor telling you that every day you must eat an apple, and you love apples. When you love apples, and somebody advises you to eat an apple daily, you can enjoy that; there is no conflict. But if you are told to take bittergourd juice every day, then you have to take it, even though you do not like it, and I do not think anybody will ever like it. Yet, you take it because it has to be taken. So, what you like is not going to be what is to be done every time, and what you do not like is not what is not to be done every time. What do you do? If you go by what you like and do not like, you will become a derelict. What is to be done you do, and what is not to be done, you avoid. This becomes *uparama*. It avoids conflicts, gives you a sense of satisfaction, and also a sense of success about yourself as a person, because you can deny yourself something you want. That is amazing. It makes you feel good, and therefore, you have a good day.

In America it is very common to say, "Have a good day." Each one has his or her idea of a good day. According to one, attending a music concert in the evening is a good day. A pick-pocket can also say, "Have a good day." What does 'Have a good day' mean? I will say that a good day is a day at the end of which, when you go to bed, you feel good. Why? Because you were able to avoid certain things which you wanted to do, but were not to be done, and you could do things that were to be done, even though you did not want to. Avoiding something that you have to, even though you feel like doing it, really makes you feel good. That capacity makes you feel good; you feel you are the master. You have reorganised your inner life and have a sense of, 'I am in charge,' which is very good.

Uparama is being in charge of your life. Then there is so much you can do, really. When you are in charge, you can help others too. Otherwise, others have to take care of you. And you are in charge when you are able to do what is to be done, *svadharma-anuṣṭhānam eva.*

Titikṣā

तितिक्षा का ?

शीतोष्णसुखदुःखादिसहिष्णुत्वम् ।

titikṣā kā?
śītoṣṇa-sukha-duḥkhādi-sahiṣṇutvam.

titikṣā kā – what is *titikṣā*?

śīta – cold; *uṣṇa* – heat; *sukha* – pleasure; *duḥkha* – pain; *ādi* – etc.; *sahiṣṇutvam* – endurance.

What is *titikṣā*? (It is) endurance of cold, heat, pleasure, pain, etc.

Sahiṣṇutva is the capacity to cheerfully, if not happily, put up with difficult situations. Why cheerfully? Because 'putting up with' is not enough. Whether you like it, putting up with something is always going to be there. Suppose the hot season has just begun, and it will get hotter in a couple of months. People will say, "Oh, it's hot, it's so hot." And if someone says that you have to put up with the heat, well, you have to put up with the heat. What can you do? If it is cold, you can wrap yourself up so that only your nose is exposed.

What is said here is that cold and heat you have to deal with – putting up with them is not exactly what is said. Cheerfully putting up with them is what is required. And that is possible. You have to learn how to put an end to this emotional sweating and shivering. Constant complaining will only increase the discomfort.

Instead, you say, "Yes this is how it is, period." It is different. Suppose there is pain. You can create further pain by what I call 'lumping'. It is like this. One person goes to the doctor and says,

"I am in great pain."

The doctor asks, "What kind of pain?"

"Oh, I have body pain."

"Is the whole body aching?"

"No, no, the whole body is not aching, it is my leg."

"Your legs are aching? "

"No, not the legs, the knee."

"Oh, the knees; both the knees are aching?"

"No, only the left knee."

Then with his hammer he goes on checking. He knows when you respond, where the pain is.

"Here?"

"There is no pain."

"Here?"

"There is no pain."

"In the centre?"

"Yes, somewhere there is the pain."

"Here there is pain?"

"Ah, yes, there is the pain."

Why do you say, "I am in pain?" Why this lumping? If you lump things together like this, you cannot have *titikṣā*. When you don't lump, you will have *titikṣā*. It is that simple. You cheerfully face an unpleasant situation, and for this, naturally, you have to learn how to avoid lumping. It is like trouble shooting.

When there is trouble, the problem has to be identified first, and then solved. Suppose, in a business there is a loss, they try to find out what is the problem, and where is the loophole. Then they find out one or two areas where there is leakage of funds, and block them. Otherwise they will be saying, 'I am losing, I am losing,' without knowing what is going on. So, you zoom in on the whole thing and do not lump anything. Yes, it is hot, but then again, it is not always hot. It is hot between twelve and three o'clock, try to avoid going out at this time; it is easy. You only have to deal with these three hours, which is easier than the generalised situation, 'It is hot, it is hot.' Nothing is difficult when you do not lump things. Certain areas are difficult; who says they are not. But then, if you pinpoint the area, if you are able to discern the area of difficulty, then you can deal with it. When you just acknowledge and act accordingly, *titikṣā* becomes easy.

When certain things are inevitable, what can you do? You accept it. When you accept, you acknowledge that this is how it is, and do what you can. Accepting does not mean that you should not do anything about it, if you can. You acknowledge it and then do what is to be done. You find there is certain cheerfulness, so you do not go about complaining all the time.

These are attitudes that make life simple. You need to simplify your living, otherwise it becomes more and more complex. Simple living does not mean you should live on a shoestring, but if it is okay for you, that may also be part of your lifestyle. Here, simple living is a life without complexities. You know the area where there is a problem, and where you have to be guarded. You guard and cheerfully put up with the inevitable, unpleasant situation.

It is said elsewhere, '*sahanaṁ sarvaduḥkānām apratīkārapūrvakaṁ cintāvilāparahitaṁ sā titikṣā nigadyate.*' *Sahanam*, putting up with, *sarvaduḥkānām*, all unpleasant situations. How? *Cintāvilāparahitam*, without anxiety, worry and complaining. Further, *apratīkārapūrvakam*, accepting gracefully what cannot be changed. Where people are involved, and you cannot change them, you give them the freedom to be what they are, and draw boundaries to take care of yourself. That is *titikṣā, sā titikṣā nigadyate.* That is how *titikṣā* is defined in the *śāstra* and this we can learn.

Śraddhā

श्रद्धा कीदृशी ?
गुरुवेदान्तवाक्येषुविश्वासः श्रद्धा ।

śraddhā kīdṛśī?
guruvedantavākyeṣu viśvāsaḥ śraddhā.

śraddhā – *śraddhā*; *kīdṛśī* – of what nature? *guru-vedānta-vākyeṣu* – in the words of the teacher and Vedanta; *viśvāsaḥ* – trust; *śraddhā* – (is) *śraddhā*.

> Of what nature is *śraddhā*? Trust in the words of the teacher and Vedanta is *sraddhā*.

Viśvāsa is trust, faith, in the words of Vedanta, *vedānta-vākyeṣu*. What is that trust here? That they are a *pramāṇa*, a means of knowledge. You give the status of *pramāṇa* to the words of Vedanta. You do not look at them as theory, speculation or philosophy, but take them as words that are an independent means of knowledge. That is called *viśvāsa.* If it is philosophy, you do not need *śraddhā,* but because these words are supposed to fulfill a purpose, naturally, you do require *śraddhā*. Like when you take Ayurvedic medicine, there is *śraddhā,* because you do not know what it is going to do. A promise is held out. Many people have taken this before and it has worked for all of them. If it has worked for all of them, there is no reason why it should not work for you. The advantage in Ayurveda is that you do not know the risks. There are no contraindications mentioned anywhere, so you take it with *śraddhā.* You get up in the morning and find that you are better. But it can prove itself otherwise. Unless it proves itself otherwise, there is faith, *śraddhā,* that it will work, and it is verifiable. However, that faith is different.

Here, it is *śraddhā* in a *pramāṇa,* which is more than verifiable; it is just you. Who you are – for this, it is a *pramāṇa.* It has to reveal itself. And therefore, it is more than *śraddhā,* really. It is surrender to the *pramāṇa* so that the *pramāṇa* can operate; that is how it presents itself. *Ātman* is to be understood by Vedanta. Vedanta is the *pramāṇa,* and Vedanta itself tells us this. What is already there, it is supposed to reveal, and you have nothing against it. This is *śraddhā.*

Śraddhā is in the attitude towards the *śāstra* – that it is true, it is a *pramāṇa.* If it is regarded as speculation, we do not have *satya-buddhi,* 'this is true.' Only with *satya-buddhi,* it becomes a *pramāṇa.* Suppose I hold up a flower and say, "This is a rabbit." When I say this, you have no *satya-buddhi* in my words. You have *satya-buddhi* in your eyes. What your eyes see is true, not what the Swami says. Why? Because what your eyes see, that sight, cannot be denied. Your whole soul, *ahaṅkāra*, ego, everything is at the altar of your eyes. So, the *satya-buddhi* is only in the *pramāṇa*, your eyes.

So too, when the words of the *śāstra* tell that you are the whole, *tat tvam asi*, it is a *pramāṇa* for you because you have *satya-buddhi* in those words. Even though you have every reason to believe that it is not true, in your question – "How can I be the whole?"– you can dismiss the whole thing, or mean, "I think I do not understand this." You give the benefit of doubt to the *śāstra*, and you enquire. When I say that you are not only the whole, you are the centre of the entire creation, *jagat*, it is a statement which is not going to be understood as it is said. It requires analysis leading to understanding, because it is an equation.

An equation is never understood just by seeing it. It is understood only when you enquire into both sides of it. The equation, which is Vedanta, is – '*tat tvam asi*, you are that.' *Tvam*, you, is one side of the equation, and *tat*, that, is the other side. *Tat* means 'that' the cause of the entire world, *jagat-kāraṇam*, Īśvara, the Lord. Now the individual, *jīva*, who is ignorant, who is of limited knowledge and limited power, is equated to Īśvara, and therefore, this equation is not tenable. But at the same time, the *śāstra* makes an equation about you.

So, you need to look into your own notion about yourself to determine whether it is true. You need to know what is Īśvara, what is the reality, etc. When you look into all this thoroughly, it becomes clear to you. Until then, you have *śraddhā*, pending understanding, in the *śāstra*.

Vedānta-vākya is taken to be true. Even though it does not seem to be true for you, you accept that the meaning is true, and you enquire and discover that. This is *śraddhā*. When there is a doubt, you do not dismiss the *śāstra*, you question your understanding. This is what you gain through *śraddhā*. If you dismiss the *śāstra*, "Oh, it says things that are not true," it is not *śraddhā*. The *śāstra* says deliberately, "You are the whole," knowing full well that you are a limited being, with a limited body, mind, and so on. All these limitations are accepted by the *śāstra*; otherwise it would not even talk to you. Why should it? Unless there is an apparent difference, there is no necessity for an equation. An equation is necessary only when there is an apparent difference, and the difference is obvious, while the non-difference is not. The non-difference is what is being unfolded. Therefore, you give the benefit of doubt to the *śāstra* and then enquire. This is called *vedānta-vākyeṣu śraddhā*.

Śraddhā is also extended to *veda-vākya*s in general. They talk about what is beyond your reason, so you have nothing against that, and therefore, have *śraddhā*. Even though you are not interested in heaven, you cannot dismiss it either. What is said by the *śāstra* is accepted as true. The whole Veda is looked upon as a *pramāṇa*. And also, in what the Vedanta teacher says, *guru-vākyeṣu*.

Guru-vākya is also important, because the *śāstra* has to be handled. The whole thing is a method, and it is held by *sampradāya*, the tradition. This tradition holds the key to unlocking the meaning of the *śāstra*, and therefore, the words of the *guru* also become important. Sometimes a custom-made approach to the subject matter is required, based on who is the student. You have to find out where the student is and take off from there. You do not take off from where the *śāstra* is, but from where the student is. So, what is not said by the *śāstra* may be said by the *guru*. For the time being, the *guru* may tell the student to follow certain *sādhana*, means, which is necessary to prepare oneself. To help the student gain a mind that is conducive for this knowledge, the *guru* may add a few things that may not be there in the *śāstra* at all. Knowing the student, he will know that it may be necessary, at this time, in this place, etc., understanding all the contributing factors to the student's mind. The ancient student had his or her own problems, and the modern student also has his or her own problems. But one thing is consistent – the mind is typical. Whatever the problems are, they have to be taken into account, to gain the preparedness, *adhikāritva*.

There is not much discussion on psychology in our *śāstra*. It only talks about simple *rāga-dveṣa* psychology; you learn to manage likes and dislikes and you will be okay. But things are not that simple, they are complex. The human mind is complex, so we have to address that too. The modern teacher has to take into account the factors that contribute to the complexity of the mind. Naturally, therefore, there may be a statement from the teacher that may not be found at all in the *vedānta-śāstra*. But it does not mean you dismiss it – so long as the main vision is unfolded and the teacher is a *sampradāyavit*, who knows the tradition of teaching. He knows not only the meaning of the teaching, but the tradition of teaching, and the method of communicating it to another person. Those who do not have the tradition always commit mistakes in their statements, and people do not grasp exactly what they say. They say one thing, and what happens in the mind of the listener is entirely different.

A *sampradāyavit* is one who has the key. So in the *guru-vākya*, in the words of the teacher, also, you have *śraddhā*.

Śraddhā means trust. This is a must because knowledge is gained only by the person who has *śraddhā* – *śraddhāvan labhate jñānam*.[5] And this *śraddhā* is entirely different from the *śraddhā* in a non-verifiable belief, like one will go to heaven. If this non-verifiable belief is the goal of a religious theology, there is no wonder that the religion is called faith.

Now, when the *guru* teaches, 'You are the whole,' you do not have any reason to disbelieve. Let us help ourselves to understand this with the 'tenth man story'. It is a story to be said here. Ten *śiṣya*s, disciples, of a *guru*, decided to go on a pilgrimage. The *guru* could not accompany, so the leader of this group of ten said, "You need not come, sir; I will take them."

"Will you?"

"Yes sir. I will take care of them. I will bring them back safe."

"Okay, be careful," the *guru* said.

These ten students have come from ten different families, and the *guru* is responsible for all of them.

---

[5] *Bhagavadgītā* 4.39

So, the ten of them start on this pilgrimage. On the way there was a small river which everybody could swim across. They swam and reached the other bank. Of course, the leader of the group, who is a responsible person, counted all of them – one, two, three, four, five, six, seven, eight, nine... "Where is the tenth man? Where is the tenth man? The tenth man is gone!" He thought he had counted wrongly, so again he counted, and again he got nine. One from the group said that he should group them and then count, so he tried eight plus one, seven plus two, six plus three, five plus four, but got nine each time. Naturally, the leader was alarmed. He cannot proceed with the pilgrimage. How can he go on without the tenth? And he cannot find this tenth man. Though he searched all over, there was no trace of the tenth man. Each one of them sat under a tree, sad as even the leader who was trying to figure out who is the missing tenth man. The tenth man is missing, but who is he? He cannot even remember his face. He tries to objectify the tenth man, but he cannot. So, this tenth man is gone, *daśamo naṣṭaḥ*. All of them were brooding over the loss of the tenth man. Then, an old man who had seen them singing and whistling, as they were coming, saw them now, all sad, sitting there under trees.

"What happened?" he asked the leader who was the nearest.

"We were ten, sir, now we are nine," said the leader. "One man is gone. We should have taken the boat, but we swam and this is what happened. One person is gone."

"Were you ten?"

"Yes, sir, we were ten." All of them have now gathered around the old man.

"You say you are nine?"

"Yes, sir, we are nine."

"Listen," he said, "the tenth man exists."

Now, 'the tenth man exists' can be a statement of some assurance, 'the tenth man exists in heaven; I see with my bionic eyes that he is there in heaven.'

"That does not really solve my problem, said the leader, "how am I going to answer my teacher?" so he asked, "Where? Where is he?"

"Here," said the old man.

"Here? The tenth man is here? Do you see him?"

"Yes I see him."

"Oh! Oh! Will you call him?"

"Yes. I will call him."

"When?"

"Now."

"Oh! Now?"

The group had a relief. From what? From the sadness of losing the tenth man. What is the relief? The tenth man exists. The old man does not say that later he will produce the tenth man. It would mean an investment of your emotions, of your life, of many things. He says, "The tenth man is here, now, and I will show him to you."

'Now, here' means there is no reason for any of them to disbelieve his words, because there is no promise held out. There is no future involved here. 'Now, here' implies only a method of discovery; he is going to call the tenth man. Let him call; there is no reason for disbelief. This is *śraddhā,* a peculiar *śraddhā.* You allow the old man to call the tenth man, to show you the tenth man. Your allowing him is called *āstikya-buddhi,* the attitude that the tenth man is around, and you are going to see him. This *buddhi* itself removes the sadness which was there in the loss of the tenth man. He was irretrievably lost, now he is not lost; he exists.

"But do you know the tenth man? Have you seen the tenth man?" "Not yet." The old man is going to show him now, here. Here no traveling is necessary, no treading the path, no *bhakti-yoga, karma-yoga,* etc. The old man is going to show the tenth man right now. The joy which will be there in the wake of the tenth man's sight is not yet born, but the sorrow that was there, because of the loss of the tenth man, has gone. There is no irretrievable loss now; there is *śraddhā,* trust, belief. Let us use the word '*śraddhā*' because 'belief' and 'trust' do not quite capture the meaning. "The tenth man exists, but I still have to see him," is *śraddhā, guru-vākyeṣu śraddhā*. And this *śraddhā* itself brings about a relief.

So too, you have been searching in order to be free from being small, and someone says, 'You are.' That itself is enough. You have found more than an assurance because the *śāstra* tells, "You are the whole." There is no reason to disbelieve that, so you allow the *śāstra* to show it to you. Like the old man is allowed to show the tenth man. And he follows a method, a very interesting method.

He asked all of them to line up, and all of them lined up. This is not obedience. Because they want to find out, they are ready to follow any method. They are ready to go through the whole process. After they had all lined up, the old man called the leader and asked him to count them. One, two, three, four, five, six, seven, eight, nine. The tenth man is not there. In fact, he did not want to count again, because he had counted so many times; that 'nine' is the most irritating number for him now. Even though he did not want to count, he still followed the method and counted, "One, two, three, four, five, six, seven, eight, nine. The tenth man is missing, *daśamo naṣṭaḥ*." Then the old man said, "That tenth man you are, *tat tvam asi*."

The leader got enlightened. But at the same time, he cannot say, 'Eureka!' like Archimedes. In fact, the tenth man cannot even talk about his story. He is humbled, really. Why? Because, he has realised. Realised what? "I have been a fool." This is the realisation. There is no other realisation. The man who was seeking the tenth man happens to be the sought tenth man. And the moment he seeks him, in the very seeking there is a denial of the tenth man. He has to stop seeking. But if he stops seeking, he will not find the tenth man. And if he seeks, he will not find the tenth man. What a situation! Therefore, deliver yourself to the hands of the old man, when you are in such a helpless situation.

What is intelligent living? Seeking help when you are helpless. This is a helpless situation, and seeking help is the intelligent thing to do. If you can help yourself, do so. When you cannot help yourself, seek help. Seeking help is an intelligent approach; you know this very well. And we may have to seek help. That is why we have prayer, etc., which is seeking help. Here, since you are both the seeker and the sought, naturally, you require some help in the form of someone to point out what you are. At least, in the tenth man story you may come across 'yourself' because it is your body. But if it is the owner of the body, the knower of everything, who is hidden in the knower as the one to be known, well, there is no way of coming across that person accidentally. No way.

What is to be known is hidden in the knower, and therefore, you require a *pramāṇa*. *Jñeya*, what is to be known, is the nature, *svarūpa*, of the knower, *jñātā*. And what is to be known is hidden in that very knower. The knower is good enough for knowing the world. Employing his perception, enhancing his perception by instrumentation, and also inferring with the backing of all his education, the knower is adequately equipped to know the world. But to know himself, he is not equipped at all. This much he has to know. Only then he can seek help from outside, and the outside help here is the *pramāṇa*. That is the *śāstra*, which is to be handled. Medicine cures but do not self-medicate; go to a specialist. Similarly here, even if one is a *śāstrajña*, someone who knows the language, etc., and can read the *śāstra*, that is not enough. Language is a necessity, but mere language will not help the person; one has to go to a teacher. One has to seek help here, and when one seeks help, one must have *śraddhā* in the source of help.

Here, it is to be seen right away. This is the safest place where you can have *śraddhā*. There is no way of it not working, because it is just talking about you, the self-evident you, being free. All your notions are falsified and their falsity is not difficult for anyone to see through; and what is said, stays. So, it is a different type of *śraddhā*. It is like the *śraddhā* in the words of the old man who said, "I will show you the tenth man now, here." When he is showing what is now, here, he does not produce anything; he only has to follow a method.

Neither by time you are away from being the whole, nor in terms of place are you away from being the whole. Then what is it that denies your being the whole? Only a method has to be followed to take care of that. That is all. Therefore, *śraddhā* in the words of the *guru* and Vedanta is required, *guru-vedānta-vākyeṣu viśvāsaḥ, śraddhā*.

Samādhāna

> समाधानं किम् ?
> चित्तैकाग्रता ।
>
> *samādhānaṁ kim?*
> *cittaikāgratā.*

samādhānam – *samādhāna; kim* – what (is)?
citta-ekāgratā – focusing the mind on one thing.

> What is *samādhāna*?
> (It is) focusing the mind on one thing.

Samādhāna is *citta-ekāgratā*. Right in front of you, *agre*, there is only one thing, *eka*. This is *ekāgra*, and *ekāgratā* is the abstract noun. The meaning of *samādhāna* is the status of your mind, *citta*, focusing on one thing at a time, *citta-ekāgratā samādhāna*. It is an accomplishment for oneself. *Citta-ekāgratā* needs to be mentioned because people may have difficulty in keeping the mind in one track of thinking. To keep the mind in a particular track of thinking for a length of time is an accomplishment, because the mind moves. The mind's nature is to move; in fact it has got to, only then can you know things. When it moves, you need to have the capacity to bring it back. This is *samādhāna*.

Everyone has this *citta-ekāgratā,* capacity to keep the mind in a given track. People often tell me, "Swamiji, I have no concentration." It is a common thing. You may say, "I have no concentration because when I read the book, my mind goes all over the place." Which book? "Sanskrit book." Suppose you are reading about a topic that you like, or the book is a novel by an author you love. There, you find concentration. You will read the whole book in one day. From where do you get this concentration? You can understand that unless you have it, you cannot apply that concentration under any circumstances. So, in what you are interested, there is concentration. However, what you are interested in, and you have a value for it, cognitively, intellectually, you may find it is not compelling, emotionally. There is no hero, no drama. Sanskrit is *rāmaḥ, rāmau, rāmāḥ.* How did *rāmaḥ* become *rāmāḥ*? It is a problem. There are *sūtra*s for that, so you not only have to know *rāmāḥ,* you also have to know how it became *rāmāḥ.* But once you begin liking it, you have concentration, because there is an emotional satisfaction in it. That must be there. Everybody has concentration, unless there is some pathological problem. When somebody says, "You must have concentration," it is another form of manipulation. Everybody has concentration; it is a question of discovering the attraction for a topic. You have to discover that. Any topic, once you get involved in it and you begin to understand it properly, elicits concentration. So, no one can say that he or she has no concentration.

Still, someone can say, "Swamiji, if I have concentration, why, when I am chanting a *mantra*, does my mind move away? It goes all over." It is the mind's nature to go all over. It should not be stagnant. Otherwise you will not be able to know anything. The thought frame must be momentary, like the frames in a movie film, unlike a polaroid. It is momentary, so you do not see a single picture. It goes on taking pictures; that is how the mind perceives motion. It has to move. "The mind has to move, okay, but why should it not chant, when I want it to? When I am repeating something mentally, my mind moves away from what I am repeating."

Here is where meditation comes. Part of the definition of meditation is bringing the mind back to the object on which you are dwelling. So, nobody can really complain, "My mind moves away." Bring it back. Bringing it back is meditation. You can no longer say that the mind moves away, because you understand the logic. Moving away is natural, but if you do not bring it back, there is no meditation. Your attempt to bring it back is meditation. "Whenever the mind moves away you bring it back," is the advice given by Bhagavān in the *Bhagavadgītā* – *yato yato niścarati tatastato niyamyaitad.*[6] That is meditation. And the capacity to bring it back is *citta-ekāgratā samādhāna.*

Samādhāna can also be taken as a mind that is not interested in too many things, or in doing many things at the same time. Trying to do many things at the same time is so common that we even have a new word for it, 'multi-tasking.' It is a habit that is not helpful in this pursuit, so you need to have *samādhāna.* And also, too many irons in the fire is a problem. When there are too many things out there to do, you need *viveka* and *vairāgya,* as already mentioned. You have only one thing in front of you, and this is what you are seeking now. It is the main, predominant occupation. "This is what I want now, this is what I am doing now, at this time in my life." So what you are doing draws your attention, has you for the time being. Now, Vedanta has you, and Sanskrit too. Nothing else has you, because you are committed to them. This is *samādhāna.*

---

[6] 6.26

Mokṣa

मुमुक्षुत्वं किम् ?
मोक्षो मे भूयादितीच्छा ।

Mumukṣutvaṁ kim?
mokṣo me bhūyāditīcchā.

mumukṣutvam – *mumukṣutvam; kim* – what (is)?
mokṣaḥ – liberation (freedom); *me bhūyād*– may I have; *iti* – thus; *icchā* – a desire.

What is *mumukṣutvam*?
(It is) the desire, 'May I have liberation (freedom).'

Mumukṣu is the person who wants *mokṣa*, the one who wants to be free, *moktum icchuḥ*. He is the one who understands exactly what he wants in life; it is very clear to him. When the desire for freedom is the main, the predominant one, every other desire subserves it naturally; it is automatic. You need not do anything about it. It is *viveka*. The *viveka* is so complete that *mokṣa* becomes the main and everything else subserves it. Such a person is a *mumukṣu*, and the status of his mind is called *mumukṣutva*.

It is not just a desire for *mokṣa*. Even curiosity can give rise to a desire, but *mumukṣutva* is not one of the desires among the many. The whole mind is full of desires, and if one of them is *mokṣa,* now and then it gets some attention. This is where *viveka* is required, which is why he uses the word, '*mumukṣutva*' – it reveals that the whole person is convinced. A *mumukṣu* is very clear about what he or she wants in life. And this pursuit does not in any way stand opposed to any other pursuit either.

Mokṣa is not like anything else. Any other pursuit of the *mumukṣu* is also linked to the pursuit of *mokṣa.* A *mumukṣu* is someone who has undergone a change, like a devotee. When a devotee takes up a job, it is the devotee who is an officer. It is not that the officer displaces the devotee. The devotee is one who has discovered devotion to Īśvara, and therefore the devotee is going to be there in the officer, in the husband, in the wife, in whatever role he or she plays; the devotee is going to be always present. So too, is the *mumukṣu* and the *mumukṣutva,* disposition of his mind. *Mumukṣutva* is a desire, a longing, *icchā.* For what? 'May I gain *mokṣa, mokṣo me bhūyāt.*' It means you have to choose *mokṣa.* And the reason you have to choose is that you are already free, *mukta.* When you are already a liberated person, it is in the choice that the pursuit begins. You have to choose.

एतत् साधनचतुष्टयम् ।
ततस्तत्त्वविवेकस्याधिकारिणो भवन्ति ।

etad sādhana-catuṣṭayam
tatastattvavivekasyādhikāriṇo bhavanti.

etat – this (is); *sādhana-catuṣṭayam* – the four-fold means; *tataḥ* – thereafter (consequent to gaining these); *tattva-vivekasya* – for the discriminative knowledge of truth; *adhikāriṇaḥ* – qualified persons; *bhavanti* – they become.

This (is) the four-fold means. Thereafter, (consequent to gaining these) they become qualified persons for the discriminative knowledge of truth.

Etad sādhana-catuṣṭayam, this is the four-fold means – *viveka, vairāgya, śama, dama,* etc., and *mumukṣutva*. *Mumukṣutva* is mentioned separately because when *mumukṣtva* is there, and if anything is lacking in terms of other qualifications, you will get that. It is like wanting to do a Ph.D. You equip yourself with all that is necessary to earn the Ph.D., because that is your goal. It is the same here. *Mumukṣutva* is the main thing. A person can have *śama-dama* without being a *mumukṣu*. And there can be a *mumukṣu* without *śama, dama, uparama*, etc., but when *mumukṣutva* is the main, it takes care of other things. So, the one who has this four-fold qualification is an *adhikārin,* an eligible student. It is this eligibility on the part of the student that makes the *vedānta-pramāṇa* very fruitful.

The teaching of Vedanta, handled by a teacher, is fruitful in enlightening a person who has this four-fold qualification. No other aid is required. *Ātman* is always ready, and if you are also ready as a person with the required mind, then the *pramāṇa* will do its job. Like opening the eyes and seeing, the exposure to the teaching will make you free from ignorance of yourself. If these qualifications are lacking in any area, the knowledge can either be denied or inhibited. Knowledge happens, but at the same time, there is some inhibition and one does not enjoy the fruits of that knowledge. With the four-fold qualification uninhibited knowledge can take place, because *pramāṇa,* the means of knowledge, is there, and the object of knowledge is also there. The teaching of Vedanta being a *pramāṇa* is proved when the person has the eligibility. Then there is nothing that can deny that, so the *adhikārin* has to be pointed out. Otherwise, people will say, "I listened to Vedanta and I did not understand that I am Brahman, therefore, Vedanta is not a *pramāṇa*." This is not valid. It is like saying, "I do not understand calculus, therefore there is no calculus." That is why one has to be eligible. After gaining this four-fold qualification, they become *adhikārins*, eligible, qualified students, *tataḥ, tattvavivekasya adhikārinaḥ bhavanti.* Qualified for what? *Tattva-viveka*, discriminative understanding of what is true. The author himself has introduced *tattva-viveka*, and now he asks this question.

Understanding realities: satya and mithyā

तत्त्वविवेकः कः ?
आत्मा सत्यं तदन्यत् सर्वं मिथ्येति ॥

tattva-vivekaḥ kaḥ?
ātmā satyaṁ tadanyat sarvaṁ mithyeti.

tattva-vivekaḥ – the discriminative knowledge of truth; *kaḥ* – what (is)?

ātmā – *ātmā* (I); *satyam* – (is) the truth; *tadanyat* – other than that; *sarvam* – all else; *mithyā iti* – (is) *mithyā*, apparent.

What is the discriminative knowledge of truth?

Ātmā, (I) is the truth; all else other than that is *mithyā* (apparent).

First, there is discriminative analysis and, finally, understanding of *tattva*. The discriminative analysis leading to understanding is called *tattva-viveka*. The analysis should be such that it leads you to the *tattva*.

And what is the *tattva*? The self is *satya* and everything other than that is *mithyā*. We need to understand these two words – *satya* and *mithyā*. There is no object called *satya*. There is a flower, there is this desk, a book, the floor, a carpet; these are all objects. Like these, you do not see an object called *satya* in the world. You cannot say, "Please bring me *satya*." Nor is there is an object called *mithyā*. You know that there is water, there is a tree, a leaf, etc., but there is no such object called *mithyā*.

When *satya* and *mithyā* are not objects, what are these words? They are words that reveal not objects, but your understanding of objects. What is meant by understanding of objects? Let us understand a desk. I ask you, "Is the desk real, *satya*, or is it unreal, non-existent, *tuccha*?" It is real, an existent thing, because you can see it. It is not non-existent, *tuccha*. Thus, you say that the desk is *satya*, and when you say that, you are talking about the reality of the desk. When I ask you whether it is existent or non-existent, you say that it is existent. So, your understanding of the reality of the desk is in terms of whether it exists or not. What exists is real, *satya*, and what does not, is non-existent, *tuccha*. *Tuccha* does not refer to an object, but to the status of an object that does not exist, like the horn or the tail of a human being. They do not exist, and therefore we say that they are *tuccha*. The human being, however, is existent, and so we understand the human being as a reality, *satya*. Let us understand that these terms are ontological terms. If we want an English word for the nature of these two terms, *satya* and *mithyā*, we can help ourselves with this word 'ontological'. An ontological term refers to the reality of something, whether it exists or does not. Therefore, while there is a flower, and there is space, and things in space, there is no object called *satya*, distinct from everything else. The existing objects that you know, you consider them to be *satya*. There are things that do not exist, and you understand them as *tuccha*.

Now, I am asking if this desk is *satya*. Yes, it is a reality. Then what about the wood that this desk is made of? If the whole thing is a desk, where is the wood? Is it outside the desk? No. Is it inside the desk? No. Then where is this wood? Wood is another thing. 'Wood' is a word for which there is an object, and you understand what that object is. It is not steel, it is not aluminium, nor is it plastic; you understand what wood is. There is a cane chair and another one is plastic, but you know that this one is wood. Therefore, by the word 'wood' you are able to appreciate an object, which is unique, and which can be distinguished from other objects like plastic, aluminium, cane, etc. The word 'wood' has its own object.

We have the object that is known as wood and the object that is known as desk. But are there two objects? No. Suppose you weigh the desk and find that it is 40 pounds. Is 40 pounds the weight of the desk or the weight of the wood? Wood, is it not? If the weight of the wood is 40 pounds, then what is the weight of the desk? The desk has no weight at all; it is a weightless desk. What does it mean? If the weight belongs to the wood, and not to the desk, then what is desk? There cannot be a zero-weight desk. It should have some weight, but it has no weight at all. How are we to understand this?

We understand that the wood is the reality in this desk; there is no desk at all, really. But we cannot dismiss the desk completely. It is not a pile of wood, or some wooden pulp. It is a desk, it exists and it is useful. So, how should we look at the desk in terms of its reality? As *satya*? No. It cannot be *satya* because it has no existence of its own; it has zero weight, like a man's horn. The weight of a man's horn is zero, because it is non-existent, so, extending this, having zero weight means something is non-existent. But a tangible thing like desk must have some weight. It has no weight, yet, it is tangible. Therefore, the tangibility and the weight belong to wood. But there is something that accounts for this wood being called a desk, or a chair, or a table. So, we need to concede a reality to the desk. This reality is referred to by the word, '*mithyā*.'

What kind of reality is *mithyā*? What exists depending upon another thing is *mithyā*. There is no object called *mithyā*. It is your understanding of the reality of an object that is called *mithyā*; it is purely cognitive. *Mithyā* is a word in your cognition.

So, what is *tattva-viveka*? Understanding what is *satya*, what is *mithyā*.

I have a flower in my hand, is it real or not? It is real. Now, I ask you what this is. A petal. If I say that it is a flower, you will not accept that because it is a petal. I want to find out where the flower is. What is this one? A petal. And what is this one? A petal, not a flower. What is this one? This is also a petal, not a flower. Let us get to the heart of it. What is this? Stamen and pollen. Pollen is not flower, stamen is not flower. Then what is flower? Where did the flower go? It did not go anywhere. We could not even establish a flower in the first place, where is the question of it going? Unless a flower is there, it cannot go. We are questioning the 'is' of it, where is the question of going? Yet, we cannot accept that there is no flower. There is a flower. What kind of flower? *Mithyā* flower.

Now you can understand what is *mithyā*. What is put-together, depending upon various factors, is *mithyā*. When we say the flower is *mithyā,* we do not dismiss the flower. It cannot be dismissed as non-existent, but neither can it be taken as self-existent. From this it is clear that *mithyā* is not self-existent. Being not self-existent, it depends upon another existent thing. Suppose that existent thing also depends upon something else; then that is also *mithyā*. If that, in turn, depends upon something else, it too is *mithyā*. How?

Let us look at a shirt. There is no shirt, really speaking, if I take the fabric away. The shirt is just fabric. Since the shirt depends upon fabric, the shirt is *mithyā*. What is fabric? *Satya,* relatively. If I refer to this shirt as *mithyā,* then what the shirt depends on becomes *satya*. So here, the fabric is *satya,* and the shirt is *mithyā*. But is the fabric, *satya*? Is it self-existent? If something is *satya,* it should not depend upon something else; it should be self-existent. Do you understand what is self-existent now? Is the fabric self-existent? No. Why?

It depends upon yarn. The shirt is fabric, and the fabric is yarn, so now the yarn becomes *satya*, and the fabric becomes *mithyā*. Then again, there is no such thing as yarn. If you untwist the threads, the whole thing becomes fibers. Therefore, what is *satya*? There is no yarn without fibers, so fiber is *satya*. We will keep analysing it and say that the molecules are *satya,* then the atom is *satya,* the nucleus is *satya,* the particle is *satya*. What is *satya*? If there is something on which the particle depends, that becomes *satya*. What is self-existent alone is *satya,* and everything else is *mithyā*.

The self is *satya – ātmā satyam*.

To understand this, the logic we are going to use is more deductive than inductive, because an opening statement is made. *Śruti* has to tell us that *ātman* is *satya,* and the author of *Tattvabodha* paraphrases the *śruti* statement here as '*ātmā satyam.*' This is just an opening statement. *Ātman* is the one who experiences everything, and in whose presence alone all experiences take place; in other words, the meaning of the word 'I'. *Ātman* is another word for 'I'. Generally, 'I' is used as the first person singular, and expressed as *aham*. *Ātman* is third person, so it is equivalent to the word 'self'. When you say, 'self', it means 'I'. When you use the first person, you say 'I' and with the third person, you refer to the self, *ātman*, but it is the same thing. In Sanskrit, the self is called *ātman*. 'I' is *aham, ātman*, because 'I' is the self. And the *upaniṣad* tells us, *ātmā satyam*.

Now, we understand that what is *satya* is self-existent. And based on what we have seen, we can appreciate that *ātman* is self-existent. But what about other things? Are they not self-existent, independent of the *ātman*? No, *anyat sarvam*, everything else, other than *ātman*, is *mithyā*. It has to be understood as *mithyā*. This is *tattva-viveka*, a discriminative analysis, an enquiry leading to the understanding of the truth revealed by the *śruti*.

The self-existent *ātman* is *satya*. It is taken for something which is not self-existent. And what is self-existent, *ātman*, is not in our cognition at all. It is not understood. When the self-existent *ātman* is not understood, then what is understood as *ātman* is not self-existent. In other words, *mithyā* is understood as *satya* and *satya* is not understood at all. What does it mean? It means there is self-confusion.

The body is not *satya-ātman*.

What is it that you consider to be *ātman*, I? Generally, the orientation is 'I' and the world. You do not take the world and the objects as you. This much clarity you have. Let us start the enquiry from here, since you do not take the mountains as yourself, or even the clothes that you wear. But you take the body as you. If the body is *ātman*, I, then what does the body become in terms of reality? *Satya*; the body, being *ātman*, becomes *satya* because the statement is *ātmā satyam*. And it says further that everything other than that is *mithyā*. If the body is *satya*, then how 'everything else' is *mithyā*? If your body is *satya*, it means everybody's body is *satya*, because they all belong to the same order of reality. In that case, everything becomes *satya*, really speaking. When everything becomes *satya*, your *satya* is small, while what it is not, is big. Therefore, no matter how big you become, still, the mountain is definitely a bigger *satya* than your *satya*. The world is overwhelming, too big; it is so much bigger than you are. 'Bigger' is not the word, because there is nothing to compare it with.

Here, there is a confusion according to the *śāstra*. The *śāstra* says that *ātman* is *satya*. Now, if the body is taken to be *ātman*, which is *satya*, then it should not depend upon anything else. But you see that the body is exactly like a flower. How? Which is this human body? Is the nail the body? You can cut the nail and throw it away, so is it the body? No. The nail is not the body. A finger is not the body, the dermis, the top layer of the skin is not the body, nor is the epidermis, the layer underneath it. Then, flesh is not the body, nor is blood, nor bone, nor even the marrow. If you have to find out a body minus all these, where is it? There is no body. Therefore, what is the body? The body is *mithyā*.

The *upaniṣad* talks about this in a different form. It gives you a model of basic constituents, elements. In one *upaniṣad* it is presented in the form of three elements, and in another *upaniṣad*, it is presented in the form of five elements, but the topic is the same. The three elements are *pṛthivī*, the earth, *āpaḥ*, water, and *agni*, fire. The body has temperature, which is fire, and it has a shape, because of water. The constituents of the body are minerals – calcium, carbon, and so on – that is earth, *pṛthivī*. This is looking at the body according to the model of earth, water, and fire. Now, you cannot say that fire is the body, nor water is the body, nor the minerals are the body. If you take away the minerals there is no body, but minerals are not the body. Take away the water, there is no body either; it will be a dehydrated packet of powder, but water is not the body. Nor is fire, the temperature, the body.

Then, what is this body? Depending upon these three, put-together intelligently in a certain form, like the flower, it is called 'body'.

Now is the body *mithyā* or *satya*? It depends on something else for its existence and it is put-together, so it is *mithyā*. If you say that the body is *satya*, you do not know the meaning of *satya*. In the vision of the *śruti*, *ātman* is *satya* and everything else is *mithyā*. 'Everything else' includes the body. This is *viveka*. Your physical body is included in everything else. Not only the physical body, but your *prāṇa*, your mind, your senses, everything is included. Other than all these, if there is something, that alone is *ātman*. If it has parts, it becomes *mithyā*, and no part is *satya*.

Consider a car. What is a car? Suppose, I do not know what a car is, but I know what is rubber, air, plastic, iron, water, and gas; I know all this. But suppose I have never seen a car, and I do not know what a car is. Then a gentleman tells me,

"This is a car, Swamiji."

"But I see rubber."

"Yes, it is rubber."

"But is rubber a car?"

"Rubber is not a car."

"Oh. Remove the rubber."

"Is car the air? "

"Air is not car. If air is car, we can keep going to places."

"Then is steel a car?"

"Steel is not a car."

"Is the plastic a car?"

"No, plastic is not a car."

"Then remove all these things, one by one, whatever is not a car. Where is the car? You still have not introduced me to a car."

And the gentleman tells me, "Swami, don't you see, this is a car!"

"How?"

"When these are all put-together, it is called a car."

"Oh! I will put them all together."

So, I put them all together. I put the four wheels, the rubber, down below to make a base, and on that I put the steel, and on the top of it the plastic, whatever was there, then on top of it all I poured water, and on top of that I poured gas, because he said the car takes you to places only if you add gas. But then, there is no motion at all. And the gentleman said, "Swami! You have to ignite it." So I lit a match and it got ignited. Does this car take you up or does it take you laterally, on the road?

Car is *mithyā*. It is a manifestation of knowledge. It is not a simple pileup of different things. It is intelligently brought together to perform a function. Similarly, this body is also intelligently put-together to perform many functions, and to achieve a common function of keeping the body alive and active. Being put-together, it is *mithyā*. It is already said that *ātman* is *satya*, and if it has parts, it will be *mithyā*, because anything that is made up of parts is *mithyā*. Therefore, for *ātman* to be *satya*, it has got to be partless. Only what is partless can be *satya*. And this is presented here.

Defining ātmā

आत्मा कः ?
स्थूलसूक्ष्मकारणशरीराद् व्यतिरिक्तः पञ्चकोशातीतः
सन्नवस्थात्रयसाक्षी सच्चिदानन्दस्वरूपः सन्
यस्तिष्ठति स आत्मा ।

ātmā kaḥ?
sthūla-sūkṣma-kāraṇa-śarīrād vyatiriktaḥ
pañca-kośātītaḥ sannavasthā-traya-sākṣī
saccidānandasvarūpaḥ san yastiṣṭhati sa ātmā.

ātmā – *ātmā*; *kaḥ* – who (is);
yaḥ – the one who; *sthūla-sūkṣma-kāraṇa-śarīrāt* – from the gross, subtle and causal bodies; *vyatiriktaḥ* – is distinct; *pañca-kośātītaḥ* – who is beyond the five levels of experience; *avasthā-traya-sākṣī san* – being the witness of the three states (of experience); *saccidānanda-svarūpaḥ san* – who abides in the form of existence, consciousness, and fullness; *tiṣṭhati* – abides; *saḥ ātmā* – he (is) the self, *ātman*.

> The one who is distinct from the gross, subtle and causal bodies, who is beyond the five levels of experience, being the witness of the three states (of experience), that which remains in the form of existence, consciousness and fullness, he (is) the self, *ātman*.

The essence of anything is *tattva*, the truth. Here, it is the essence of everything. This discriminative enquiry leads to the vision of the *śruti* that says, *ātman* is *satya*, and everything else is *mithyā*.

The difference between *satya* and *mithyā* is this. *Mithyā* cannot exist without *satya*, but *satya* exists by itself. Putting it the other way, while *satya* does not need any other thing for its existence, *mithyā* cannot enjoy the same status. It depends upon *satya* for its very existence.

Therefore, that which does not depend upon anything else is *satya*, while anything that depends upon *satya* for its existence is *mithyā*. And the statement here is *ātmā satyam*. Body, *ātman* confusion is there because *mithyā* is not separate from *satya*.

If *ātman* is *satya*, then what is the *viveka* here? The *śruti* can make a statement, *ātmā satyam*, but can I understand *ātmā satyam* because *śruti* tells me? No, because *ātman* is not totally unknown. If it is totally unknown, and the *śruti* tells me about it, I can take *śruti*'s word for it. But here, *ātman* is known to me. As what? As fat, tall, short, lean, black, white, male, female, young, old. *Ātman* means 'I' and it is known to me. And when I analyse what is known as *ātman*, I find that it is not *satya*, but *mithyā*. If I say that I am tall, or short, I definitely mean that I am equal to the body; the tallness of the body is my tallness. This means that *ātman* is equated to the body. If that is so, the body should be *satya*. But we have seen that it is not. It also depends upon something else.

The entire body can be viewed according to different models. If you consider the biological model, it can be reduced to cells. That is all it is – a bunch of cells. But you do not call a bunch of cells as the body. You know what a body is, but minus the cells there is no body. So, in this model the body is reduced to cells.

If you look at it from the standpoint of another model, the body is just minerals. It is calcium, carbon, and so on. The body can be reduced to simple minerals, but minerals are not the body. In your body there is certain amount of carbon, calcium, iron, phosphorous, iodine, etc. If you put all these elements together, in the quantities and proportions that they have in the body, can someone say that this is the one I want to marry? It is very clear that the body, which seems to have its own existence, is reducible to all these minerals. And therefore, this body is as *mithyā* as the flower we saw earlier. Thus, there is confusion here.

The reason for the confusion is that *mithyā* is not independent of *satya*. Where *mithyā* is, there *satya* is. You do not search for *satya* when you confront *mithyā*, any more than you search for water when you confront a wave. When you confront a wave, you do not search for water because in the very sight of the wave is the sight of water. Where there is wave there is water, but water need not be a wave.

Similarly, this physical body is *mithyā*; being so, it is definitely never independent of *satya*. If *satya* is the *ātman*, then that *satya* is very much present in the *mithyā* body, which is why you can mistake the body for *ātman*. The body is taken for *ātman*; *ātman* is taken for the body, and the limitations of the body are taken as the limitations of *ātman*.

This problem of confusion is connected to being self-conscious. If this body is the body of a cow, there cannot be a sense of limitation, if we understand a cow as one that does not have the degree of self-consciousness to have a complex that will lead to any kind of opinion about itself. Self-ignorance is there, but the confusion is very minimal. A human being, however, who has confusion can be enlightened. The person who can have confusion is also someone who is capable of freeing himself or herself from that confusion. That is the advantage of a human being. And the confusion is there, because *ātman* is present in anything that we call *mithyā*, and is, therefore, available for committing a mistake.

Confusion about ātman is universal

This mistake is inevitable because we are all born ignorant. Ignorance is not going to begin at a given time; it is our capital. We start with ignorance, including self-ignorance, and therefore, *ātman* is a sitting duck. For what? For being mistaken.

A mistake is generally personal. You may mistake the rope for a snake, while another person may not. But here, it is not a personal mistake, which is generally psychological. This is a basic mistake which is universal, because each individual has a physical body, a set of senses, and a mind. And each individual is conscious of himself or herself as a person, and is born with self-ignorance. So, we have all the ingredients for committing a mistake. And the mistake will be uniform.

This universal confusion about *ātman* is, 'I am a mortal,' because the physical body is universally mortal, unless you have a special, eternal body. Think of what an eternal body would be. If it is eternal, it should not have parts, because anything that has parts will fall apart. Whether the parts are nuts and bolts, or some organic joints, or even a cell that has its own parts, it will fall apart. There is no physical body that is eternal; anything that has parts cannot be eternal, and anything that is put-together in time is not eternal. That is why the dead ones form the majority, now and always. So, we all know that this body is mortal. Therefore, 'I am a mortal, subject to illness, ageing, pain, and death,' are universal conclusions.

Then again, the body being one and everything else being separate from this body, naturally, there is a conclusion about location too. With reference to the pervasiveness of the body, I am going to see myself wanting. If I am here, I am not there. If I am there, I am not here. There is a sense of incompleteness with reference to pervasiveness. And again, there is inadequacy with reference to abilities, skills, and so on. Thus, we have varieties of limitations centred on the physical body; so the problem, and therefore, the mistake is universal. Being universal, I need to make an enquiry into, and thereby recognise, understand, the *ātman* as *satya*. How to resolve the confusion, he is going to say.

Methods of analysis to resolve the confusion about ātman

There are various methods of analysis known as *prakriyā*s in Vedanta. A *prakriyā* is a method of enquiry, analysis, to help us understand what is what. One *prakriyā* is the *śarīra-traya-prakriyā*, a *prakriyā* wherein there is the distinguishing of the *ātman*, or recognising the *ātman*, as independent of the three *śarīra*s, bodies. And when the three bodies are divided into five layers, for the purpose of analysis, it is another *prakriyā*. These three bodies are divided into five layers because at every layer there is a mistake about *ātman*. The layers are from the standpoint of our own experience, and we find there are five common levels of experience that we mistake for *ātman*. To sort this out we have the *pañca-kośa-prakriyā*.

Every individual has these three states of experience – waking, dream, and deep sleep. We analyse these and find out what exactly is the *ātman* here. Is *ātman* a waker, or dreamer, or deep sleeper? This is the *avasthā-traya-prakriyā*, presenting the three states of experience, and analysing them to find out what is *ātman*, and what it is not. Then we have a *kāraṇa-kārya-prakriyā*, cause-effect method of analysis. These are the Vedanta *prakriyā*s, methods of analysis, because at all these levels there is confusion about *ātman*.

Ātman is other than sthūla-sūkṣma-kāraṇa-śarīra

Sthūla-sūkṣma-kāraṇa-śarīrāt vyatiriktaḥ, is the three-body *prakriyā*. We will analyse later what the three-fold body is, but now we will just understand the meaning of the words. *Vyatiriktaḥ* means that which is distinct. *Śarīra* means body, and *sthūla-śarīra* means the physical body, as *sthūla* means gross. Therefore, *ātman* is distinct from the physical body, *sthūla-śarīrāt vyatiriktaḥ*. Note that he does not say that the physical body is distinct from *ātman*, but that *ātman* is distinct from the body. Like water is distinct from a wave. It does not mean that the wave is distinct from water, but water is definitely not the wave. This is what he points out here.

Here again, some people commit a mistake, thinking that we can separate *ātman* from everything. I say, one is true and the other is not true. When I say wave is water, I do not say that water is wave. B is A; A is not B. It is like an actor and the role he plays. The role is the actor, whereas the actor is not the role, otherwise he would not be able to act at all. As a role, he can even assume the role of a beggar. The beggar, B, is the actor, A. B is A, but A is not B. Even at the time of acting the role of a beggar, A is not B. Otherwise it would be a problem. If there is that kind of self-confusion, he shouldn't get into the theatre at all. B is A, but A is not B, wave is water, while water is not the wave. Here also, we say that *ātman* is distinct from *sthūla-sūkṣma-kāraṇa-śarīra*.

Why do we have to say this? Suppose I ask you, "What is pot?" I just want to know what a pot is. And I get the answer, "A pot is not an elephant; a pot is not a camel; a pot is not a rat." What are you talking about? I ask what a pot is, and you say that it is not this, and it is not that. Please tell me what a pot is, but you are telling me what a pot is not.

Confusion necessitates negation, *prasakta-pratiṣedha*. Here, I want to know what is *ātman*. The question is, *ātmā kaḥ*? And he answers – Distinct from the physical body, *sthūla-śarīrāt vyatiriktaḥ*, distinct from the subtle body, *sūkṣma-śarīrāt vyatiriktaḥ*, distinct from the causal body, *kāraṇa-śarīrāt vyatiriktaḥ*. Why does he say this? Because you take *ātman* as the *sthūla-śarīra*, and so on. You can understand now why we need to negate. This is an occasion, *prasakti*, for which negation, *pratiṣedha*, is necessary, because there is a mistake committed. Otherwise, there would be no necessity for a negation. If you mistake a pot for an elephant, then we have to say that the pot is not an elephant. But if a pot is not known to you, there is no mistake committed, and there is no need to say that the pot is not an elephant. It would be the same if *ātman* were totally unknown to you, *svargādivat*, like heaven, etc.

If *ātman* is totally unknown, you do not require the statement that *ātman* is *sthūla-sūkṣma-kāraṇa-śarīrāt vyatiriktaḥ*. But because *ātman* is you, and whatever you know about yourself is what *ātman* is taken to be, while in the vision of the *śruti, ātman* is other than what you take it to be, you require such a sentence. And the mistake is universal. Everyone considers *ātman* to be as good as the body, to be mortal, and therefore, it is said, *sthūla-śarīrāt vyatiriktaḥ, ātman* is distinct from the *sthūla-śarīra*. Then, *ātman* is taken to be the mind. And to this he says, "No, *ātman* is distinct from the subtle body, *sūkṣma-śarīrāt vyatiriktaḥ*." If you say that you are ignorant, that you are subject to *karma*, he says that *ātman* is distinct from the causal body, *kāraṇa-śarīrāt vyatiriktaḥ*. *Ātman* is neither subject to ignorance and *karma*, nor a mental condition, nor does it have the attributes of the physical body. Now you can understand why the enquiry is called *viveka*. If a wave is self-conscious, and takes itself to be just a wave, ignorant of its content, water, which is the truth, *satya*, of itself, the wave is the loser. If the wave is enlightened, then there is no small wave, big wave. There is only water. And the wave can say, "I am the ocean." *Ātman* is *sthūla-sūkṣma-kāraṇa-śarīrāt vyatiriktaḥ*.

Ātman is pañca-kośātīta

In this *prakriyā*, the same three *śarīra*s are analysed in a way that covers the human experience. The experience of being tall, short, black, white, is one experience. Another experience is that of being hungry, thirsty, healthy, ill, etc. Then there is the experience of being agitated, angry, sad and so on. "I did this. This is mine," is another type of experience. And there is the experience of being ignorant. All these experiences are covered by this statement that *ātman* is *pañca-kośātīta*.

Kośa means a sheath, that which covers something. Is *ātman* covered? That is how it is construed – *ātman* is covered, and you have to remove all the covers. There is no such thing. *Ātman* is *satya*. Every sheath is *mithyā*. Is water covered by the wave? The wave does not cover the water, nor does *ātman* have any cover. It cannot hide. In fact, *ātman* is the only one that cannot hide, much less disappear. It is always present. But ignorance can accomplish varieties of things. Due to ignorance, *ātman*, which is the truth of every *kośa*, seems to be covered at every level, *kośa*. The physical body is a *kośa* because *ātman* is mistaken for the body. Similarly, *ātman* is mistaken for *prāṇa* when you say, "I am hungry, thirsty." At each level, there is a distinct experience, each of which reveals the *ātman*. And that experience seems to be the attribute of the *ātman* itself. This is why we have this sentence here, *pañca-kośātītaḥ*, that which is distinct from the five *kośa*s.

Ātman is avasthā-traya-sākṣin

Using another *prakriyā*, *ātman* is analysed from the standpoint of the three states of experience, *avasthā-traya*. Should I take the *ātman* to be the waker, or the dreamer, or the one who sleeps? Since the waker is me, and the waking state is for myself, should I take *ātman* to be a waker? Or is *ātman* the dreamer? And who wakes up? Is *ātman* the one who sleeps? Is it basically a sleeper, and then becomes a dreamer, and then a waker? Or is it distinct from all the three? There is a method of analysis here, which we will introduce later, and through this method, we are going to distinguish and recognise *ātman* in all the three – whether it has the attributes of the waking state to assume the status of being a waker, or it has the attributes of the dream to become the dreamer, or sleep to be the sleeper, or is it free from all these attributes? And here the statement is, it is free from all the attributes of these states, and is a witness to all three states of experience, *avasthā-traya-sākṣin*. Then, we will also analyse the cause-effect, *kāraṇa-kārya-prakriyā*.

What is *ātman*? Definitely, it is free from all this, so he says *sthūla-sūkṣma-kāraṇa-śarīrāt anyaḥ avasthā-traya-sākṣī pañca-kośātītaḥ*. It is free from these so called five sheaths. There is nothing to cover *ātman*; it is only your mistake that is called a cover. So, free from the five sheaths, *pañca-kośātīta,* and free from the three bodies, *sthūla-sūkṣma-kāraṇa-śarīrāt vyatiriktaḥ,* and that which is the witness in all three states of experience, *avasthā-traya-sākṣin* – that is *ātman,* free from all this. But what is *ātman*?

Now he gives a set of words to define *ātman.* Any definition requires a minimum number of words, and those he gives here. A definition implies a statement that reveals only that object, not any other. If any other object can be defined by the same words used in defining a given object, then that is not a definition. If you say, the one who has two legs is a human being. Is that a definition? What about a crow, or a crane, in fact, every bird? It is not a definition at all. A definition must be such that the meaning of the words can reveal only one object, not another. And also, the words should reveal the object. Suppose, I say that *ātman* is '*caccha poccha gogghaa,*' these three words do not reveal any other object. But they do not reveal *ātman* either. Therefore, the words that define should not cover any other object, and at the same time, reveal the given object completely. So, we require certain words from the language to reveal *ātman,* and these words are *sat, cit, ānanda.* This is what our understanding of *ātman* should be.

Negating what it is not, what it is mistaken to be, the words reveal what it is. Both are important. It is not mere negation; after negating we reveal. In fact, it is how these words can work. Only when we take care of what it is not, do these words have meaning. The words reveal, but the negation aspect is equally important because of the confusion that is there. Then, after negating, the words used with a certain method serve the function of revealing. Even in the revelation there is a method of looking into the words. Thus, he says here that the one who is *saccidānanda* is *ātman*, *saccidānanda-svarūpaḥ sann yaḥ tiṣṭhati sa ātmā*.

Negation of not-I

To begin with, let us look at all that is here as what is known to you, and unknown to you. Not just what is known, but what is known to 'you'. So, 'you' is one element, and what is known, what becomes evident to you, is another. This is how we start the enquiry. Now, what about unknown things? They are knowable, that is, they may be known later. Either way, they are other than you. What is known to you, having become evident to you, and what is potentially known, but now unknown to you – these will form what we call the not-I, *anātman*. Everything that is known and unknown is other than you, the self, *viditam aviditaṁ sarvam ātmanaḥ anyat*.[7]

Then what is 'you'? That which is not an object of knowledge. To whom? The one for whom knowledge of objects takes place, that is *ātman*. Therefore, in this world, how many things are there? Broadly, from what we have understood now, we can say that there are two things, to begin with. This is only to begin with; mark my words 'to begin with'. We have two things. One is you, the other is everything else. Everything else also includes things that are not known to you. Because the unknown can become known later, they are also included in everything else. It can include the heaven too, and *devatā*s like Indra, Varuṇa, Agni, who are all separate from you – all of them are included in what is to be known.

So, there are only two things, *padārtha*s, to begin with – I, the knower, and the other is whatever is known to the I. And the known is not the knower. 'I' means the one who has the sense, I am the knower, and there is a world, which I am not. In this situation, that there is a world is known to you, and your conclusion that you are not the world is also very clear to you. This is universal.

---

[7] *anyadeva tadviditād atho'viditādadhi* (*Kenopaniṣad* 1.4)

You are the knower, and this knower is recognised as one who is distinct from the world that is known.

Here, you need to make a note – you are able to say that there is a world because it is known to you. The Swami exists, and is an object of your knowledge, known to you, evident to you. Therefore, the known Swami is part of the world that you know, and is not taken to be yourself, the knower. So too, any object that is known to you implies you being the knower, and the known not being you. Whether it is the earth, sun, moon, stars, or a black hole, anything that is known to you is not you. You make this very clear. A pot,[8] being known, you are the knower of the pot; you are not the pot – you draw a line between the knower and the known. The known is not mistaken for the knower because the line is very clear. The clothes that you wear, very close to your physical body, are known to you. They are objects of your knowledge, and are not taken to be yourself. You may have certain relationship with reference to various objects that you know, like, "This is not mine, this is mine," but whether it is in your possession, or belongs to somebody else, the object

---

[8] Whenever we require an example of an object we use a pot, so that the moment the word 'pot' is used, you know we are discussing an object.

is always taken to be other than yourself – my house is not me, my child is not me, my father is not me, mother is not me. Each one of them is not me. So, this special relationship also reveals the object to be only a known object, and the knower, you, to be entirely different.

Extending the knower-known boundary

Now, the *śāstra* wants you to extend this knower-known situation. Universally, where do you draw the line that separates the knower, you, the *ātman*, from the known, the world, the not-I? That line runs along the perimeter of your physical body, the dermis. Up to this alone you are, and beyond this, is the world. If anything touches this skin, the outer skin, it is touching you. It is clear that the line is drawn there. This is the line not only for you, but for me, for everybody.

Here, we can very easily see one problem. When you draw the line, you put my body in the sphere of what we call not-I, the world. When I draw the line, without any kind of a doubt, I also include your body in my world, as not-I, because it is very clear to me that the line between me and the world only runs along the physical body. Everything else is an object for me, an object of my knowledge, and therefore I consider it not-I. And you include my body in your not-I. However, you do not include your body in not-I, and I do not include my body in not-I. Since we have a common confusion, both of us pass as normal, and we require a third person to point out that we are confused. A non-confused person is required because both of us are committing the same mistake, if it is a mistake. It looks to me like it is a mistake, since my not-I includes your body, and in your not-I my body is included. If, for you, this body is not-I, how is it going to become 'I'? It is an object for you, so how does it turn into a subject? How is it going to become *ātman*? Well, there seems to be a basis for confusion, and this itself is enough to make us enquire.

What is the criterion to conclude that this world is not-I? It is known to me. There is no other criterion. Being the knower of an object, and understanding that an object that is known cannot be the knower, you conclude that since this is known, it is not the knower. The *śāstra* tells that you should extend this a little further.

Existence of the known is established by a means of knowledge, *pramāṇa-siddha*.

Let us understand that if an object is understood to exist, it has got to be known. For you, the existence of an object is not evident unless it is known to you. Any object has to become evident to you in order to prove its existence. In other words, you, the knower, employ an appropriate means of knowledge, *pramāṇa*, and, thereby, come to know its existence. Now, the Swami is considered to be here, not because the Swami is self-revealing. I am not a radiant Swami who reveals himself to you, like an isotope. This physical body has to be bathed in light and it has to reflect light. Then again, that reflecting light has to be received by your eyes. Whether it is sight or some other means, you have to employ a means of knowledge, only then can you say that this body exists. You cannot say that this body exists without it being known. Therefore, anything that exists, that 'is', is something that is known to you. It may exist for somebody else, but for you it is as good as non-existent, if it has not come to your knowledge. An object 'is', because it is known to you; it is *pramāṇa-siddha*, directly or indirectly.

Again, what is known as an object cannot be the knower. If it becomes an object that is evident to you, you cannot have your I-sense in that known object. Then what kind of sense will you have in it? No matter what that object is, whether it is a pot, or a flower, or a body, the sense that you have towards it is this-sense, *idaṁ-pratyaya-viṣaya*. It is definitely not an I-sense, because it is known.

The knower, 'I' is the place where you can place your I-sense, and anything known, being an object of your knowledge, cannot be the recipient of the I-sense. On the other hand, it will be an object of this-sense. Both, a known and an unknown object become the recipients of this-sense, *idaṁ-pratyaya-viṣaya*. Any object of knowledge never enjoys an I-sense.

The Swami exists, the Swami 'is' because the Swami is known to you. Being known to you, he becomes the object of this-sense. And being an object of this-sense, the object should be taken as not-I. Now, do you have a body or not? Of course, you say, "Yes," which means this body 'is'. How do you say that the body 'is'? Whether it is by inference or perception, is the body known to you, or unknown to you? If it is known to you, then it becomes an object of this-sense. If it is an object of this-sense, how can you say, "I am tall, I am short, I am mortal, I am white, I am black?"

You may say, "Swamiji, it is true. This body is an object of my knowledge and should be referred to only as not-I, because it is 'this' body. But Swamiji, even though it is 'this' body, I have some intimacy with this body. My sense of 'this body' does not extend to any other body. It only goes up to this body. There is an intimacy with this body; me and this body are together. When the body was born, I was born, or, when I was born, this body was born. And wherever the body goes, I am there, where the body sits, I sit. If the body leaves, I leave, and wherever the body is, I find myself there. This is not so simple. This body and I – even though it is 'this' – have some special feature, a *viśeṣa*. Like there are people and people, but this one is my mother; and there are children and children, but this is my child. There are houses and houses, but this is my house. So too, there are bodies and bodies, but this is my body." This is okay, and there is a reason for it, which we will look into later, but now we are trying to find out where we should draw the line between 'I' and not-I. Where does the not-I begin, and this 'I' stop?

From what we have seen, you definitely cannot say that where your nose ends the world begins. No, it is clear that this physical body also is to be included within the field, *kṣetra*, of not-I. And if it is included in the not-I, then you have to draw the line somewhere else. Somewhere the 'I' should stop. What is 'I' then? With reference to the body, I am tall, I am black, and so on. That is fine. It is purely an incidental status for 'I'. But where do you draw the line?

We draw it according to our experience. I am tall, short and so on, is one experience. I have understood that this body, as an object of knowledge, is an object, like any other object. And just as I have a special relationship with certain objects in the world, the not-I, even though this body is also within the not-I field, yet, I have a special relationship with it. Then, my experience is also that when there is hunger, I am hungry. Suppose, this experience is the basis for a conclusion, then, using our Sanskrit term here, I would say that I am *prāṇa*. *Prāṇa* here, as a general term, stands for the entire physiological function – respiration, digestion, etc.

But hunger is known to you. Where do you draw the line now? The line goes further; from the anatomy it travels to the physiology, and from there, it proceeds further.

Maybe I am the group of senses. The senses can be 'I' because when the eyes see and the ears hear, I say that the seer, the hearer is 'I'. Therefore who is 'I'? The senses, the five senses. Why not? This group of senses stands for 'I', *indriya-samūhaḥ ahamasmi*.

You say that your eyes see. How do you know the eyes see? I see that my eyes see. Suppose a blind person says, "Sir, I am blind."

"How do you say that you are blind?"

"Because I see, sir."

"What do you see?"

"I see that my eyes do not see."

That my eyes see, or do not see, I know. This is the important truth about the way the *pramāṇa*s operate. The eyes operate, the ears operate, and behind these eyes and ears there is an 'I', who is able to say that the eyes see and the ears hear. Therefore, I cannot say that the senses constitute 'I', because there is an 'I' who employs the senses, who is aware of the senses and their function, their non-function, and malfunction. Whether the functions are sharp or dull, or do not do what they are supposed to do, it is known to the 'I'. It comes back to you again. Where do you draw the line?

Perhaps, you can say that the mind is the self, *manas eva ātmā*. What do you mean by the mind? Emotions or a given thought? In fact, like the eyes and ears serve as instruments, the mind also serves as an instrument, *karaṇa*. To see that there is a flower here, what happens? The eyes see. But then, something has to happen in the mind. And whatever is happening in the mind we call it a *vṛtti*. We are not interested in how this is seen, and so on; that is not our area. But then, a change has to take place in the mind, and the change is in keeping with the sight, the information gathered by the eyes. That is converted in the form which we call a *vṛtti*. There is a necessity for that mental change, *vṛtti-apekṣa*, for sight to occur. A modification of the mind is required for every cognition.

Let us just look at it the other way. Suppose, you do not require any relevant mental change in order to see an object. What would be the outcome? You would see either everything at once, or, you would not see at all. But the fact is that you see a given object – now the flower, now not the flower, but the hand, etc. From this it is clear that the mind assumes a change, and in that change, whatever is perceived, you know it is exactly the object that is there.

For every perception there is a change in the mind relevant to the object of perception. Now, that changed mind, is it seen by you or not? You have to see it. In fact, what you see all the time is what is happening in your mind, not what is happening outside, really. Whatever form the mind assumes, that is what you see. If outside there is a rope, and you see a snake there, then what is it that you see? Do you see the object outside or the object inside? You do see the object outside, which is why you say that it is a snake and not an elephant, but then, whatever occurs in your thought is what you are going to say you see. What do you understand from this? All the time what you come across is only what is happening in your mind. So, you encounter the world only through the counter of the mind.

The mind undergoes change, called a *vṛtti;* for a pot, a pot-*vṛtti*, for a flower, a flower-*vṛtti*. And you are the knower, the witness of these *vṛtti*s. Now, where should you draw the line? Not at the mind. All the emotions are also included here. It is with reference to the emotion that you say, 'I am loving, I am hateful, etc.' And to say, 'I am understanding or not understanding,' is, again, with reference to what is happening in the mind. So, where do you draw the line? Somewhere you have to draw it. Perhaps you can say, "I am the knower, the subject." Let us say it is the subject. The mind includes emotions, memory, cognitions, all mental activities, and the one who is conscious of these mental activities is 'I'.

Now, what does not-I include? Let us just look back and see all the things that are not-I. We start with the external world, the mountains, earth, stars and so on. Then your body, my body, is included in the not-I.

If, in your vision, your body is not included in the not-I, then that is where correction is needed. That is what the *upadeśa* is.

Lord Kṛṣṇa says, "Arjuna, this body is called a 'field'. The one who knows this (field), is the knower of the field; thus say those who know that."[9]

The physical body, which is the locus of confusion, should be included in the physical world. This is not some kind of a ghostly body but a tangible, solid, physical body, and therefore it cannot stand outside of the physical world. If the physical world is something that is not-I, my physical body is included therein. Naturally, my *prāṇa* is also included therein. Within this physical world, wherever there is a living organism enjoying a physical body, there is some *prāṇa* making it tick with life. And that is also *idam*, an object of this-sense.

Then, time and space are included because they are also objects of this-sense. Every cognition and object of cognition is included. The cognitions remembered by me, recollected by me, which were originally gathered from the world, are all included.

---

[9] *idaṁ śarīraṁ kaunteya kṣetram ityabhidhīyate*
etadyo vetti taṁ prāhuḥ kṣetrajña iti tadvidaḥ (*Bhagavadgītā* 13.1)

And the emotions I objectify are also included. Everything is included in not-I.

Now, what is left out? Whatever is left out is to be analysed. We need to understand what negation, *neti neti*, is. We are not negating anything here. People say Vedanta is a negative philosophy. Vedanta only negates our erroneous thinking; it is not negative or positive. This is how things are.

The invariable consciousness 'I' is ātma-svarūpa

If we look at any cognition, we can see that there is something invariable. The object which you refer to as 'this object' is an object of your knowledge. We can say it a little differently; it is an object of consciousness, like pot-consciousness, cloth-consciousness – each is an object of consciousness. Pot-consciousness is a given form-consciousness, as is flower-consciousness. From the standpoint of each of the senses we have form-consciousness, sound-consciousness, smell-consciousness, taste-consciousness, touch-consciousness. What is invariable? Consciousness is invariable. Similarly, if your physical body is an object of your knowledge, you can say this-body-consciousness. This body is an object of consciousness. So, we have body-consciousness, hunger-consciousness, thirst-consciousness, thought-consciousness, an emotion-consciousness, a recollected-object-consciousness, and so on. Whether it is with reference to the form outside, or the form that is seen by you as a corresponding thought inside, there is no difference, really. In fact, the thought-consciousness is what the form-consciousness is. What is present in all of them is *saṁvit* – it is a word for consciousness. It is invariable, *saṁvit ekā*. The objects are always variable, while consciousness is invariable.

It is the same for time-consciousness and space-consciousness. You are aware of space in terms of distance, so there is space-consciousness. And you are aware of time, so there is time-consciousness – past, present or future-time-consciousness. And if you recognise your own ignorance of any given subject matter, or any object, then there is ignorance-consciousness. Both ignorance and knowledge are included as object of consciousness. Your memory is also included as memory-consciousness. When you say, "I am angry, I am hungry, I am thirsty," the anger, hunger and thirst are objects of consciousness. In all these, what is present is one consciousness. Is consciousness objectified by you?

Consciousness is not an object and cannot be displaced

I now ask you to do the following. I will say a few words, and as I say them, just keep seeing the object. An apple, a book, your pen, consciousness..., your neighbour, desk, consciousness..., tree, crow, rose, consciousness..., bus, car, a bike, consciousness. For the word 'consciousness' what did you see? You did not see anything. Can you say, 'therefore there is no consciousness?' When I said the word 'consciousness' you did not see an object. Is there no meaning? No. You are the meaning of consciousness, I, *ātman,* the content of the seer, hearer, knower, doer.

Think of a cow, then think of a horse. The cow is displaced, and the horse is there now. Think of a tree, think of a crow. The tree is displaced by the crow. So, one object displaces the other. Now, when I ask you to think of a tree, does it displace consciousness? No. Think of Russian ignorance; is consciousness displaced? No. Think of English language, which you know. Is consciousness displaced? No. Remember something, recollect something. What did you eat for breakfast? Does it displace consciousness? No. Think of the past. Does it displace consciousness? Think of the future; does it displace consciousness?

What displaces consciousness, I? Nothing really displaces consciousness, I. You see a form, you are there; you hear a sound, you are there; you pick up a smell, you are there; any given emotion, you are there; hunger, you are there; thirst, you are there; recollection, cognition, you are there. You are there all the time.

What does not require to be objectified is 'I'. And that is what consciousness is. Everything is bathed in consciousness, is the object of consciousness. There is only one thing that is 'like' consciousness, and for that we use the word *cit*. Previously I used *saṁvit*, and another word is *cit*.

Consciousness alone is self-revealing, referred to by 'I', and everything else needs consciousness to get revealed. To help you understand this, an imagery is used in our *śāstra*, the *upaniṣad*s, which are our source books. This is just from the standpoint of your eyesight. To see an object with your eyes, the essential requirement is light. If the object is luminous, like the sun, or a glow-worm in the night, or the stars, or a lamp, then you do not require a light to light it up. The object is either luminous, or reflects light for it to be seen. We use two words here to express that – *bhāti*, the third person singular of the verb '*bhā*, to shine,' and *anubhāti*, 'shines after,' reflects. So the sun, a star, *bhāti*. But the moon *anubhāti*, 'shines after,' reflects.

The Swami is sitting here; you see the physical body. Does it *bhāti* or *anubhāti*? *Anubhāti*. Every opaque object that is not self-luminous is *anubhāti*, whereas, a luminous object like the sun, and so on, *bhāti*. This is the situation that you know. The *upaniṣad* takes this particular fact and uses it as an imagery to launch into this process of cognition of what is.

Now, when the sun shines, I use *bhāti*, granted, but can the sun reveal its existence, its luminosity, if my eyes are closed? The imagery here is with reference to visual perception. Therefore, the sun shines, is luminous, depending upon what? Upon my eyes. The sun is luminous, I can say, only when my eyes light up the sun. The eyes have to light up the sun, the moon, the stars, all objects, whether they are opaque or luminous. All objects shine after the eyes. Therefore, the pair of eyes *bhāti* or *anubhāti*? *Bhāti*. Without the eyes, even the light cannot reveal itself, and so, in this imagery, all forms and colors, including the sun, shine after the eyes.

Can the eyes shine, *bhāti*, without a mind backing them? No. The pair of eyes, is it *bhāti* or *anubhāti*? *Anubhāti*. And the mind *bhāti*. But the mind itself shines after whom? After 'I.' Then what shines? I shine; shine all the way.

I shine whether the mind shines or not. When the mind goes to sleep, I shine, to get up and say, ' I slept well.' When the mind dreams, I shine, lighting up the dream world. When I am awake, and my eyes are open, things are seen, then I light up the mind, and with the mind, the eyes light up all the forms. So, in every perception, whether it is a form-perception, sound-perception, smell-perception, taste-perception, touch-perception, or cognition of an inferred object, what is invariably present is the self-evident 'I'. The 'I' shines all the time, all the way. Time folds up, space folds up, as it happens in sleep, while 'I' shine. Then time and space are manifest, and 'I' shine. In fact, the 'I' consciousness lights up everything.

Let us understand this further. The 'I' is self-evident, *bhāti,* and everything else, this entire world, *anubhāti,* shines after, is evident to you. The world of form becomes evident because of your eyes, the world of sound becomes evident because of your ears, and the world that is inferred by you, like a black hole, etc., which is part of the world, becomes evident through your reasoning. Anything inferred is also there because it becomes evident to you.

When everything is evident to you, shining after consciousness, 'I', what is not evident to you?

There is nothing that is non-evident. The only 'object' in this world that does not require any evidence for its existence is 'I'. And without the 'I' being self-evident, can there be anything to become evident to you? Look at this process. The Swami 'is', because you see. The Swami talks, because you hear. Your body is, your eyes see, because you see. Your mind is thinking about this because you see it; you see what is going on. There is always a 'because'. Now tell me, do you exist or not? Suppose someone says, "Let me consult and tell you." Do you have to consult anybody? Do you have to consult your senses? Now you can understand what it means to say that the self is beyond the senses. It is not an object of the senses, in the sense that you do not need to prove the existence of your self. Are you here? If, to answer that question, evidence is required, for whom is it required? Where does this evidence resolve, resulting in the cognition of the existence of you? What is the altar of resolution?

In this world, *jagat*, there is only one thing that is self-revealing, without requiring to be revealed. That is only consciousness. In every revelation, consciousness has to be present, just as in every visual perception light has to be there. That is the imagery, but the light of the imagery is given up here, and we go to another light, the light of consciousness, *jyotirjyotiḥ*, the light of light, which is always there in every revelation, and revealing itself all the time. There is never a time when this is absent.

Now, please tell me, is *ātman* to be experienced, or recognised as it is? Recognised, because it is always there. People who talk about experience, and so on, do not understand even this much. The consciousness by which every experience is revealed is present all the time. All the teaching is about this consciousness, which happens to be 'I'.

We have three words to correct three mistaken conclusions about *ātman*. We will look into these three words.

That which is not an object of consciousness is the self that is self-revealing, self-evident. If consciousness is the nature of 'I' and is not recognised as such, then it is seen from the standpoint of the common mistaken conclusions about 'I'. Let us analyse these common conclusions that human beings have about themselves.

If you see from the struggles in life, everyone has the wish, "I want to live, and live a day more." There is always the fear of death. People commit suicide because they do not see that they can be happy in the future. That is also a conclusion. So, it is very clear that, 'I not only want to live, but I also want to live happily.' Wanting to live happily is as powerful an urge as wanting to live. Because it is a common urge, it is universal. Wanting to live is an urge of every living organism; it is the instinct for survival. There is always a struggle to be, and the human being is not an exception. He wants to live, live a day more, and live happily; these two are equal.

Then, as a human being, there is one more thing and that is, 'I cannot stand being ignorant.' The moment you come to know what you do not know, there is an urge to know. You can make anybody miss his or her sleep just by telling the person, "I have a great secret to tell you. Do not tell anybody." When the person wants to know what it is, you tell, "Tomorrow I will tell you." That is enough to lose one's sleep. So, the love to be knowledgeable is also common among human beings.

On the basis of this, we can put the whole struggle of human life in one sentence – I want to live, and live happily, without being ignorant. These three urges come from the three conclusions that I am a mortal, I am unhappy, inadequate, or imperfect, and

I am ignorant. These three conclusions are addressed by Vedanta.

If I am a mortal, I am a mortal. Nobody is going to change that. The physical body does not say, 'I am a mortal' and suffer from that. The physical body does not really concern itself about death, even though a live body wants to live. Therefore, the problem and the conclusion, 'I am a mortal,' belongs to the self-conscious 'I'. I am a mortal, and therefore I want to live a day more at any time. Then again, the conclusion, 'I am unhappy,' ' I am ignorant,' is also centred on 'I'. The body does not say, 'I am ignorant' and it does not say, 'I am unhappy' either. These three conclusions are centred on 'I'. If the 'I' is subject to mortality, unhappiness and ignorance, and if they are really the attributes of 'I', then there is no solution to the problem.

This is what many theologians think about the *ātman*. According to them, the attributes of mortality, limitations in terms of knowledge, and so on, accounting for ignorance, and also the limitation in terms of your intake of happiness, are real limitations of the *ātman*. And when they are real, we can only hope for some palliative because there is no cure for a reality. If they are intrinsic attributes, there is no cure. They also promise you that in heaven you will be okay.

Due to the interference of the Lord's grace, you will go there and be happy. This is able to attract people, because the conclusion that these attributes are intrinsic to the self is well-entrenched. So, a theology that maintains that the Lord will take care of you is very appealing. If you are able to trust that he will take care of you, that is a great relief. Thus far popular religion can go. It cannot really give you anything more than that.

Discerning what is real

Vedanta has something different to say. This three-fold conclusion centred on 'I'– I am a mortal, I am unhappy and I am ignorant – is it real? If it is real, there is no solution. Even if you go to heaven, and be very near Bhagavān, you are going to be the same. The smallness that you experience about yourself will not go away. That is *saṁsāra,* and the sense of being a *saṁsārin* will not go away from you.

We saw that in every piece of knowledge there is the presence of consciousness. Nobody can touch that. In every revelation of an existent object, there is the presence of consciousness, like the presence of light in sight. What is seen is variable, but the invariable in every sight is the presence of light. Similarly, what is revealed is manifold and varied, and what is present in every revelation is consciousness. If there is anything that is self-evident in this world, it is only you.

Now, are you ignorant? Or are you consciousness? 'I am ignorant' is a conclusion, and so is, 'I am knowledgeable.' I am knowledgeable with reference to what I know, and I am ignorant with reference to what I do not know. The consciousness reveals both what I know and what I do not know, that is, I am neither ignorant nor knowledgeable. If I conclude that I am knowledgeable, I cannot avoid the conclusion that I am ignorant. If I think that I am ignorant, of course, I cannot avoid the conclusion that I am knowledgeable, in a limited way – even to say that I am ignorant, I must be knowledgeable. Since I do not say, 'I am ignorantee, or ignorantal or ignorantest,' to that extent I am knowledgeable. When I say, 'I am ignorant,' definitely there is some knowledge involved, and consciousness is invariable. Ignorance is an object; how can I put my 'I' in the object? But I do put it there, and say that I am ignorant. It can be a point of view. But to have a point of view, you must have the view, otherwise there is no point of view.

A point of view requires a view. There is no point in pointing out a point of view, if the view is not clear.

If the point of view is a view without knowledge of the total, it is not a point of view; it is a distortion. What is, is not clear. And in a point of view, definitely, the truth is involved. So, in every conclusion I make, I am very much involved. That is why I make the conclusions that I am a mortal, I am ignorant, etc. But then, I am ignorant from a standpoint, knowledgeable from another standpoint. The very fact that I am knowledgeable and ignorant shows that I am neither ignorant nor knowledgeable. Both are points of view. And they are points of view only if the view is clear. What is the view? I am the invariable consciousness that is present, revealing the ignorance and knowledge.

There is nothing wrong in saying, 'I am ignorant' as long as the view is clear. Then you are not saying that 'I' is subject to ignorance. The revealed ignorance and the revealed knowledge are not 'I'; neither of it is the view. Therefore, when I say, 'I am ignorant' I have a wrong conclusion. 'I am limited in knowledge' is also a wrong conclusion; it is the source of the need to become knowledgeable. And that can never be fulfilled, because the more I know, the more I come to discover how much I do not know. Pursuing knowledge that way is the life of a *saṁsārin*. But, there is moving away from *saṁsāra* when I begin to question very intimately whether this 'I' is subject to ignorance. And I find that it is not. In fact, the pressure to be knowledgeable is because I am not ignorant, in reality, and I want to get back to myself. I cannot stand the conclusion that I am ignorant, because I am not, and I can be at home only being myself.

Being yourself is just understanding. It is not going and sitting somewhere, or being someone. It is just you. Never are you away from yourself, which is why you cannot stand this conclusion; it is against your nature.

Ātman is not mortal but the truth of time

The conclusion, 'I am a mortal' is corrected in the recognition of the self being self-revealing consciousness, which is not subject to time. Anything that exists in time is something that has a beginning and an end. Some things have no traceable beginning, but they end, and therefore exist in time. Consciousness is not subject to time. We make an assertion here that consciousness exists in all three periods of time – past, present and future.

There are many ways of looking at this. One way is this. Think of the past, think of your last birthday. When you think of this past event, do you think of it in the present or in the past? Whether it is the current thought of the stone age or of 1993 or of yesterday, it is all now. You think of the past now. All right, let us think of the future. Think about six months from now. When do you think about the future? Now or in the future? Now. So, the future is now, and the past is also now. Therefore, if you really want to know anything about time, you should know about the now.

Let us find out what is the 'now' in now. Does your concept of now imply time, a length of time? When you are conscious of a length of time, understand, there is time-consciousness. Keep that recognition of consciousness going. If you analyse the length of time involved in the present, you say that it is the present century, then the present year, the present month, the present week, the present day; then the present hour, the present minute, which has 60 seconds. So the present second is the present. Then the present second has one million microseconds, so a microsecond is the present. Now, mathematically you can go on and on, and you will never arrive at the present. But you think of any length of time, and in that length of time there is consciousness – consciousness of that length of time. As you look into it, the length of time erases itself, and what is present is consciousness alone. Therefore, consciousness does not come, does not go, *na udeti nāstam eti.*

In fact, you do not have to keep it going; it keeps going and you have to recognise that. When you think of time, there is time-consciousness. And time-consciousness is now-consciousness. In this now-consciousness, what is the length of time in 'now'? There is no length of time. This is what is called *sat*. It is not bound by time, but is the truth of time. The truth of time is now, and now is consciousness, *cit*, which is *ātman*. Therefore, *ātman* is what? *Sat*.

We have two words for *ātman*. One is *cit*, consciousness, the other is *sat*, so *ātman* is *sat* and *cit*, invariable consciousness. The word 'consciousness' is our translation for the word '*cit*' – it does not mean any other like social consciousness, environmental consciousness, but the consciousness of environmental consciousness, of social consciousness, etc. We have to use an English word, and we have chosen this one. In Sanskrit, too, we have the same problem of releasing the word '*cit*' from its limitations. Consciousness is a word for which there is no object, as we have seen. But at the same time, without being an object, it is recognised as invariable presence because of which all objects are cognised.

Being invariable, it does not rise, *na udeti;* it does not go, *nāstam eti;* it does not increase, *vṛddhiṁ na yāti*. That is the nature of consciousness. Coming and going is possible only in terms of time. Something was not there before, it is there now, and it will not be there later. Consciousness, *svayam vibhāti*, itself shines, not subject to time. It is *sat* and *cit*.

So, the conclusion, 'I am a mortal,' is wrong. Consciousness alone can be 'I', and everything else becomes an object of consciousness. Therefore, when you say, 'I am,' what do you mean? 'I', consciousness, am, is; consciousness 'is'. Any concept of 'was' or 'will be' is consciousness. Now you can understand the mistake also. In 'I am mortal,' the 'I am' is fine, but 'mortal' is an erroneous conclusion, and that conclusion is the basis for the fear of death. If you say that not-I is mortal, who says it is not? Not-I is mortal. That the body is mortal is not what causes the problem; the problem is, 'I am mortal'.

That the body is mortal, nobody is going to change. It is mortal, it is time-bound; you cannot stop its ageing and its dying. What is subject to death, dies, and what 'is' is. And before death, if I can understand this, then I do not mind the body being mortal at all. This self-confusion is the locus of all the problems of the self-conscious human being.

Ātman is free from unhappiness

Someone can say, "I am *sat-cit* alright, but that only makes me more sad. I thought sadness would go away some time, but now you say that I am eternal. In all three periods of time I exist, and therefore, I am going to be eternally sad. It does not solve my problem. In fact, you have caused a new problem for me. Previously, at least, I had a hope that I would go to heaven and be happy. But you have convinced me, it is a temporary place. So, heaven as a solution is gone, and therefore, Swamiji, I am eternally sad."

'I am sad' is also a conclusion. I have a question. Are you always happy or occasionally happy? If you say the you are occasionally happy, it means that otherwise you are sad. So, happiness is an event that takes place in your life. It comes and goes away, but never remains. Maybe, it is an additional attribute to the sad person, which the sad person picks up. Happiness seems to happen and then dissipate, like a metal which is heated. For the time being it is hot and glowing, and then, after some time the glow is gone, but the heat is there; later that also is gone. Similarly, there is a glow of happiness, then afterwards, the warmth of the cheerful mind; then that also goes away, leaving cold feet, fear, etc. Like the heat that is an adventitious attribute to the metal, the sad person also gains the added attribute, *viśeṣa*, of the glow of happiness. There seems to be a dissipation, what we call 'entropy'.[10] And again, I have to warm myself up, for which some music, a workout music, is necessary. All this is necessary so that I can be something. Therefore, it looks to me like happiness is an incidental attribute that is assumed by this sad individual, and then dissipates again. If 'I' is eternal, is this also going to be eternal? It means I will be like this all the time, and I have to depend upon situations to be happy.

The problem is, you keep on covering situations. One situation is new and eye-catching, and afterwards, it does not give the same kick. It is like the law of diminutive utility. A situation is no longer as arresting as it was before. You become familiar with it, and it does not produce the same happiness; you look for a new situation. This is *saṁsāra* and it is going to be there in all three periods of time, *trikāle'pi tiṣṭhati.* It means you are eternally booked to be the same.

However, you also told me that occasionally you become happy. That is enough for me. When that

---

[10] Entropy is a measure in thermodynamics of the unavailable energy in a closed system

occasion arises, when you become happy, does the sad person gather the happiness? If the sad person gathers the happiness, the sad person continues to exist. It is something like wearing a hat. When you wear a hat it is a new attribute to you, but do you disappear under the hat? No, this hat is only an addition. So too, if the sad person gathers happiness, like donning a hat, the sad person should continue. If, under the hat of happiness, the sad person continues, what does it mean? It means there can never be a moment of joy, which is pure happiness, so you can never laugh heartily. It will always be a wry, enigmatic smile. On one side, there is a smile, and on the other side, you do not know what it would be. But you do laugh heartily, and when you do, you do not seem to care for anything. Your concern for the future or the burden of the past, seems to have just disappeared.

Further, happiness is not an object. If it were, all of us would try to get that object and keep it with us. Though we covered this, we can just briefly look at it again. In the world we do not see an object called 'happiness,' nor do we see happiness as an attribute of an object. Nor is happiness an attribute of your mind. If it is, to whom does the sadness belong? Is there a mind when you are happy? Yes. Is there a mind when you are sad? Yes. Which is true? It is clear that happiness is neither an object, nor an attribute of an object. A particular time is not a source of happiness, much less a particular place. With this, the world is gone – time, place, situation, object. That is all the world is.

You need to understand that the world is neither a source of happiness, nor is it a source of unhappiness. The world is not capable of producing unhappiness or happiness. It can cause some physical pain, and it has a balm for that too. The world has opposites, but it cannot cause unhappiness. Therefore, who is the source of unhappiness? Let us understand this. We have established that there is no source of happiness outside.

Am I the source of unhappiness?

I can be both happy and unhappy. If I am the source of unhappiness, who is the source of happiness? I am the source of happiness too. Of these two, which is true, which is not true? If it is not true that I am the source of happiness, then the one who is unhappy has to become happy. The one who is unhappy becoming happy is just a contradiction. The happy person becoming unhappy is also a contradiction. If I am that very happiness, my becoming unhappy is equally a contradiction.

Between these two contradictions, let us see which one we like. If I am happy and then become unhappy, that contradiction seems to be one I can manage. Why? Because if I am the source of that very happiness, my unhappiness is due to wrong thinking, and that I can correct. If I am unhappiness, happiness is not possible at all. If I am happiness, even my wrong thinking cannot keep me from my being happy.

One good thing about thinking is that it does not last. Thinking exists when the thinking 'is', and, like moving clouds, it can never be stationary. The process of thinking is always moving. No thought can stay, and you should thank God for it, because if thoughts were to stay, you would not be able to see things discretely. If you were to see a car, and afterwards an elephant, you would see the elephant on the car. That a thought is momentary is a blessing for you, and it is a blessing all the way. Suspension of thought, *apohana*, is Bhagavān's grace.

As a simple person without knowledge of anything, no knowledge of *ātman*, or God, one is able to laugh for a moment. And if that is not there, one will not live. The human species would be dead and gone; nobody would be there to write some history, because no human being can stand interminable pain.

And there is no other grace which is as powerful, as meaningful, for a human being as this, and that is the capacity for one to suspend all one's opinions for the time being and just be oneself. It is not that one is enlightened; one is just lightened, for the time being.

Every self is loaded; it has a history. And that history also involves a projection of the future. The future is loaded with all the plans, and the past, of course, is loaded. So, with all this, the fears and anxieties, it is just impossible to laugh. But then, it is made possible by this grace called *apohana*, your capacity to suspend the whole personality so that only the person is there.

That person who says, "I am sad," which is a conclusion born of history, is suspended. If something amuses you, heartily you laugh, and all that is there is *ānanda*. In this *ānanda*, the object is in front and also the person who confronts the object. But there is no confrontation. The subject seems to swallow the object, loves the object. Being pleased with the object, the subject strikes harmony with it, and finds nothing wanting in the object. In fact, there is nothing found wanting in the person, really speaking. What I want you to understand is that when you are happy, what is there in front of you does not evoke in you the wanting person, the dissatisfied person, the disturbed person.

What does it mean to be the pleased person? The wanting person is quelled, for the time being. Everyone has these imps, the imps of a wanting person. There are so many imps inside, and if not one imp shows its head, you are pleased and find this experiential happiness called *sukha* or *ānanda*. These are words to point out who you are, because in that experience of happiness alone your own nature is revealed, according to the *śāstra*.

On enquiry it becomes clear that the source of happiness is not outside. Nor is it inside. Neither the liver nor kidney is a source of happiness; the kidney is for stones, the liver for cirrhosis. The mind is also not a source of happiness. What is left is only me. I am the source of happiness. But I am also the source of sadness. The world is not a source of sadness either, only I am the source of sadness. If sadness is my nature, I cannot be happy, and if sadness is not my nature, no sadness can stay forever, denying me the happiness that I am. Understand that this is how the situation is.

Unhappiness is against one's nature

I am sad is, after all, a thought, like any attribute is a thought. A thought is a point of view. You have to remember – I am sad, I am a failure, I am useless, etc. You have to remember all your conclusions from childhood, or, you have to be reminded of them. What we need to understand is that these are incidental attributes. It is very clear, then, that they do not belong to you, which is why they have to be remembered. And to remember is to employ your faculty of memory. That is a wonderful arrangement.

If all that you have gathered is always on the screen of your mind, nothing new can be registered. In order to ensure that we can know things, this capacity is given to us to suspend everything, and keep the mind free. And the capacity to suspend it all and learn something is also truly amazing. This is grace.

It is because of this alone that I am able to see myself as happy occasionally. And I love to be that person, not the sad person, waiting for this happy person to come.

That you have to see the happy person, later, is because of the conclusion, 'I am unhappy.' If that is true, you should be happy being unhappy, honestly, because that is your nature. If it is your nature, it will never become a matter for complaint. But you cannot stand being unhappy, nor can you get tired of being happy. Suppose someone complains, "I am too happy these days." How will anyone say that? If anybody does, then the problem is different. The truth is, you are happy being happy. That proves the point that even though both happiness and unhappiness are not from outside, but are from you, still, one is something you want to be, while the other is something you do not want to be. You are happy being happy; you are not happy being unhappy. It means unhappiness is alien to you.

Nothing alien will be accepted by your system. Your own constitution does not accept it, and you also do not accept anything alien to yourself, as a person. It is not that unhappiness is something that is alien to you in the sense of being unfamiliar. It is too familiar, but is alien in the sense of being against your nature. You do not want to be unhappy. And if you are unhappy, it is like having an insect in your ear – a live insect, a very enterprising insect, and at the same time, a dumb insect, which does not know how to come out. It is alien, and can drive you crazy; it has to get out. Unhappiness is exactly the same.

Many times your old grief has to get out only by grieving. You cannot handle that grief because it is alien, still it is inside and it has to get out. Unhappiness is against your nature. I am not saying that you should not be unhappy. This is not what I am saying. We are just trying to look at ourselves to see what is true, so that we can allow that truth to rule our life. And whatever has to go will go. The word '*ānanda*' is used to point out that at the moment of happiness what is there is just you.

Ātman has no spatial limitation

If *atman* is *saṁvit, cit,* consciousness that is invariable in all cognitions, in all situations of your experience, then it is also not subject to *kāla,* time. If it is not subject to time, is it subject to any spatial limitation? It is not.

Anything spatially limited has to have a form of some kind. Even if it has no visible form, it still exists only in a given place, like air, which is only in the atmosphere. It is not all-pervasive even though it has no particular visible form. In our model it does have form, and because it has constituents, it occupies certain place, so there is a place where it is not. Within the atmosphere you can create a vacuum by removing the air, and beyond the atmosphere there is no air. So, we have to understand what we mean by form. Anything that occupies a given place has a form.

Does space, then, have spatial limitation? No, it does not. Space is not in a particular place, space being space, is not spatially limited. Now, is consciousness spatially limited? If consciousness is spatially limited, then space will become the basis of consciousness, and consciousness would necessarily become an object. It would become variable, but that is not the case. As you are aware of time, you are also aware of space; there is space-consciousness, just like there is time-consciousness. Further, time-space-consciousness is there, and is also not there. Both time and space disappear in deep sleep. There is no space-concept, no time-concept, and at the same time, you are very much there.

Here, the method of analysis we are using is called *anvaya-vyatireka*, the co-presence and absence of a thing. *Anvaya-vyatireka* is a method to determine reality. In order to arrive at the reality of a given thing, we see whether the features of a given thing are always present. For instance, when I see a pot made of clay, I see, at the same time, clay. Now, there are two things here. One is clay, the other is a pot. These are two different words for two different things. When I use the word 'clay,' you do not think of a pot, and when I say, 'pot,' you need to think of clay or some other material. This is *anvaya*. If the pot is broken, gone, does the clay go? No. It means there is no *vyatireka*, helping us understand that clay is the reality of pot. This method of analysis is used all the time in scientific research. By this method of analysis we understand that the pot is not an intrinsic attribute to clay. And therefore, the clay becomes *satya,* that is, the reality of that pot. The pot has its own meaning, which is a particular form of clay, or any other material, that we call 'pot'. And not only is it a particular form, it has a purpose to serve too. The form includes the purpose.

So too here, when I look at what exactly is the 'I', in every experience there is the presence of consciousness. In experiencing a form, there is form-consciousness, in experiencing colour, there is colour-consciousness; so too, sound-consciousness, smell-consciousness, taste-consciousness, touch-consciousness. Then, time-consciousness, space-consciousness, emotion-consciousness; whatever is there, consciousness is present. If the whole waking state is dismissed, and I get into another dimension of reality, the dream state, then in that dream state, also, I find that consciousness does not go away.

In the dream there is a dream world and dream-world-consciousness. From this it is clear that the waker is a status that I assume, as is the dreamer.

When I go into deep sleep, I do not find the dreamer status or the waker status; both are gone. Then what status do I have? A sleeper status, wherein the individuality is not totally dismissed, but goes into an unmanifest condition, in the sense that in this state I have no experience of myself as a person with problems, etc. Perhaps that is the saving grace for the individual to protect him or her from insanity. That is the time when the individuality with all its problems is largely unmanifest. It is not totally unmanifest because the *ahaṅkāra*, the ego, is there in a rudimentary form. 'I am here' consciousness is not there; it is unmanifest, but consciousness is not gone. So, I am conscious of not experiencing anything particular. That is why I can relate the experience in the morning and say, 'I slept well.' In fact, deep sleep is defined only as an experience wherein there is no particular experience of an object. But *ātman*, 'I' consciousness, is not gone. I am there very much, because I slept.

Consciousness does not go to sleep, does not dream or wake up; it does not undergo any intrinsic change. Without undergoing any intrinsic change, with reference to a particular state we call the *ātman* a sleeper, a waker, or a dreamer. That invariable presence, without being a waker, dreamer, or sleeper, is *ātman*, consciousness.

If consciousness is the nature of *ātman*, which is invariably present in all three states of experience, then it is not bound by time and space. It has no form. Space is, consciousness is. Space has its existence in consciousness, while consciousness is self-existent. From the standpoint of *ātman*, consciousness, *cit*, there is no spatial limitation, because it is formless.

If this is so, then what is the distance from consciousness to anything in space? What is the distance between you, consciousness, and anything in space that you are conscious of? Between the pot and clay what is the distance? Between the wave and water what is the distance? Between space and consciousness what is the distance? Space is consciousness. Time is consciousness. Therefore, between space and consciousness there is no distance, because there is no space and consciousness. The moment you are aware of space, there is space-consciousness. The moment you recognise time, there is time-consciousness. There is no distance between time and consciousness, and there is no distance between space and consciousness.

If I ask you what is the distance between my two hands, you will say that it is about two feet. Suppose, I ask you what is the distance between my left hand and space. There is no distance. Distance is between two points in space. Now, is there distance between a point and space? The distance is nil. There is no distance between an object in space and space, which is why we say that space is all-pervasive.

Nothing is away from ātman

If this is so, between you and me what is the distance? You can say that between that physical body and this physical body there is a distance, if the word 'I' refers only to the physical body. Then between these two bodies, which exist in space and therefore provide two points in space, distance is inevitable. There is empiricality here. The distance can be covered by effort, then speed, time; in fact, everything comes into the picture. And this empiricality is relative in the sense that we compare our speed, etc., to the speed of light, which seems to be a constant. It is not true, totally, but our concept of speed is purely empirical, that is, it works. What we need to understand here is that between two objects in space there is a distance, a measurable distance, and that distance can be covered by effort.

Let us see the distance between me and you – the word 'you' transcends your body, your mind, your senses and refers to you as consciousness, which assumes the status of being a witness to everything else. And from that you, consciousness, to me, the physical body, what is the distance? This body, as we have seen, is this-body-object-consciousness. Between consciousness and the object-consciousness what is the distance? Zero. Think of a star, it is the same. When you say, "I see the star," the whole thing is a thought. The distance, the star and everything else is a thought. Then between the thought and consciousness what is the distance? That is the distance between the consciousness and the star there. Between the wave and water, what is the distance? That is exactly the distance between a thought-wave and consciousness.

Where are you? The question itself is wrong, because the question stems from the conclusion that there are places where you are not. There is no distance between you, consciousness, and any object in space. Between space and consciousness what is the distance? If you cite a distance, that distance is space, is it not? Between space and consciousness there is no distance whatsoever.

Ātman is *cit* consciousness. *Cit* is the only word which tells what *ātman* is. That it is a mortal, as

I thought, is not true; it is *sat*. It is *ānanda*, which means it is limitless spatially, *sat-cit-ānanda*. Here, we need to note that *ānanda* is not bliss. *Ānanda* is a word that reveals the limitlessness, the spatial limitlessness, of you.

So, *ātmā kaḥ*, what is *ātman*? *Saccidānanda-svarūpa*. In this *saccidānanda-svarūpa*, the *ānanda* is experienced by you. When? When you are aware of the object, because the limitlessness of consciousness is not something that has to surface. Spatial limitlessness means there is nothing that is away from it. That is what wholeness is. The limitlessness is wholeness, and experientially it is called fullness or happiness. In your usual experience of happiness, there is this fullness, limitlessness. And the limitlessness does not come, does not go, because, if consciousness does not come and go, its limitlessness also does not come and go. Its existence does not come and go; therefore consciousness is *sat-ānanda*.

Ignorance denies recognition of being limitless

If this is so, why do I experience that fullness, limitlessness, only occasionally? More often than not, I have no experience of that. Why? In fact, I ask you, "Why?" "That is because I do not know."

You have said it. It is ignorance. Even though you experience fullness now and then, you do not know it as yourself. The notion that you are an individual, and so on, is not there in sleep. That is why it is such an inviting experience, a welcome experience. You are never tired of going to sleep. Why? Because the notion, 'I am a small, insignificant, wanting, unhappy person,' is not there in sleep. Not only is it not there in sleep, it is not there occasionally, because of *apohana*, this great grace, the capacity to suspend the notion that you are the wanting person.

You can still be a subject, experience the object and be happy experiencing the world. Looking at the stars you can be happy, looking at a child, you can be happy. At that time, the child is the world. The world means whatever you confront. Even microbes can be the world. If what you confront is a child, and the child does not evoke in you the wanting person, you are happy. To the extent that the presence of the wanting you is there, to that extent the fullness is going to be edited and abridged. And, there are situations where that wanting you is totally taken care of. That is the time when you recklessly laugh, even though, generally, you do not do so.

This fullness is not something that comes between the fulfillment of a desire and the rise of another desire. You become happy without fulfilling a desire. And you become unhappy even after fulfilling a desire. If you become happy after fulfilling a desire, then you should be happy once you have married the person you wanted to marry. You should be happy all the time. Married? Happy! That is not true. Both ways it is not true. It is not true that after fulfilling a desire and before the rise of another, you are happy. You are not sure when you will be happy. How does it happen? If you do not feel like whipping yourself, you will see that you are limitless.

Therefore, the question, 'When will I be limitless?' is meaningless, because the 'I' is limitless. Where is the question of losing it at any time? If you think you have lost it, that is what we call ignorance. It is amazing. It can rob, it can cover everything, and make you think that you become limitless for some time. In other words, you become eternal for a few minutes. How ignorant is that!

Wholeness is never lost

The 'I' is always *ānanda*, unbroken *ānanda*. That is the nature, *svarūpa*. We are not talking of bliss. Bliss is an experiential word that does not communicate anything. If we say that it is bliss, the next question will be, "Swamiji, I know that I am bliss. How can I experience it?" In fact, in every blissful experience what is present is you, and that is to be cognised. We are not waiting for a new experience. We are analysing our own experiences of waking, dream, and deep sleep to understand what is invariable in all this. And that limitlessness is you, which is not gained only on the fulfillment of a desire. With the desire it is whole, without the desire it is whole. With the individuality it is whole, without the individuality it is whole. In sleep, where there is no individuality, it is whole, and in the waking state, with the individuality, it is whole. The wholeness is never lost for the 'I'. Knowing it, everything is a plus.

Otherwise, we wait for this wholeness to happen. This is like saying when will the sugar be sweet, the poor sugar does not know. If the sugar cube asks, "When will I be sweet?" "When you give up the notion that you are bitter." So too, all that is required is that the notion, I am small, goes, then the fullness rules.

Further, a thought, being a thought, is not permanent, so happiness can happen any time, without fulfilling any desire. And you do not need to be made happy, because that is just you. The manifest experience is happiness, and it reveals the fullness of you. It shows that you do not need to fulfill your wants in order to be happy. Does it not?

It seems logical that all your likes and dislikes have got to be fulfilled in order to be happy. If you are a wanting person because of all your wants, then you will be non-wanting only when all your wants are fulfilled. And it is impossible to fulfill all your wants. Therefore, it is logically impossible for you to be happy – to be happy and at the same time wanting is a contradiction. If you have to be happy, you have to be free from being wanting, and when are you going to fullfill all your wants? Your wants also include that others change, and if that is so, you are not going to be happy any time; you cannot change anybody.

The very fact that you are able to laugh reveals that you do not need to fulfill your wants in order to be happy. If, without fulfilling your wants, you see yourself happy, as you often do, what does it mean? It reveals that without fulfilling wants, you are happy. That is, you do not need to get into the process of 'becoming' to be happy. In fact, when you are in the process of becoming, you are unhappy, and when you give up the process of becoming, you are happy.

And you give up the process of becoming whenever you are happy. How do you give it up? Not cognitively but experientially. Without knowing anything, something captures you and you become happy. You do not know why you become happy, really speaking.

That moment of happiness only reveals the fact that the subject and object become one whole. This is wholeness, *pūrṇa*. When you are looking at the stars, and you are happy, you are whole. If you are unhappy, also, you are whole, but there is a sense of separation. When you are happy this separation is gone. The wanting-wanted separation is gone. That is why, any situation which does not evoke the wanting you is always a desirable situation. When you see the mountains, or nature of any kind, generally it does not evoke any demand. There is no rule, however, that when you see the mountains they will not evoke in you the demanding, wanting person. The blue sky generally does not create any problem for you. You do not want the sky to be different, the mountains to be different, the clouds, if at all, to be different. You accept that they are what they are. You are a non-demanding person and things are bright and beautiful. If things do not evoke in you the wanting person, there is a wholeness.

It is very simple, and that is what you need to understand. When I talk of wholeness, do not imagine some 'whole'. In fact, the imaginer and the imagined, the subject and the object, is the whole. There is no other whole. Whatever you do, it is just the whole, all the time. When does your wholeness go? It can never go. The subject and object form the whole, *sat-cit-ānanda*. This is you. All additions are within this *sat-cit-ānanda*. And if you remove all that is added, it will be *sat-cit-ānanda*. You add anything to space, it is space; you remove anything from space, it is space. In your understanding of wholeness, it is the same thing.

Ānanda is ananta – limitlessness

The definition of *ātman* is *saccidānandasvarūpa*. Elsewhere, there is a definition of Brahman, *satyaṁ jñānam anantaṁ brahma.*[11] This *satyam* is what we call *sat*, *jñānam* is *cit*, and *anantam* is *ānanda*. *Ānanda* has no other meaning except *ananta*. Any other meaning is not the meaning in this context. Therefore, '*ānanda*,' like the other words, is only a *lakṣaṇa*. They reveal, by implication, what that *ātman* is.

In *ānanda* there is a subject and there is an object. When you are happy because of something, that

---

[11] *Taittirīyopaniṣad* 2.1.1

something becomes the object, and there is a subject *ātman*, the individual. This individual subject and the object do not have any kind of wanting-wanted division, and when that is not there, the division-born unhappiness is also not there. When you find that the object is wanting in any way, you become a wanting person. And the presence of this wanting-wanted dichotomy creates a division, purely by your thought, in the already established wholeness, which is the nature of *ātman*. The wholeness means limitlessness, which is both subject and object. There is no other limitlessness. If the subject, you, and the object in front are one and the same, then there is limitlessness. And that is the nature of *ātman*, the *caitanya*, consciousness. It is never lost at any time. Even when you are wanting and there is an object wanted, then too, it is the same. But experientially, you will not be able to have that fullness in a wanting-wanted situation. If cognitively you have no appreciation of this limitlessness, then you can only wait for an experience in which the object pleases you and does not evoke the wanting person – onlythen you are happy. And that happiness is, therefore, a *lakṣaṇa* for *ātman*.

Why is *ānanda* mentioned if *ananta* is more accurate? There are two reasons. One is that it is a *lakṣaṇa*, because in the experience of happiness what obtains is the wholeness that is you. Thus, *ānanda* becomes the *lakṣaṇa* for *ātman*, which is *ananta*. That is what is said here in *anantaṁ brahma*. The second reason is that *ānanda* is something that everybody wants to have. That is, everyone wants to be happy. You want happiness, rather, you want to be happy. The happiness that you are seeking, even in experience, is just yourself. It is your fullness alone. But your seeking happiness makes it a kind of *puruṣārtha*. When we say that *artha-kāma* is a *puruṣārtha*, it means that it is something that is sought after by all. And this experiential happiness, the happy person, which is set up as a goal by everybody, is not separate from you. Why? Because you cannot be more than what you are. You can only be limitless, and you cannot improve what is limitless. It is to be cognitively gained. So, when *ānanda* is used in the place of *ananta*, you should see only the meaning of *ananta* in the meaning of *ānanda*, especially if *ānanda* goes along with *sat* and *cit*. This is called *svarūpa*. It is not experiential *ānanda*, *anubhūta-ānanda*, but rather, *svarūpa-ānanda*.

Svarūpa-ānanda and Experiential-ānanda

The difference between *svarūpa* and *anubhava*, experience, is this. The *anubhūta-ānanda* is due to a particular mental condition, *vṛtti-viśeṣa*. It is because of the *vṛtti-viśeṣa* that the mind assumes a certain form conducive for the experience of *ānanda*. But then, in that *ānanda*, the fullness that is experienced is the very nature of *ātman*. Therefore, *ānanda* stands for fullness or limitlessness, which is the meaning of *ananta*. This difference must be understood.

Limitlessness is something that you can cognitively own, whereas *ānanda* will keep you seeking. Because the *ātmānanda*, the special *ānanda* of the *ātman*, has to be proven to be something different from simple ice-cream *ānanda*, disco *ānanda*, rock *ānanda*, etc. All of them give you some *ānanda*, but they will say that it is not the *ānanda* they are talking about. It is some special *ānanda*, and therefore they call it 'Bliss' and spell it with a capital 'B'. Thinking that simple happiness is not an adequate word, they think they should use some special word because there is a special *ānanda*. Therefore, they will say that *sat-cit-ānanda* means existence-knowledge-bliss. Naturally, you are going to look at this 'Bliss' as something that is special, and you would wait for it to come. Suppose, there is out of the ordinary experience of happiness, how would you know, 'this is it'?

You need to have certain frame of mind to understand, to just see *ātman*, and that seeing is only cognitive. When it is cognitive, you have to gain it cognitively, *brahmavid āpnotiparam.*[12] *Vid* means there is a knower; the knower of Brahman gains *param*, the limitless. And *tarati śokam ātmavit,*[13] the knower of *ātman* crosses sorrow. This is how it is. The whole pursuit is cognitive. The truth is communicated until the other person sees it; that is teaching. All that is here is *ātman*.

"If that is so, then why I do not know?" The 'I do not know' is exactly what is addressed by Vedanta. You cannot say, "I studied Vedanta and now I am trying to do something else to know *ātman*, because Vedanta did not work for me." It has to work for you; you have to make it work by equipping yourself adequately. If the eyes do not see, you cannot say, "My eyes do not see colours, therefore I am going to use my nose or ears." You cannot do that. You have to correct your eyes. This kind of approach towards the *śāstra* and the teaching, is the appropriate attitude for understanding what is.

---

12 *Taittirīyopaniṣad* 2.1

13 *Chāndogyopaniṣad* 7.1.3

Now, with this, we must understand that *ananta* is the meaning of *ānanda*. Therefore *sat-cit-ānanda* means consciousness that is not subject to time and which is the content of everything, *sat*. On what basis do you say that *sat* has the meaning of the content of everything? Because it is *ananta*, it is limitless. This is the nature of *ātman* that is *sat*.

How do you recognise *ātman*? It is recognised first just as yourself, as purely consciousness, because you are a conscious being, and this consciousness is self-revealing. Then, about this consciousness you discover certain facts in terms of correcting your notions, 'I am mortal, time-bound,' and so on, by seeing that consciousness cannot but be timeless. This is how the word '*ananta*' helps you understand *sat*. Since *sat* is *ananta*, it is not an existent object in time, but is limitless in terms of time and space. Therefore, the word *ananta*, which is *ānanda*, is so very important.

We require these three words as the minimum number to address the three problems – that I am ignorant, that I am mortal and that I am unhappy. All these are solved by knowing *ātman* because all three problems are due to non-recognition of *ātman*.

Sthūla-śarīra

The author now explains every word in his definition of *ātman* in a question-answer form.

स्थूलशरीरं किम् ?
पञ्चीकृतपञ्चमहाभूतैः कृतं सत्कर्मजन्यं
सुखदुःखादिभोगायतनं शरीरमस्ति जायते वर्धते
विपरिणमत अपक्षीयते विनश्यतीति
षड्विकारवदेतत्स्थूलशरीरम् ।

sthūla-śarīraṁ kim?
pañcīkṛta-pañcamahābhūtaiḥ kṛtaṁ
satkarmajanyaṁ sukha-duḥkhādi-
bhogāyatanaṁ śarīram asti jāyate vardhate
vipariṇamata apakṣīyate vinaśyatīti
ṣaḍvikāravad-etat-sthūla-śarīram.

sthūla-śarīra – gross body; *kim* – what?
etat – this; *śarīra* – body; *kṛtam* – made of; *pañcīkṛta-pañca-mahā-bhūtaiḥ* – the grossified five basic elements; *satkarma-janyam* – (which is) born due to good *karma*; *sukha-duḥkhādi-bhogāyatanam* – (which is) the counter for enjoyment of pleasure, pain, etc.; *ṣaḍvikāravad* – which has the six-fold modifications (such as); *asti* – exists; *jāyate* – is born; *vardhate* – grows; *vipariṇamate* –

undergoes changes; *apakṣīyate* – degenerates; *vinaśyati* – perishes; *iti* – thus; *sthūla-śarīram* – (is) the gross body.

> What is the gross body?
>
> This body (that is) made of the 'grossified' five basic elements, born due to good *karma*, (which is) the counter for enjoyment of experiences of pleasure, pain, etc., which has the six-fold modifications (such as) exists, is born, grows, undergoes changes, degenerates and perishes, (is) the gross body.

Let us first look at *sukha-duḥkhādi-bhoga-āyatana*. *Āyatana* means a place to which something is restricted. This physical body is an *āyatana*, a dwelling place, for experiencing *sukha* and *duḥkha*. Every object that you experience does not necessarily give you *sukha* or *duḥkha*, pleasure or pain; it can be just an object of indifference. This is the *ādi*, in *sukha-duḥkha-ādi*.

The physical body, *śarīra*, is where you gather experiences, pleasant, unpleasant, and also in between, when you are awake.

And what is that *śarīra*? Etymologically, the word '*śarīra*' is derived from the passive of the verb *śṛ* which means to be shattered, to decay. Because by nature it is decaying, it is a *śarīra*, *śīryamānasvabhāvatvād iti śarīram*.

This is something which has various parts that are put-together, and therefore, it is subject to disintegration. This assemblage of varieties of things is what is called the *śarīra*, and the anatomy is called the *sthūla-śarīra*.

All right, how is it put-together? What does the anatomical body consists of? You can say a hundred different things. It consists of cells, it consists of limbs, of organs; we can talk about this in terms of so many different models. Here, we have a model called the *pañca-mahābhūta*, just to help us understand this.

A model should be understood as a model, not something that is absolute. It is a point of view. This is a book that talks about what is said in the *upaniṣad*, so naturally, it is going to present only the model presented by the *upaniṣad*. And the *upaniṣad*'s aim is only to point out what is true, the *vastu*, not to point out what are the basic elements, and how things function, etc. That is not its purpose. It is purely concerned with the reality. And in presenting this reality, it has to deal with the empirical reality that you face everyday. Your experiences have to be explained. The concern of the *upaniṣad*s is to show what is the content of all experience, naturally they have to take into account all human experiences. They cannot point out the reality without including these experiences and also explaining them.

If you say that *ātman* is distinct, *vyatirikta*, then *ātman* is one thing and everything else is omitted. And if everything else is omitted, what is omitted has to be assimilated again. Otherwise, how are you going to integrate that to *ātman*? So first, what is to be omitted is to be omitted in your understanding of *ātman*. When you want to know what *ātman* is, naturally, you have to negate all those that are superimposed upon *ātman*. First, we negate the physical body made of five elements. The whole *jagat* is covered within these five elements.

Let us look at the whole thing in a five-fold way. In this body we have five sense organs, and five organs of action. The five senses correspond to five sense objects, *śabda*, sound; *sparśa*, touch; *rūpa*, form; *rasa*, taste; *gandha*, smell. And these five sense objects that we experience through the five senses are nothing but the manifestation of the five basic elements called *mahā-bhūtāni*. Here, *mahā* is basic and *bhūtāni* is elements, the five basic elements. In physics they enumerate a number of elements in the periodic table, but here we are talking about basic elements that include space also. In physics, they will not consider space as an element, but here we do. Then *vāyu*, air, is an element, water is an element, fire is an element, and earth is an element. These are the five basic gross,[14] or physically manifest, elements. They are 'grossified,' really speaking, which is indicated by the word '*pañcīkṛta*.'

This physical body is made up of the five 'grossified' elements, *pañcīkṛta-pañca-mahābhūtaiḥ kṛtam*. It is viewed as a combination, an assemblage, of five gross elements. Not only this physical body, but any body is made of these five elements. It occupies space and there is air, oxygen, throughout; we are talking about a live body here. And there is *agni*, fire, indicated by the temperature. Water is there; the whole shape of this body is because of water. And then, the carbon etc., the minerals that comprise the body are the earth. So, this physical body, and every body, consists of five elements. Your body is five elements and my body is also five elements. Yet, you know the difference between this body and that body, due to particular parentage and so on, decided by *karma*. Otherwise, all bodies would look alike, being made of the same five elements. First there is parental selection

---

[14] Gross is not to be understood in its normal sense here, but is a technical word indicating that an element is physically manifest and can be perceived by one or more of the five senses.

that is set up by *karma*, accounting for a *jīva* being born in this particular body. Selection of place, time, etc., is also determined by *karma*. Even a snail is born of *karma*.

And why a human body? *Sat-karma-janya*. It is born of some *sat-karma*, which means *puṇya-karma*. Not pure *puṇya*, because then it would be a *deva-śarīra*, a celestial body. Pure *pāpa* will give an animal *śarīra*, and there again, there are different types of *pāpa*, so there is a snail-life, a frog-life, etc. And, some special *puṇya* with certain other *pāpa* will give you a human life. Thus, we have this *puṇya-papa*, and in this, what is responsible for a human body is some *sat-karma*, *puṇya-karma*, which is why it is called *sat-karma-janya*. 'Among the living beings, a human birth is difficult to gain, *jantūnām narajanma-durlabham*.'[15] There are so many options available. Why should the *jīva* take this human body? Well, because of some good *karma*, *sat-karma-janya*. This human body, which is *sat-karma-janya*, is *sukha-duḥkha bhogāyatana*, a hutment of enjoyment, a counter to encounter the world. And it is *ṣaḍvikāravat*, endowed with six-fold modifications – *jāyate*, *asti*, *vardhate*, *vipariṇamate*, *apakṣīyate*, *vinaśyati*. This is common for all. First, it is born, *jāyate*. It has to be alive;

---

[15] *Vivekacūḍāmaṇi* verse 2

only then will all other things follow. Once born, and born alive, it lives, *asti*. Then it grows, *vardhate*. At first it cannot move by itself, then it learns to move on its own force, and afterwards is slowly able to stand on its legs. This is growth, *vardhate*. Next, *vipariṇamate*, it undergoes change. The child becomes fourteen, fifteen; the whole physical body has become an adult, *vipariṇamate*. Then what happens? The *śāstra* does not worry about what happens to you for a few years. The next stage it counts is *apakṣīyate*, decline. You live an adult life, and slowly you begin to hold the book further and further away; it means, *apakṣīyate*. Then, one grey hair appears somewhere – *apakṣīyate*. Every joint makes its presence felt, they make a cracking sound – *apakṣīyate*. What comes next is *vinaśyati*, and one is history. These are the six modifications. We have to accept this; it is called *bhāva-vikāra*. Anything that is alive will undergo this six-fold change. That which has this six-fold change, *ṣaḍvikāra*, is *ṣaḍvikāravat*.

The *sthūla-śarīra*, physical body, undergoes all these changes, and is called *ṣaḍvikāravat*. Though it is a live body, we are only talking about anatomy here. What makes it alive is the *sūkṣma-śarīra*, which will be discussed. The live *śarīra* is the one that undergoes all this change. This *sthūla-śarīra* is also called *annamaya*, a modification of food; it is another way of looking at it, which is mentioned later. It is born of a modification of the food eaten by the parents, is maintained by food, and when it dies away, it becomes part of the elements. So, the *sthūla-śarīra* is called *annamaya*.

The *ātman* is *sthūla-sūkṣma-kāraṇa-śarīrād vyatiriktaḥ*, distinct from the *sthūla-śarīra*, the *sūkṣma-śarīra*, and the *kāraṇa-śarīra*. This has to be said because the *sthūla-śarīra*, etc., are not separate from *ātman*, whereas *ātman* is not any of them. That is what is pointed out here. *Viveka* is required because the attributes of the *sthūla-śarīra* are taken to be the attributes of *ātman*. To negate those attributes it was pointed out that *ātman* is distinct from the *sthūla-śarīra*, as is the *sūkṣma-śarīra*.

The *sthūla-śarīra* is the live anatomy, and the *sūkṣma-śarīra* is what makes it alive. Next, he points out what is the *sūkṣma-śarīra*.

Sūkṣma-śarīra

सूक्ष्मशरीरं किम् ?

अपञ्चीकृतपञ्चमहाभूतैः कृतं सत्कर्मजन्यं सुख-
दुःखादिभोगसाधनं पञ्चज्ञानेन्द्रियाणि पञ्चकर्मेन्द्रियाणि
पञ्चप्राणादयो मनश्चैकं बुद्धिश्चैकैवं सप्तदशकलाभिः
सह यत्तिष्ठति तत्सूक्ष्मशरीरम् ।

sūkṣma-śarīraṁ kim?

apañcīkṛta-pañcamahābhūtaiḥ kṛtaṁ satkarmajanyaṁ sukha-duḥkhādi-bhoga-sādhanaṁ pañca-jñānendriyāṇi pañca-karmendriyāṇi pañca-prāṇādayo manaścaikaṁ buddhiścaikaivaṁ saptadaśa-kalābhiḥ saha yattiṣṭhati tat sūkṣma-śarīram.

sūkṣma-śarīra – subtle body; *kim* – what?

yaḥ – that which; *apañcīkṛta-pañcamahābhūtaiḥ kṛtam* – is made of the five elements (that have not undergone the five-fold process of grossification); *satkarma-janyam* – born due to good *karma; sukha-duḥkhādi-bhoga-sādhanam* – the means for enjoyment of pleasure, pain, etc.; *pañca-jñānendriyāṇi* – five organs of perception; *pañca-karmendriyāṇi* – five organs of action; *pañca-prāṇādayaḥ* – five *prāṇas; manaḥ ca ekam* – plus one, the mind; *buddhiḥ ca ekā* – plus one, the intellect; *evam* – thus; *yat tiṣṭhati* – which abides; *saptadaśa-kalābhiḥ saha* – with seventeen factors; *tat sūkṣma-śarīram* – that (is) the subtle body.

What is the subtle body?

The subtle body is that which is made of five elements (that have not undergone the five-fold process of grossification), born due to

> good *karma*, the means for enjoyment of pleasure, pain, etc., with the seventeen factors namely, the five sense organs, five organs of action, five physiological functions, the mind and the intellect.

The *sūkṣma-śarīra* provides an important link between *ātman* and the *sthūla-śarīra*. It is a body that is *sūkṣma,* which means subtle. It is not available for physical perception, but at the same time, its presence cannot be missed. If I can give an example, what is *sūkṣma* for the fan is the energy. Energy is not visible, but at the same time you cannot miss it. And if energy is not there, the fan stops. So, what makes this fan work is the presence of energy. Similarly, anything that dies has a physical body which is alive. And that which makes it a live physical body is the *sūkṣma-śarīra*.

The *sūkṣma-śarīra* is always in keeping with the anatomy. Think of it. Suppose, there is a frog *sthūla-śarīra*. The hind legs are longer than the front legs, and it has a particular form. But if this frog has a *sūkṣma-śarīra* like that of a human being, what will be the lot of the frog? It will not be a frog. It will have all kinds of complexes, or it may even get enlightened! A frog must have a *sūkṣma-śarīra* in keeping with a frog's body and the life it has to live. And the human being must have a *sūkṣma-śarīra* in keeping with the human body. Therefore, there is something peculiar to the given physical body, which is indicated by calling it an *upādhi*. For the *sūkṣma-śarīra,* there should be an appropriate *sthūla-śarīra*. In nature we find that the *sthūla-śarīra* and the *sūkṣma-śarīra* combine very well. Only in a human body do we have this faculty of choice, of certain level of thinking, and so on. So, we understand that without the *sūkṣma-śarīra,* no living organism is alive. Without the *sūkṣma-śarīra* there may be a physical body but it is not alive; it cannot respond to the external world. That which makes the *sthūla-śarīra* respond to the external world, and makes it otherwise alive, is the *sūkṣma-śarīra*.

We find this *sūkṣma-śarīra* in different stages of evolution. Whether it is by evolution or by nature, we find different degrees of awareness to the external world. The monkey seems to be more aware of the external world than other mammals. It can use a weapon; a gorilla can take a stick in its hand and fight. A human being is more evolved, because he not only takes a stick in hand, but many other things too.

Sūkṣma-śarīra is not available for our visual perception, or any other form of perception. We can only make an inference. Inferentially we know; because it is alive, the *sūkṣma-śarīra* is there. Even the doctors declare death purely by inference. They shine a flashlight in the eyes of the patient, and the person does not respond. Then they try to detect the pulse, and there is no response, so they say that the person is gone. How did they conclude that the person is gone? Inference, because they do not see the person going. The *sūkṣma-śarīra* walking out is not seen; it is not visible, which is why it is called *sūkṣma*. Its going away is not seen, but you cannot miss its presence, and you cannot miss its absence either. That which makes the body alive and the departure of which is the death of the body is the *sūkṣma-śarīra*. In the absence of the *sūkṣma-śarīra* this human body no longer functions.

What are those functions provided by the *sūkṣma-śarīra*?

Sense perception by the senses, *jñānendriyāṇi*, and activity by the organs of action, *karmendriyāṇi* are because of the *sūkṣma-śarīra*. He tells what they are. The vocal apparatus, hands etc., are organs of action, each of which has a function. And if the organs of action do not function, at least the senses function, and if they also do not function, the mind functions. This is the *sūkṣma-śarīra*. In dream, the senses and organs of action do not function, but the mind functions. *Prāṇa*, the physiological activity, continues, so breathing continues and the mind is also active. When you go to sleep, the mind does not function, but *prāṇa* does, and because the *prāṇa* functions, the *sūkṣma-śarīra* is still there and the body is alive. Even though you have gone to sleep, or are in a state of coma you are there, because the *prāṇa* still functions. Therefore, *prāṇa* is a very important part of the *sūkṣma-śarīra*. That which gives life, which makes the body alive is the *prāṇa*. As long as *prāṇa* functions there is energy available for this body. All the physiological functions are called *prāṇa*, and when the body's *sūkṣma-śarīra* leaves, which means the body is dead, then the *prāṇa* does not function. Otherwise, a dead body would require breakfast, etc. When the *prāṇa* does not function, there is no digestion, absorption, circulation, and no respiration. The presence of *prāṇa* is the minimum requirement for life; there is always a minimum. There is also a minimum requirement in the anatomy, *sthūla-śarīra*, for this *sūkṣma-śarīra* to function. At least one kidney has to be functioning, half the liver, and at least thirty percent of the heart. If that minimum is there, the *sūkṣma-śarīra* will be here in this body. If the *sthūla-śarīra* does not have the minimum amount of functional organs, when there is a rupture there, the body dies. So, they are mutually dependent. The *sthūla-śarīra* should fulfill certain requirements, and then the *sūkṣma-śarīra* will function.

This physical body is a *bhogāyatana*, a tenement for experiences. And in this tenement, there is an indweller. Suppose, the person is lying down and I call him, "Rāma, please get up." He does not get up. Then I shout, "Get up." Rāma does not get up. Then I shake the person, still he does not get up. Perhaps, he is really in a deep sleep, so I sprinkle some water on his face. There is no response at all. Then, finally, I check the pulse. Till then I had some hope, but after checking the pulse, what do I say? Rāma is not locally available; he is gone. It means the tenement is vacated. The only difference between the bricks and mortar tenement and this tenement is that somebody else can occupy that tenement, but not this one. Once the tenement is vacated, it is useless; it was meant only for that person. Why? Because it is *sat-karma-janya*, born of some good *karma* done by that person. The physical human body is *sat-karma-janya*, and the *sūkṣma-śarīra* has to be in keeping with that, so it is also *sat-karma-janya*.

The physical body is *sukha-duḥkha-bhogāyatana*, the counter for the experience of pleasant and painful experiences, and the *sūkṣma-śarīra* is *sukha-duḥkha-bhoga-sādhana*, the means of gathering these experiences. The mind is a means to encounter the world, as are the senses and so on. They are the means to bring in the data of the world. That by which you gain something, gather something, do something, is *sādhana – sādhyate anena iti sādhanam*. The organ of speech is meant for expression, as are the hands etc. These organs of action, *karmendriyāṇi*, are *sādhana* for expression. So, either you express yourself into the world through the organs of action, or you let the world walk into you by means of the sense organs. Even the mind, as a necessary component of sense perception, or inference, is a *bhoga-sādhana*. Therefore, the entire *sūkṣma-śarīra* becomes *sādhana* for all experiences, *bhoga-sādhana*. *Bhoga* here does not mean enjoyment, but any experience. That is why it is *sukha-duḥkha-bhoga*. Experience is common, though it may be pleasant or unpleasant. To go through the experiences, and also to accomplish various ends, the *sūkṣma-śarīra* is the means, *sādhana*, and the *sthūla-śarīra* is the counter, *āyatana*.

This *sūkṣma-śarīra* is *apañcīkṛta-pañcamahābhūtaiḥ kṛtam*, made with the 'non-grossified' intangible form of the five basic elements. He will discuss this in detail later. This subtle body consists of the five senses of perception, *pañca-jñānendriyāṇi,* the five organs of action, *pañca-karmendriyāṇi,* and the five beginning with *prāṇa, pañca-prāṇādayaḥ. Prāṇa* here is respiration, and then we have *apāna,* elimination; *vyāna,* circulation; *udāna,* ejection; *samāna,* digestion. These are the five physiological activities, also called *prāṇa,* in general. So, three groups of five make fifteen, and to these are added the mind, *manaś* and the intellect, *buddhi.*

Though it is the same mental faculty, why do we make a separation between *manas* and *buddhi*? When there is a desire in the thinking faculty, or an emotion, or a doubt, we call it *manas,* mind. When there is a change to register a perception, that is also *manas.* The thought form that occurs when you see the Swami is a function of the *manas;* we can say it is a Swami-thought. Then, there is also the knowledge that this is the Swami, which is the function of *buddhi.* The mind in the form of determinate knowledge or ascertainment is called *buddhi, niścayātmika-antaḥ-karaṇa-buddhiḥ.* It is the same mind, but when there is a conclusion, when there is resolve, and when there is will, that is *buddhi.* Your *ahaṅkāra,* ego, is also included in the *buddhi.* It can also include recollection and memory, but if it is recollection of an emotion, or a recollection that leads to an emotion, it is *manas.* If it is just a recollection of an object, like what you ate for breakfast, and there is no emotion involved there, it is *buddhi*. If that recollection brings an emotion, then it is *manas*. Every mental function is included here in *manas* and *buddhi*. That which is there, *yat tiṣṭhati*, in this body, with these seventeen factors, *saptadaśa-kalābhiḥ saha*, is called *sūkṣma-śarīra*. This is also a product, something that is put-together.

There are different things here, put-together in a subtle form, created by the subtle elements, *apañcīkṛta-pañcamahābhūtaiḥ kṛtam*. These subtle elements are the same five elements, not 'grossified'. You can now understand that *pañcīkṛta* means grossified and *apañcīkṛta* means not grossified. These five elements that are not grossified, which are purely subtle, constitute the *sūkṣma-śarīra*. It is something like energy. In a light bulb there is a tungsten wire. That is the part that matters. And that matter is nothing but energy, but it is in a gross or material form; it is grossified energy. Energy in a gross form is matter, and in a subtle form is energy. When both are combined there is a light wave. We can understand that energy is the *sūkṣma* form of matter. Similarly, the five *sthūla* elements constitute the physical body, and their *sūkṣma* counterparts constitute the *sūkṣma-śarīra*. There is some arrangement here.

Both of them are born of five elements, one is *sūkṣma, apañcīkṛta-pañcamahābhūtaiḥ kṛtam,* and the other is *sthūla, pañcīkṛta-pañcamahābhūtaiḥ kṛtam.* The subtle body is made up of these five subtle elements with certain peculiarities brought about by some genetics. Therefore, there is a selection of parentage.

To be born with a human body requires a selection on the part of the *jīva*'s *karma* to give the human parentage. That is how the arrangement is. There again, the *sūkṣma-śarīra* is in keeping with the *sthūla-śarīra,* so the human form is *sat-karma-janya.* Of course, all the subtle bodies are made up of five elements, but there are certain peculiarities brought about by the selection of parentage, etc., which is done by *karma.* And that *karma* gets unfolded in this life. The old *karma* sometimes presents to you situations that you never worked for, and so you find yourself helpless. After all, this parentage that you have, you definitely cannot help now. You cannot change your parents. Even if you want to, you cannot replace your mother or your father. That is an already accomplished fact, and like that, there are many things that you cannot change.

In life you find many situations, without asking permission from you, get unfolded. If certain events have to take permission from you, you will never have a headache, never catch a common cold, you will have no hip pain or joint pain. Everything will be exact and proper. But, these things do not ask you at all, which is why we say that they are *karma* unfolding.

That which exists in a given physical body with these seventeen factors, the departure of which marks the death of the physical body, is *sūkṣma-śarīra*. It is not the *sūkṣma-śarīra* that departs, but the *ātman*, as the *jīva*, conditioned by the *sūkṣma-śarīra* that walks away. The *sūkṣma-śarīra* is not an entity. It is a composite that the *ātman* identifies as itself, therefore, seemingly limits it, *sūkṣma-śarīra-avacinna-caitanya-ātman*. So, *ātman* with this *sūkṣma-śarīra*, called *jīva*, walks away. And this walking away will be there until the person gets *mokṣa*. This is the *śāstra*.

Now, he is going to tell us what are the five sense organs, *pañca-jñānendriyāṇi*, and the five organs of action, *pañca-karmendriyāṇi*. This is the book in which all these terms are explained in detail, which is why we read it first.

Pañca-jñānendriyas, their function and presiding deities

श्रोत्रं त्वक्चक्षू रसना घ्राणमिति पञ्चज्ञानेन्द्रियाणि ।

śrotraṁ tvakcakṣū rasanā ghrāṇamiti pañca-jñānendriyāṇi.

śrotram – the ear (sense of hearing); *tvak* – the skin (sense of touch); *cakṣuḥ* – the eye (sense of sight); *rasanā* – the tongue (sense of taste); *ghrāṇam* – the nose (sense of smell); *iti* – thus; *pañca-jñānendriyāṇi* – (these are) the five organs of perception.

> The five organs of perception are: the ear (sense of hearing); the skin (sense of touch); the eye (sense of sight); the tongue (sense of taste); the nose (sense of smell).

Here, we must make a note of a peculiarity. The eyes are located, as are the ears, sense of smell, sense of taste. They have their locales. But, one sense organ is not located in a particular place in this body; it is all over the body. This is very significant and because of this alone, you have total identification with this body. The one sense organ that is all over this physical body is the sense of touch. Even the organ of taste initially registers the sense of touch. Taste comes later. This sense organ, the tongue, serves two senses, taste and touch. If you drink something piping hot, like milk, you will understand whether it is sense of taste or touch.

The sense of touch is all over the body. Only then can you take care of the body. Imagine, otherwise, if like the eyes, nose, and so on, the sense of touch is not in your fingers, hands or legs, but only at one point in the body. You may come home without your hands or legs! It is not like this, and cannot be like this. The whole body must be a sense of touch, because the *sūkṣma-śarīra* is present all over this physical body. Every cell has the presence of the *sūkṣma-śarīra*, and thus, the whole body is conscious.

Next, he tells us what are the five *karmendriyāṇi*, but before that let us look into a very interesting connection. You will understand this more profoundly when we cover more, but now we can look at it at this level.

You are here, in the scheme of things, and you are not isolated. Not only are you a part of everything, there is a certain symbiosis. Your presence is important for some others, and their presence is also important for you. There is an inter-dependence. There are many things like this. The bees require the flowers for nectar and the flowers need the bees for pollination. The trees give you oxygen, and you give them the carbon dioxide. So, you have a symbiotic existence. In this way, you are connected to this whole universe. Whether you know all of it, you are a part of the whole. If the physical world can be taken as one physical whole, then your physical body is part of it. The good thing is that you can still have certain independence in that scheme. The body has certain independence, because it is a living organism, and not mere forces. There is something more.

In this physical world, there are many forces, all of which are connected to each other. Within this physical world is another order of reality, which makes certain physical forms alive. That is what we call *sūkṣma*. Therefore, there is a *sūkṣma-prapañca*, a subtle world. Here, in this body, there is a *sūkṣma* level, and in an ant also there is a *sūkṣma-śarīra*. It follows the same principle. The *sthūla-śarīra* behaves in a certain manner, because in keeping with the *sthūla-śarīra*, there is a *sūkṣma-śarīra*.

This *sūkṣma-śarīra* consists of varieties of functionaries. Each one has a function, and every function is due to a collective law. For instance, a gland in your body, such as the pancreas, and any pancreas elsewhere, all behave the same; all of them fail, all of them work, all of them overwork, all of them produce insulin in the same way. Thus, you have a pancreatic collective. Then there is a thyroid collective, a pituitary collective, and so on. Because you have these collectives, you can study them and specialise in a given area, like the pancreas. So, we have all these laws – a pancreatic order, a hepatic order for the liver, etc. That is why if anything works on a frog, it should work on a human being. They first test a new drug or procedure on a frog, then on a rat, on a monkey, and if it has also worked on a monkey, then next they jump to a human being. They are so sure about this. This is what we call order.

We need to understand this order. Our *śāstra* is very much aware of this universe, the *samaṣṭi*, which is why everything is Īśvara for us. So there is nothing that we can approach irreverentially. There is nothing that does not evoke reverence, because everything is Īśvara. I am only making a provisional statement; we still have to prove that. And you cannot really appreciate Īśvara unless you appreciate this intelligent order. In every function there is intelligence, because the functionary is made in a peculiar form. In every functionary there is so much knowledge.

Each organ is just cells, but there is difference, and that implies knowledge. It is made to function in a particular way and that means it is a functionary. If it is a functionary, it follows certain order, which means there is some kind of a law. When we say that there is a law it means Īśvara is there, because we look at the law as not separate from Īśvara.

Each sense organ functions because of a law. This is what I call the order. The ears, for instance, uniformly only hear; they do not see. The eyes only see, they do not hear. What does it mean? There is an order here. There is a law, and because it is common, it is an order. This is what we call the collective. When we conduct research, we try to find out what is common, because in the commonality there is a law. The eyes see, and sometimes they do not. When they do not, why is it they do not? So, they look into the eyes to try to find out the mistake. Then they correct the mistake. That is how research proceeds. They try to find out what is the defect and how it can be corrected, then how that correction can be improved upon; it goes on. And it all indicates that there is a law.

These laws are viewed from the standpoint of the total. As I told you provisionally, the whole thing that is here is Īśvara. If all that is here is Īśvara, then Īśvara from a given standpoint, viewed as a phenomenon, is called a *devatā*.

Looking at Īśvara from the standpoint of the functioning *jñānendriya*s, he says:

श्रोत्रस्य दिग्देवता । त्वचो वायुः । चक्षुषः सूर्यः । रसनाया वरुणः । घ्राणस्याश्विनौ । इति ज्ञानेन्द्रियदेवताः ।

śrotrasya digdevatā, tvaco vāyuḥ, cakṣuṣaḥ sūryaḥ, rasanāyāḥ varuṇaḥ, ghrāṇasyāśvinau, iti jñānendriyadevatāḥ.

śrotrasya – of the ear; *devatā* – the deity; *dik* – Dik, the directions; *tvacaḥ* – of the skin; *vāyuḥ* – Vāyu; *cakṣuṣaḥ* – of the eye; *sūryaḥ* – Sūrya; *rasanāyāḥ* – of the tongue; *varuṇaḥ* – Varuṇa; *ghrāṇasya* – of the nose; *aśvinau* – the Aśvins; *iti* – thus; *jñānendriya-devatāḥ* – are the presiding deities of the five organs of perception.

The presiding deities of the organs of perception are: of the ear is Dik; of the skin, Vāyu; of the eye, Sūrya; of the tongue, Varuṇa; of the nose, the Aśvins.

The ears are presided over by the deity called *Dik*. For the sense of touch, the *devatā* is Vāyu. Vāyu here is not air, but the *devatā*. Air is the physical form, so what is the *devatā*? It is exactly like you. There is a person there, who is not the physical body, and that person is the *devatā*, *vāyu-devatā*, who presides over the sense of touch.

For the eyes, the *devatā* is the Sun. It is not the sun as such, but the Sun *devatā*. The Lord in the form of the Sun is called Sun *devatā*, the deity who is presiding over sight, who is the law of sight. When we have problem with sight, we not only go to the ophthalmologist, but we also pray to the Sun *devatā*. The ophthalmologist has to diagnose properly and also treat properly. He is not God. And so, we have special prayers, one of which is *āditya-hṛdaya*, a few verses in praise of the Lord Sun. If you have a problem with sight, and you read that, you will get better sight. It has worked. I had given the meaning of *āditya-hṛdaya* to somebody who was losing his sight, and after reading it for some time, he got back everything. It works.

Now, for the sense of taste the *devatā* is Varuṇa, the Lord of water. Next, the two Aśvini *devatā*s form the presiding deities of the sense of smell, in the left and right nostrils. These are the *devatā*s of the *jñānendriyāṇi*. I will talk about these further later, but now let us just understand what they are.

श्रोत्रस्य विषयः शब्द-ग्रहणम्। त्वचो विषयः स्पर्श-ग्रहणम्। चक्षुषो विषयो रूप-ग्रहणम्। रसनाया विषयो रस-ग्रहणम्। घ्राणस्य विषयो गन्ध-ग्रहणमिति।

śrotrasya viṣayaḥ śabda-grahaṇam
tvaco viṣayaḥ sparśa-grahaṇam
cakṣuṣo viṣayo rūpa-grahaṇam
rasanāyā viṣayo rasa-grahaṇam
ghrāṇasya viṣayo gandha-grahaṇamiti.

śrotrasya – of the ear; *viṣayaḥ* – the sphere; *śabda-grahaṇam* – (is) receiving sound; *tvacaḥ* – of the skin; *viṣayaḥ* – the sphere; *sparśa-grahaṇam* – (is) receiving touch; *cakṣuṣaḥ* – of the eye; *viṣayaḥ* – the sphere; *rūpa-grahaṇam* – (is) receiving colour (form); *rasanāyāḥ* – of the tongue; *viṣayaḥ* – the sphere *rasa-grahaṇam* – (is) receiving taste; *ghrāṇasya* – of the nose; *viṣayaḥ* – the sphere; *gandha-grahaṇam* – (is) receiving smell; *iti* – thus.

Thus, the sphere of the ears is receiving sound. The sphere of the skin is receiving touch. The sphere of the eyes is receiving sight. The sphere of the tongue is receiving taste. The sphere of the nose is receiving smell.

Grahaṇa means reception, receiving. What kind of *grahaṇa* is it? He defines the sense organ in terms of the object, *viṣaya*, it receives. For the ear, the object that is received is sound, *śabda-grahaṇa*. The perception of sound is the reception of sound, and receiving a sound is the purpose for which the ears exist. The ear lobes may be meant for many things, but as a sense organ, the ear is meant only to receive sound. Next, the sphere of skin is receiving touch. That is the purpose for which the *tvak* is there. *Tvak* is not just the skin, but the sense of touch that is all over the physical body. Then, the *viṣaya*, the object, of the eyes is receiving forms and colours. The purpose for which the eyes exist is the perception of forms and colors. The tongue as an organ of perception is the sense of taste, *rasa-grahaṇa*, and the presiding deity is Varuṇa. It also serves as an organ of speech. Bhagavān was also trying to minimise everything, and as far as possible put two or three things together. Everything is well-connected with the minimum number of materials. There are many organs in the human body, and they are all placed there after good planning, because these many are necessary to be a human being with a self-conscious mind. This is the minimum requirement for that. Lastly, we have the sense of smell for which the object is odor, *gandha*. It is located in the nose, which is not only meant for the perception of smell, but also for breathing.

Pañca-karmendriyas, their function and their presiding deities

Now, he discusses the five organs of action, the *indriyas* that help you perform actions called the *karmendriyāṇi*.

वाक्पाणिपादपायूपस्थानीति पञ्चकर्मेन्द्रियाणि ।

vākpāṇipādapāyūpasthāni iti pañcakarmendriyāṇi.

vāk – the organ of speech; *pāṇiḥ* – the hands; *pādaḥ* – the legs; *pāyūḥ* – the organ of evacuation; *upasthaḥ* – the organ of procreation; iti – thus; *pañca-karmendriyāṇi* – (these are) the five organs of actions.

The five organs of action are : the organ of speech, the hands, the legs, the organ of evacuation and the organ of procreation.

Vāk, the organ of speech; *pāṇi*, the hand; *pāda*, the feet, *pāyu*, the organ of evacuation; and *upastha*, the organ of procreation. These are the five organs of action, *iti pañca-karmendriyāṇi*. And they also function because of *devatā*s. They are:

वाचो देवता वह्निः । हस्तयोरिन्द्रः । पादयोर्विष्णुः । पायोर्मृत्युः । उपस्थस्य प्रजापतिः । इति कर्मेन्द्रियदेवताः ।

vāco devatā vahniḥ, hastayorindraḥ, pādayorviṣṇuḥ, pāyor mṛtyuḥ, upasthasya prajāpatiḥ, iti karmendriya-devatāḥ.

vācaḥ – of speech; *devatā* – the deity; *vahniḥ* – (is) Fire; *hastayoḥ* – of the hands; *indraḥ* – (is) Indra; *pādayoḥ* –

of the feet; *viṣṇuḥ* – (is) Viṣṇu; *pāyoḥ* – of the organ of evacuation; *mṛtyuḥ* – (is) Mṛtyu; *upasthasya* – of the organ of procreation; *prajāpatiḥ* – (is) Prajāpati; *iti* – thus; *karmedriya-devatāḥ* – (these are) the (presiding) deities of the organs of action.

> The (presiding) deities of the organs of action are: Fire for organ of speech, Indra for the hands, Viṣṇu for the feet, Mṛtyu, Lord death, for the organ of evacuation, and Prajāpati for the organ of procreation.

Agni is the presiding deity of speech, *vāk*, the one because of whom there is speech. The fire god is the deity of speech. Why? Because when you speak, you throw light upon a topic. Some say that heat is also generated, but that is not what is meant here. The *devatā* is purely in the form of light, *prakāśātmika*. When we talk of fire here, it is as the source of light, not heat, because speech implies that you are revealing something. Only then should you speak.

This is reflected in the names for the three grammatical persons in Sanskrit – first person, *uttamapuruṣa*; second person, *madhyamapuruṣa;* and third person, *prathamapuruṣa*. The meaning of *prathamapuruṣa* is 'first person,' but it is the third person, he, she, it.

Why? Because, before you talk find out whether you have a worthwhile topic. You must have material, a subject matter to talk about, and that subject matter is *prathamapuruṣa*. If you talk about Rāma, Rāma will form the *prathamapuruṣa*. Talk about a pot, pot will be the *prathamapuruṣa*. The subject matter will be in the third person, *prathamapuruṣa*, the foremost person.

Then, when you talk, make sure there is somebody to listen to you. That somebody who is available is *madhyamapuruṣa*. Respect him also. Do not waste his time and do not intrude upon his privacy. Just because you want to talk, you do not push the person to sit and listen, even if what you have to talk about is worthwhile. This is *tapas*, discipline, and you need to learn this. So, what you talk about is worthwhile, *prathama-puruṣa*, and you have respect for the listener, *madhyama-puruṣa*. Then comes the *uttama-puruṣa*. *Uttama* means last, and lastly, you come into the picture, *uttamapuruṣa*.

It is amazing how grammar shows the thinking behind the whole culture. People just talk because they want to talk. It is different from speaking to throw light upon a topic that is in your head. It has to manifest for which we have language. Language can include gestures, or even sign language. Whichever means you use, that is what we call communication, and if you are using the organ of speech, the *devatā* is Agni. Therefore, Agni *devatā* is meant here only as a source of light. And from this we understand that our speech should throw light, not produce heat.

For the hands, which represent strength etc., the presiding deity is Indra. For the feet, the presiding deity is Lord Viṣṇu. Being all-pervasive, he is the Lord for your legs and feet, with which you are able to move around. The lord of clearance, Yama, is the presiding deity for the organ of evacuation, *pāyu*. When the kidney is in trouble, Yama *devatā* is invoked, because the kidneys, etc., are very important for the clearance of waste. The creator, Brahmāji, is the *prajāpatiḥ*, the *devatā* for the organ of procreation.

He now gives each organ's sphere of action, *viṣaya*.

वाचो विषयो भाषणम् । पाण्योर्विषयो वस्तुग्रहणम् ।
पादयोर्विषयो गमनम् । पायोर्विषयो मलत्यागः ।
उपस्थस्य विषय आनन्द इति ।

vāco viṣayo bhāṣaṇam, pāṇyorviṣayo
vastu-grahaṇam, pādayorviṣayo gamanam,
pāyorviṣayo mala-tyāgaḥ, upasthasya
viṣaya ānanda iti.

vācaḥ – of speech; *viṣayaḥ* – the sphere; *bhāṣaṇam* – (is) speaking; *hastayoḥ* – of the hands; *viṣayaḥ* – the sphere; *vastu-grahaṇam* – grasping objects; *pādayoḥ* – of the feet; *viṣayaḥ* – the sphere; *gamanam* – movement; *pāyoḥ* – of the organ of evacuation; *viṣayaḥ* – the sphere; *mala-tyāgaḥ* – elimination of waste; *upasthasya* – of the organ of procreation; *viṣayaḥ* – the sphere; *ānandaḥ* – pleasure; *iti* – thus.

> The sphere of activity of the organ of speech is speaking; of the hands, grasping things; of the feet, movement; of the organ of evacuation, elimination of waste; of the organ of procreation, pleasure.

The sphere of the organ of speech is *bhāṣaṇa*, speaking. The hands, from scratching onwards, have their scope in grasping things, *vastu-grahaṇa*. It means receiving an object, dropping an object, everything that our hands can do. The area of the legs and feet is *gamana*, moving around, which includes kicking a football. The province of the organ of evacuation is throwing out waste. The *upastha* is the organ of procreation, and there is a particular pleasure, *sukhaviśeṣa*, in that.

With this, the *sthūla* and *sūkṣma-śarīra*s are explained in some detail.

Kāraṇa-śarīra

कारणशरीरं किम् ?
अनिर्वाच्यानाद्यविद्यारूपं शरीरद्वयस्य कारणमात्रं
सत्स्वरूपाज्ञानं निर्विकल्पकरूपं यदस्ति
तत्कारणशरीरम् ।

kāraṇaśarīraṁ kim?

anirvācyānādyavidyārūpaṁ śarīra-dvayasya kāraṇa-mātraṁ satsvarūpājñānaṁ nirvikalpaka-rūpaṁ yadasti tat kāraṇa-śarīram.

kāraṇaśarīram – causal body; *kim* – what (is)? *anirvācya-anādi-avidyā-rūpam* – of the nature of indefinable, beginningless *avidyā; śarīra-dvayasya* – of the two bodies (gross and subtle); *kāraṇa-mātram* – as merely the cause; *satsvarūpa-ajñānam* – ignorance of one's nature; *nirvikalpaka-rūpam* – in the form of total non-differentiation; *yad asti* – which is; *tat* – that (is); *kāraṇa-śarīram* – the causal body.

What is *kāraṇa-śarīra*?

Kāraṇa-śarīra (causal body) is that which is of the nature of indefinable beginningless *avidyā*, as merely the cause of the two bodies (gross and subtle), ignorance of one's nature, and of the nature of total non-differentiation.

The whole analysis we are doing now is *tattva-viveka*, a discriminative analysis conducted with the help of the *śruti*. We conduct this enquiry because there is a basis for it, and that is *aviveka*. When *viveka*, discriminative analysis, is applied, there is necessarily *aviveka* providing as basis for it, and we have seen this basis adequately. Our experience also gives us the basis to understand that there seems to be some confusion about realities. Then the *śruti*, of course, tells us that there is confusion, when it tells us what we should know about ourselves. Therefore, this enquiry is done by the one who has *aviveka* with reference to *ātman*, which is mistaken for *anātman*, and *anātman* is taken for *ātman*. *Ātman* is taken to be the body-mind-sense complex, and everything else is regarded as different. And because of this *aviveka*, wrong conclusion, this analysis is a necessity.

That wrong conclusion stems from self-ignorance. The ignorance of reality happens to be self-ignorance, the reality being the self. First, you want to know the truth, and slowly it ends up in wanting to be yourself because the truth is you. That is why truth-finding becomes a trip, an endless trip, if you exclude yourself. The truth happens to be you, and therefore, knowing the truth is knowing oneself. The self-confusion has to go, and it can go. What goes is only self-ignorance, called *avidyā* from the standpoint of your enquiry here.

Avidyā is anādi – beginningless

This *avidyā,* the self-ignorance, does not begin; it only knows how to go. Why do we say it does not begin? Any beginning implies its prior absence. If it begins, it was not there before, and unless it was not there before, it cannot begin. If ignorance begins, which means it was not there before, then what was there before it began? If light was not there before, what was there? Darkness. Similarly, if ignorance was not there before, it means that knowledge was there. And knowledge and ignorance cannot co-exist. *Avidyā* cannot be there if its opposite, *vidyā,* is there. If *vidyā* is there, *avidyā* cannot begin. You can understand why we say that *avidyā* is *anādi,* beginningless. But it comes to end. Therefore, it is also *mithyā.* Our definition of reality is that which has no beginning, no end. And *avidyā,* which is *anādi,* is the *kāraṇa śarīra.* It is called a *śarīra,* being an *upādhi,* an adjunct, because of which the *saccidānanda-ātman* is a *jīva,* an individual who has the sense of doership, does *karma,* gathers *puṇya-pāpa,* which form the cause to be born again and again. So, there is no beginning for it, and it does not exist by itself.

With regard to the *svarūpa* of *ātman*, there is *ajñāna*. What exactly I am is not known to me, but that 'I am' is known to me. 'I am' is evident, in fact, self-evident, and that I am *saccidānanda* is not known to me at all. What is known to me is, I am a doer, an enjoyer, I am limited, a *saṁsārin*. This is very well known to me.

There is confusion, which is why the enquiry starts. If the confusion is not there, if the mistake is total and there is no element of doubt, then there will be no self-enquiry at all. The very self-enquiry is because I have variable notions about myself, and this confusion is also *ajñāna*.

Avidyā is anirvācya

Now, if this *sat-svarūpa-ajñāna*, which is *anādi*, and in the very form of ignorance, *avidyā-rūpa*, has a reality, then we have a problem here. One reality is *ātman*, and *avidyā* would be another reality. If you say that due to *avidyā* a person becomes a *jīva*, then you are presenting two parallel realities. If it is so, *avidyā* cannot do anything to *ātman*, and *ātman* will not be mistaken for something else. If there is another reality other than *ātman*, that reality can only create something that has no connection with *ātman* at all. But that is not how it is. Therefore, *ātma-ajñāna*, like everything else, does not exist independently of *ātman*. Any ignorance, whether it is ignorance of an object or ignorance of *ātman*, does not exist independently, but depends upon *saccidānanda-ātman*. *Ātman* is the *āśraya*, the basis, that gives reality to this very ignorance.

So, *ātma-avidyā* is neither independently existent like *ātman*, nor it can be dismissed as non-existent. You need to concede that it is in between *sat* and *asat;* this is what we call *mithyā*. It is neither independently existent, *sat*, nor is it non-existent, *asat*, but it has some kind of existence, *yat kiñcit bhāvam asti*. As long as it exists, it exists. It is something like a dream. Is dream real or unreal? If you say it is unreal, non-existent, then you will not experience it, and if you say it is existent, then you cannot shake it off on waking up. And therefore, dream is in between. Not only is dream in between, everything else is also in between.

We need to understand this 'in between'. It is called *anirvācya*. That which can be categorically stated is *nirvācya*, and that which cannot be categorically stated is *anirvācya*. The meaning of the word is not as we often come across in Vedanta books. If it is inexplicable, the discussion is over. Why make an attempt to explain if it is inexplicable? It is meaningless.

Therefore, to say that it is not categorically definable is really explaining it properly. We can all understand that. A pot cannot be stated to be existent, nor it can be dismissed as non-existent. Its status of being in between these two is what is called *anirvācya*, that which cannot be categorically accepted as real or unreal.

Ignorance, being what it is, does exist, because it creates a problem for me. The problem, I am happy, I am sad, *ahaṁ sukhi, ahaṁ duḥkhi*, is there, and the cause of that is *sat-svarūpa-ajñāna*. This *ajñāna* cannot be dismissed as non-existent, because I see the product. Nor I can say it is existent, because in the wake of knowledge it goes away. Also, it is not independently existent apart from *ātman*. So, he says, *sadasadbhyām-anirvācya-avidyā*. It is that which is not available for categorical appreciation, *nirvaktum-ayogya-anirvācya-avidyā*. Here, no diagram can help. What kind of diagram can you give for the reality of a pot? The whole *śāstra* is a reality *śāstra*. And *ātman* is not available for a diagram. It is limitless. What can you do? There is no attribute, and everything else is not available either this way or that way. Therefore, this *ajñāna* is that which cannot be diagrammatically expressed, or categorically stated, and at the same time cannot be dismissed as non-existent. It is *anirvācya-anādi-avidyā-rūpaṁ satsvarūpa-ajñānam.*

Further, the *kāraṇa-avidyā*'s own form, until the product arises, has no *vikalpa*. It is free from any kind of division, *nirvikalpaka-rūpa*. Pure ignorance, when its product is not there, when the error is not there, is called *vastu-agrahaṇa,* purely non-recognition of the *vastu*. And that kind of experience is there in sleep or when your mind resolves in a situation where there is no division. Whether you are able to resolve the knower-known difference, for the time being, or notice that between two thoughts there is no knower or known, it is *nirvikalpa*. That *nirvikalpa* is exactly the state of ignorance and the *ātman*. Between thoughts what obtains is nothing but *ātman* plus ignorance, as long as it is there. If it is not there, then it is *ātman* without thought, and *ātman* with thought. It is all the same. The clay with the form of a pot and clay without being a pot are both the same clay. With a pot it is clay, without a pot it is also clay. In the form of a pot it is useful, without the form of a pot, well, it is not immediately useful. You can make a pot out of it. Similarly, if ignorance is there between two thoughts it is *nirvikalpa*. *Ātman* is *nirvikalpaka-rūpa*, and ignorance of it also has no features, so there is no experience of duality.

If ignorance is there, however, it will continue to be there, because ignorance is not opposed to consciousness.

If somebody says that when all thoughts go away, only pure consciousness is there, I will ask, "When did it become impure?" It is like saying that when all waves go away, pure water will be there. When did it become impure? When the waves were there, was it impure? When a thought is there *ātman* is there. When a thought is not there *ātman* is there. *Ātman* is always the truth of everything, and therefore, it is always there. So, the *ajñāna* that denies knowledge of the nature of oneself, *ātman*, is *anirvācya*, that which cannot be categorically stated as real or unreal. And its beginning cannot be arrived at, *anādi*. The *jīva* himself, who is exploring, is a product of that ignorance, and he cannot really arrive at the cause of ignorance. He need not, because we are not exploring to know what ignorance is, we are exploring what we are ignorant of.

Further, the cause of the two bodies, subtle and gross, is that because of which there is the experience of not thinking, not objectifying anything, like in sleep or in a resolved frame of mind, *nirvikalpaka-rūpaṁ śarīra dvayasya kāraṇam yadasti*. Because it is the cause of an experience, it is called *śarīra*, and that is the cause, *kāraṇa*, for the *jīva*. This is called *kāraṇa-śarīra*.

Now *ātman* is independent of these three *śarīra*s, *sthūla-sūkṣma-kāraṇa-śarīrād vyatiriktaḥ*, though all three are not independent of *ātman*. Because of these three *śarīra*s, we have three distinct states of experience.

Avasthā-trayam

A state of experience is called *avasthā*. *Ātman* is that which is present in all three states of experience, and without which these states of experience are not possible. *Ātman* is unaffected by any state of experience – it never sleeps, and never wakes up, either partially or fully. *Ātman* is always present. It has no eyelids. When you say, "I slept, I dreamt, I am awake," 'I' is *sākṣin*. But, while the sleeper is *ātman*, the dreamer is *ātman*, and the waker is *ātman*, *ātman* is neither sleeper, dreamer, nor waker. This is what we call *avasthā-traya-vicāra*, analysis of the three states of experience.

अवस्थात्रयं किम् ?
जाग्रत्स्वप्नसुषुप्त्यवस्थाः ।

avasthātrayaṁ kim?
jāgrat-svapna-suṣuptyavasthāḥ.

avasthā trayam – the three states of experience; *kim* – what (are)?

jāgrat-svapna-suṣupti- avasthāḥ – the waking, dream and deep sleep states.

What are the three states of experience?

(They are) the waking, dream and deep sleep states.

The next question is:

जाग्रदवस्था का ?
श्रोत्रादिज्ञानेन्द्रियैः शब्दादिविषया ज्ञायन्त इति यत्सा जाग्रदवस्था । स्थूलशरीराभिमान्यात्मा विश्व इत्युच्यते ।

jāgradavasthā kā?
śrotrādi-jñānendriyaiḥ śabdādi-viṣayā jñāyanta iti yatsā jāgradavasthā, sthūla-śarīrābhimānyātmā viśvaḥ ityucyate.

jāgradavasthā – the waking state; *kā* – what (is)?

yat – that (in which state); *śrotrādi-jñānendriyaiḥ* – by the organs of perception such as the ear, etc.; *śabdādi-viṣayāḥ* – the objects of cognition beginning with sound, etc.; *jñāyante* – are cognised; *sā jāgradavasthā* – that is the waking state; *sthūla-śarīra-abhimānī-ātmā* – 'I' *ātmā*, identifying with the gross body; *viśvaḥ* – *viśva*; *iti ucyate* – is called.

What is the waking state?

That (in which state) the objects, of cognition beginning with sound, etc., are cognised by the organs of perception such as the ear, etc., that is the waking state. 'I' *ātmā* identifying with the gross body is called *viśva.*

What is the waking state? *Śrotrādi* is (the five sense organs) beginning with the ears. With these sense organs, their respective sense objects – beginning with sound – are known; they are perceived by you. This state is waking, *jāgradavasthā*.

With the sense organs exposed to the sensory world, you gather experiences of the world, such as sound, *śabda*, and so on, through the sense organs such as the ears, *śrotṛ* etc. Naturally, it includes your actions in the world. When your sense organs bring in the world to you, you are going to respond to the world. When you are awake, experiencing this world and expressing yourself in this world, it is *jāgradavasthā*, and *ātman* is called *viśva*. The *avasthā*, the state of experience is waking, and the one who goes through that experience is the waker, *ātman*.

Without *ātman* there is no experience whatsoever. The *svarūpa*, the nature, of *ātman* is consciousness, and every experience implies consciousness. Since the presence of consciousness is always there in an experience, *ātman* is there, but it is qualified. The qualification here is this waking experience. So, we call *ātman*, the waker. And when *atman* is waker, the *jīva* is *viśva*. Here, *viśva* means you are complete, as a *jīva*, because here alone you can use your free will. In dream you cannot; you are only an experiencer, *bhoktṛ*. Therefore, there is *kartṛtva*, doer-ship, only in the waking state. And here alone the *puruṣārtha*s are possible. Anything new that you want to gain here is accomplished only by your free will. You are complete as a *jīva*, an individual, in this incarnation only when you have identification with your physical body. After all, you are born with this physical body. If you are complete without it, why should you be born with the physical body?

You have come to this physical body; that is why the waker is called *viśva, sthūla-śarīra-abhimāni*, the one who identifies with the physical body. This implies identification with the other two bodies, *kāraṇa* and *sūkṣma*. We have to make a note of this so that we do not commit the mistake here of thinking that the identification is only with the *sthūla-śarīra*. The person who identifies with these three bodies – *sthūla-sūkṣma-kāraṇa-śarīra abhimāni* – is called *viśva*, a complete manifest *jīva*.

Next, is the dream state and the dreamer is *taijasa*.

स्वप्नावस्था का इति चेत् ?
जाग्रदवस्थायां यद्दृष्टं यच्छ्रुतं तज्जनितवासनया निद्रासमये
यः प्रपञ्चः प्रतीयते सा स्वप्नावस्था ।
सूक्ष्मशरीराभिमान्यात्मा तैजस इत्युच्यते ।

svapnāvasthā kā iti cet?
jāgradavasthāyāṁ yaddṛṣṭaṁ yacchrutaṁ
tajjanita-vāsanayā nidrā-samaye yaḥ prapañcaḥ
pratīyate sā svapnāvasthā,
sūkṣma-śarīrābhimānyātmā taijasa ityucyate.

svapna-avasthā – the dream state; *kā iti cet* – (if it is asked) what is?
jāgrad-avasthāyām – in the waking state; *yad dṛṣṭam* – what was seen; *yat śrutam* – what was heard; *tad-janita-vāsanayā* – (projected) by the impression born of that; *nidrā-samaye* – while in sleep; *yaḥ prapañcaḥ* – which world; *pratīyate* – is experienced; *sā svapna-avasthā* – that is the dream state; *sūkṣma-śarīra-abhimānī-ātmā* – 'I' *ātmā*, identifying with the subtle body; *taijasaḥ* – *taijasa*, the effulgent one; *iti ucyate* – is called.

(If it is asked) what is the dream state?
(It is) the world which is experienced while in sleep, (projected) by the impression born of

what was seen, what was heard in the waking state. 'I' *ātman* identifying with the subtle body is called *taijasa,* the effulgent one.

This is a very interesting statement, '*nidrā-samaye yaḥ prapañcaḥ pratīyate*, the world which appears at the time of sleep.' *Samaye* means at the time of, and *nidrā* is sleep, so during sleep, the kind of world which is experienced by you is dream. Whatever world appears to you as an experience at the time of sleep, that state of experience is called a dream. Why do we say *nidrā-samaye*? Why should we not say that when you are not awake you are dreaming? No. From the waking state, there is no direct connection to the dream. In the waking state, there is an order of reality that involves identification with this physical body, and with this identification you cannot go to the dream state. It is impossible, for dream is another order of reality. There is no sudden dropping of the waking state and getting into the order of dream reality. So, you completely die to this order of waking state. And dying to this order of reality is going to sleep. In sleep, all this is gone in terms of your experience. When the waking experience is gone, and there is no other mental activity, that is called sleeping. And from sleep, you wake up half to dream. If you wake up straight away to the physical body, which means identifying with the physical body, then you are a waker, *viśva*. During the waking there is only day dream possible which is not dream. Therefore, the mention '*nidrā-samaye*, during sleep.' Modern research has confirmed this.

The dream-reality-experience is the same as in the waking state. When you dream, your expression there is complete, in that you are affected by the world and you affect the world. In dream you do not think, "After all, this is a dream. Why should I bother?" If you think like that, it is part of the dream. In the waking state also, you may say, "After all, this is *māyā*," without knowing what it is. Similarly, while dreaming you may say that it is a dream, but it is part of the dream reality. It may be some kind of a trigger to wake you up. Therefore, in dream the reality-experience is exactly as it is here.

The dream state is a great help to us, even though dream analysis is not necessary at all for us to understand what is *ātman* and *anātman*. There is no necessity for analysis of sleep either. It is analysed because we go through these experiences, and we need to account for these experiences. We are purely concerned with realities. We are trying to find out whether 'I' is waker, dreamer or sleeper. And the analysis of these three states of experience reveals the presence of *atman*, but it is not any one of the three.

Whenever you are awake, the varieties of experiences that you go through leave behind on the slabs of memory certain impressions, *vāsanā*s. These memories of experiences in which you were very much involved, are what you experience in a dream.

The experience may not appear in the same form, but in a symbolic form it is known to you; it is never unknown. This is why here we have, 'Whatever was seen in the waking state, *yaddṛṣṭaṁ jāgradavasthāyām*.' And not only what was seen here, but also what was heard. Sometimes you can go through the experience of a narrative of an epic like Rāmāyaṇa or a class in biology. Therefore, whatever was seen or heard of, stands for all forms of experience during the waking state. This recollection called *vāsanā* is of waking experience. With the help of the impression, the memory, born of experiences one had gone through, *tajjanita-vāsanayā*, there is a *prapañca*, a world of experience, and that state of experience is called dream. In our model, this is how we define it. In another model, they will explain it in terms of certain *nādi*s, which have a physiological/ physical aspect. Neurologically, also, you may have another model.

Further, in dream you undergo an experience in which there is a *sūkṣma-śarīra,* but no identification with the *sthūla-śarīra.* You do not identify with the senses, but at the same time, you undergo sensory experiences with the *sūkṣma-śarīra.* The mind along with the *prāṇa* is active, which is why *prāṇa* is important. If it ceases to be, there is no *sūkṣma-śarīra* activity, and the *jīva* has moved away. The *kāraṇa-śarīra* will also be gone.

This *sūkṣma-śarīrābhimāni,* one who identifies with the memory, etc., who undergoes the experience of dream, is *taijasa,* the effulgent one. Why effulgent? Because he is purely in the form of thoughts, which are all one effulgent *jyotis,* he is called *taijasa.* The *upaniṣad* gives a meaningful name. *Viśva,* the name for the waker, as we saw, is the one who is complete. The dreamer is *taijasa, sūkṣma-śarīra-abhimāni,* and *kāraṇa-śarīra-abhimāni.* And who is *taijasa*? When you say he is a dreamer, that 'er' is *ātman.* The 'er' is common in all three. Whether it is seeing, hearing, or speaking, 'er' stands for the person as we see in the seer, hearer, and speaker; the 'er' is *ātman.*

Here, we have to note that there is a mistaken notion being propagated that the waker is not *ātman,* dreamer is not *ātman,* and the sleeper is not *ātman.* What is *ātman*? It is beyond, it is the fourth, and that is *ātman.*

That is conciousness, please. Understand, consciousness is not a state; it is the 'er' present in waking, dream, and in deep sleep. But all these three states of experience do not affect the *ātman*; they are incidental. That is what is pointed out by this analysis of the three states of experience. What is present in all the three states is *ātman*, and *ātman* itself is not any one of them. This is the *phala*, the result, of this enquiry. A given method of analysis that helps you understand the topic in discussion is called *prakriyā*.

Continuing with his definitions of the three states, the author asks:

> ततः सुषुप्त्यवस्था का ?
> अहं किमपि न जानामि सुखेन मया निद्रानुभूयत
> इति सुषुप्त्यवस्था ।
>
> *tataḥ suṣuptyavasthā kā?*
> *ahaṁ kimapi na jānāmi sukhena mayā*
> *nidrānubhūyata iti suṣuptyavasthā.*

tataḥ – then; *suṣupti-avasthā* – the deep sleep state; *kā* – what?

aham – I; *kim api* – anything; *na jānāmi* – do not know; *sukhena* – happily; *mayā* – by me; *nidrā* – sleep; *anubhūyate* – is experienced; *iti* – thus; *suṣupti-avasthā* – the deep sleep state.

> Then what is the deep sleep state?
>
> 'I do not know anything. Happily the sleep is experiened by me.' Thus, (this is) the deep sleep state.

Then, what is the deep sleep state? You cannot say that *suṣupti avasthā* is the one in which there is snoring; one can dream and also be snoring. It is common experience that in sleep, there is no subject-object relationship. Waking up you say, "I did not know anything particular." In sleep when nothing is happening, you cannot say so at that time. Only on waking up you can say, "I slept well, *sukham aham asvāpsam*." The word '*sukha*' is added here to prove that in sleep you have given up your individuality, and with that, all the problems of the individuality. Note that only the individuality is gone, not the individual. The individual is there in sleep, because the experience, I slept, is there. But the individuality is gone, and when that is gone, all the problems of limitation are gone. There, the experience is a happy one; there is no problem because there is no *vikalpa*.

Now, you can understand what *nirvikalpa* is. It means there is no *vikalpa*. There are many *vikalpa*s, but whatever the *vikalpa*, it indicates duality, a subject-object duality. Then again, there are varieties of objects that the subject experiences; none of these are there in deep sleep. The subject also does not undergo any change to become a hearer, seer, thinker, etc. All these *vikalpa*s are absent in sleep – and you love it. You love it so much that you extend your sleep by another half an hour in the morning, when you can. This is also why people love *nirvikalpa-samādhi*. In sleep you have *nir-vikalpa,* no *vikalpa,* no duality, and in the experience of *samādhi* also, there is no *vikalpa*. It is the absence of duality that you love in both, and in this there is no difference between the two. The difference is that in *samādhi,* the mind is awake. There is nothing wrong with it, if you want that, but the problem is you will emerge from it, and then say, 'I **was** *nirvikalpa.*' Śāstra tells you, 'You **are** *nirvikalpa* inspite of subject-object difference.'

The analysis of the three states of experience reveals this fact that *ātman* is free from all states of experience while the states are not without *ātman.*

Next he says:

कारणशरीराभिमान्यात्मा प्राज्ञ इत्युच्यते ।

kāraṇa-śarīrābhimānyātmā prājña ityucyate.

kāraṇa-śarīra abhimānī ātmā – 'I' *ātman,* identifying with the causal body; *prājñaḥ* – *prājña; iti ucyate* – is called.

I, *ātman*, identifying with the causal body is called *prājña*.

The *kāraṇa-śarīra abhimānī ātman*, the sleeper, who is totally identified with the *kāraṇa-śarīra*, is called *prājña*. Why is *ātman* called *prājña* here? When he is awake he is not *prājña*, he is *ajña*; he says, 'I am ignorant.' This is very interesting. In the *śāstra*, it is pointed out that when a blind man goes to sleep, he is no longer blind. Why? There is no conclusion, 'I am blind.' Even though he is blind, he is no longer blind in deep sleep. So too, the *rāja*, the king, is no longer a *rāja*, the beggar is no longer a beggar, and the musician is no longer a musician. When you are awake you recognise the limitations of your knowledge. The moment you go to sleep you drop that sense, 'I am *ajñaḥ*.' And in that way you are a *prājñaḥ*, because the sense, 'I am of limited knowledge,' is not there at all. This is the meaning for *prājñaḥ*. Whether a baby is sleeping, or a great *paṇḍita* is sleeping, in sleep both of them are *prājñaḥ*. Here, it is just a name; there is no other meaning for it in this context.

The *sthūla-sūkṣma-kāraṇa śarīra*s, each gives you one state of experience. Identified with the *sthūla-śarīra*, for instance, *sthūla-śarīra-abhimāni-ātman*, one is a waker.

Therefore, these three are *upādhi*s for *ātman*. An *upādhi* is that which brings about a seeming change to something. A crystal can appear to have orange colour, if an orange cloth is behind it. The orange colour does not belong to the crystal; a crystal is always clear. So, what makes it orange? Its *upādhi*. The orange cloth becomes an *upādhi* for the crystal, and the crystal appears to be orange. If you take the crystal for an orange coloured stone, that is an error. And there are people who think they have to remove the colour from the crystal. You can understand what is cognitive. You do not need to remove anything from the crystal, but you should watch it in different situations. Suddenly it assumes a different colour, now red, now yellow, and now without any colour. From this we understand that the crystal has no colour at all. This is cognitive. The method is *anvaya-vyatireka*, co-presence and absence. By seeing the variable nature of the colour, we understand that the crystal never gives up its purity. So too, *ātman*. Even though it appears to be sleeper, dreamer and waker, it is free from all of them. But *ātman* is mistaken to be the three states of experience. Once the original mistake is there, all other mistakes occur, and in them there is certain uniformity. That is why we can state them all here.

Mistakes are not generally universal. Here, they are; therefore, everyone has to correct the mistake. That is why Vedanta will not be popular, and is never popular. And it need not be popular. We can make it available for everybody, because it is relevant for any person, but we need not popularise Vedanta.

The mistake is universal because there is a basic ignorance of oneself. And as a human being, every *jīva* has these three *śarīra*s, *sthūla-sūkṣma-kāraṇa*. These three *śarīra*s account for five, what I would call, layers, where we can commit a mistake. There is only one mistake, and that is with reference to *ātman*. But that single mistake is experienced in a five-fold way, at five different levels, uniformly.

Five basic levels of error about ātman

You have a physical body. I have a physical body. Both of us are born with ignorance; therefore, *ātman* can be taken as the physical body. One becomes a confined person, a conscious being who is as good as this body. One takes oneself to be as good as the physical body – I am mortal, I am male, I am female, I am young, I am old, I am black, white and so on. Attributes of the body are taken to be the attributes of the self, *ātman*. This is one mistake.

Then there is another mistake – I am hungry and thirsty. If I am hungry, *ātman* should always be hungry. The truth is, I am hungry now, I am not hungry now, I am thirsty now, I am not thirsty now. Yet, I identify with hunger and thirst. It is another level of error. I am ill, I am healthy, is all with reference to what we call, in one word, *prāṇa*. And it is also uniform, collective. Then, we have conclusions with reference to the senses, I am blind, I am deaf. It is not that the ears are deaf or the eyes are blind – I am deaf, I am blind. Therefore, the deafness or the blindness which belong to the senses are taken to be the attributes of 'I,' and I suffer. Again, the condition of the mind is my condition. The emotional condition of my mind, like anger, and so on, is my condition. And that forms a level of error. If I like something, I am a liker. If I dislike something I am a disliker. These are the mind in the form of *rāga-dveṣa*, mistaken for I, *ātman*.

Then, I have another level – I did this, and I am guilty. This happened to me and I am hurt. The guilt and hurt belong to the ego, but the conclusion is, I am the agent, *kartṛ*; I am the experiencer, *bhoktṛ*. That is the ego, not I.

We have a further level of error – 'I am ignorant, I am happy, *sukhi*, I am sad, *duḥki*.

So, these are the three different levels in which we commit mistakes – the three *śarīra*s are providing us with three types of mistakes. Hence, the three *śarīra*s are viewed as five *kośa*s. It is a *kośa* because it covers, like a sheath, *kośavat ācchādakatvāt kośaḥ*. At each level you commit a mistake. So, we have five types of mistakes corresponding to the five levels of experience. They are common to all, and are considered *kośa*s that cover *ātman*.

However, *ātman* cannot be covered by anything. You cannot even cover your knowledge. Suppose a person has a scar, or some birth mark, and does not like it, so he or she covers it with some cosmetic stuff. The patch is covered, but can his or her knowledge that there is a patch be covered? It cannot be covered. You cannot cover knowledge, much less can you cover consciousness. There is no *kośa* for *ātman*, therefore it does not have any of the attributes of these *kośa*s, it is *pañca-kośātītaḥ*.

> पञ्चकोशाः के ?
> अन्नमयः प्राणमयो मनोमयो विज्ञानमय
> आनन्दमयश्चेति ।
>
> *pañca-kośāḥ ke*
> *annamayaḥ prāṇamayo manomayo*
> *vijñānamaya ānandamayaśceti.*

pañca-kośāḥ – the five sheaths; *ke* – what (are)?

annamayaḥ – the food (modified) sheath; *prāṇamayaḥ* – the vital air sheath (the physiological functions); *manomayaḥ* – the mind sheath (the mental states); *vijñānamayaḥ* – the intellect sheath; *ānandamayaḥ ca* – and the sheath of happiness; *iti* – thus.

What are the five 'sheaths'?

The food (modified) sheath, the vital air sheath (the physiological functions), the mind sheath (the mental states), the intellect sheath, and the sheath of happiness.

Every level is a *kośa*. For instance, *annamayaḥ cāsau kośaḥ*; it is *annamaya* and it turns into a *kośa* because like a *kośa* it covers, in the sense that it is a place where people commit a mistake. Because this mistake is uniform, it is called a *kośa*. And there are five of them, which are enumerated in the *śruti* as *annamaya*, etc. *Annamaya* means *anna-vikāra*, a modification, or transformed form of food. There is also another meaning for this suffix, *mayat*; it has the meaning of predominance, saturation, like saturated with water would be *jala-maya*. When you say *annamayaḥ yajñaḥ*, it means a Vedic ritual in which food distribution is abundant. So, *mayat* has these two meanings, and we have to see which is appropriate. Here, in *annamaya*, there is no difficulty at all. But, there seems to be a difficulty when we see the translation of *annamaya* as 'food-sheath.' First he enumerates the five *kośa*s, and then talks about each one of them.

Annamaya-kośa

अन्नमयः कः?
अन्नरसेनैव भूत्वान्नरसेनैव वृद्धिं प्राप्यान्नरूपपृथिव्यां
यद् विलीयते तदन्नमयः कोशः स्थूलशरीरम्।

annamayaḥ kaḥ?
annarasenaiva bhūtvānnarasenaiva vṛddhiṁ prāpyānnarūpapṛthivyāṁ yad vilīyate tadannamayaḥ kośaḥ sthūlaśarīram.

annamayaḥ – food (modified) sheath; *kaḥ* – what (is)? *sthūla-śarīram* – the gross body; *annarasena eva* – by the essence of food alone; *bhūtvā* – having come into existence; *vṛddhiṁ prāpya* – having gained growth; *ānnarūpa pṛthivyām* – in the earth that is in the form of food; *yad vilīyate* – which resolves; *tad* – that (is); *annamayaḥ kośaḥ* – food (modified) sheath.

What is the food (modified) sheath?

The gross body, having come into existence by the essence of food alone, having gained growth, (and also) which resolves in the earth that is in the form of food, is food (modified) sheath.

The first is *annamaya*. What is eaten is *anna, adhyate iti annam*. Even though the word '*anna*' has come to generally mean rice, anything that is eaten is *anna*. Now, the essential form of this *anna* eaten by the parents becomes the cause for the child to be conceived, *annarasenaiva bhūtvā*. Then, having come into being, the child in the mother still grows by the essence of food alone, *annarasenaiva vṛddhiṁ prāpya*. After conception, the food that the mother eats, nourishes the foetus, then it grows, and is born. Once it is born, it continues to grow by what? *Anna-rasena eva*; only, *eva*, by the essence, *rasa*, of *anna*.

We eat a lot of things, but a lot of it is thrown out. These are things that the system rejects, and what is essential the system retains. That is called *rasa*. By this *annarasa*, the body grows, and having grown, it dies away. Where does it go? Well, nothing is lost really speaking. All these five elements forming the tangible *sthūla-śarīra*, go back to the same earth, *pṛthivī*. And what kind of earth? *Annarūpa-pṛthivyām*. The *pṛthivī* itself is considered to be *anna*, because all food comes from there. Food is vegetarian. Even if somebody eats non-vegetarian food, finally speaking, even that animal depends entirely upon what comes from the earth alone. The earth is the producer of food, is the source of food. So, that which gets resolved into the *pṛthivī*, which is in the form of food, *annarūpa-pṛthivyāṁ yad vilīyate*, that physical body, *sthūla-śarīra*, is called *annamaya*, a modification of food. Being born of food, it is called *annamaya*.

Why does he call it a *kośa*? It is a *kośa* only when it is a locus for committing a mistake. Otherwise, it is not a *kośa*, it is only *annamaya*. *Annamaya* becomes a *kośa*, because it covers our understanding of *ātman*. Our interest is in whether *ātman* is *annamaya*. It is not. If it is not *annamaya*, why do we bring in *annamaya* at all here? If I ask you, what a cow is, you need not tell me that a cow is not a horse, not a dog, etc., because the cow is not me. Unless I have a doubt whether I am a cow, you do not need to say that I am not a cow. You just have to tell me what a cow is. But then, if the cow is mistaken for a horse, you do have to say, "This is a cow, not a horse."

Similarly, *ātman* is mistaken for *annamaya*. Since *ātman* is taken to be as good as this physical body, you have got to say that *ātman* is not *annamaya*. And again, why do we say that it is not *annamaya* instead of saying that *ātman* is not the physical body? That should be good enough. No. There is a *viveka* being pointed out here.

When you see the food outside, whether it is a piece of bread, or cooked vegetables, do you have *ātma-buddhi* in any one of them? Do you take the bread as yourself? No. However, when they become a part of the physical body, your attitude changes. You do not say that the physical body has weight, you say, 'It is my weight.' When you are weighing vegetables, and rice, etc., it is 'that' weight, but when it comes to the weight of the body, then you say it is 'my' weight. Therefore, we need to correct it. This weight is the weight of the body. Period. There is nothing more to it. If at all there is anything more, it is only Bhagavān. Bhagavān puts these things all together to make this body, and then makes it alive.

Prāṇamaya-kośa

प्राणमयः कः ?
प्राणाद्याः पञ्चवायवो वागादीन्द्रियपञ्चकं प्राणमयः कोशः ।

prāṇamayaḥ kaḥ?
prāṇādyāḥ pañca-vāyavo vāgādīndriya-pañcakaṁ prāṇamayaḥ kośaḥ.

prāṇamayaḥ – *prāṇamaya; kaḥ* – what (is)?

prāṇādyāḥ pañca-vāyavaḥ – the five physiological functions beginning with respiration etc.; *vāgādi-indriya-pañcakam* – the five organs of action beginning with speech and so on; *prāṇamayaḥ kośaḥ* – the sheath that is a modification of air.

> What is *prāṇamaya*?
>
> *Prāṇamaya*, the sheath that is a modification of air, is the five physiological functions beginning with respiration etc., and the five organs of action beginning with speech and so on.

Prāṇādyāḥ pañca-vāyavaḥ – *prāṇamaya* is the five 'airs', beginning with *prāṇa*. 'Five airs' is purely an expression, extended from the respiration that implies air, *vāyu*. Respiration is very important in your life; only as long as the breathing goes on are you alive. That is *prāṇa*, and is *vāyu*, respiration, the main function necessary for keeping this body alive. It has nothing to do with air, as we understand it; *vāyu* here is respiration. Because of respiration there is life, and because of that life, there are some other activities that are also called *prāṇa* or *vāyu*. And there are five of them. There can be more, or fewer, but in our model there are five. It is purely a model. These five include all the glandular activities, which are very important. These glands are small things which control everything. If a tiny gland in the ear is not functioning, you cannot stand up; you will wobble. So, they can cause all kinds of problems.

In another model, there are *marmas*, centres, which regulate bodily functions. If they press those points, the person will reel in pain. In fights they used to do that. Even today, in Kerala, there are people who know this discipline. And they use it to cure – accupuncture and accupressure are said to have come from this *marma-vidyā*. But in our model, the *śāstra* talks about this five-fold function, *pañca-prāṇa*, of our entire physiological activity. Sometimes, *prāṇa* stands for all five, but when it is mentioned separately, as it is here, *prāṇa* is purely respiration. Then *apānā* becomes evacuation, *vyāna*, circulation, which implies your heart and the whole circulatory system. All arteries and veins come under circulatory system. Then, *samāna* is digestion. You have to digest and assimilate what is necessary for the body. Everything that is eaten is converted into chyle first, and then cycled into the whole metabolic pathway, converting to energy. This process is what we call *samāna*, and necessarily includes the liver, stomach, pancreas, and so on.

All of them are included in *samāna*. Lastly there is *udāna*,[16] *ud-giraṇa-kara*, that which reverses the process, like vomiting. These are the *pañca-prāṇa – prāṇa, apāna, vyāna, udāna, samāna* – that account for the entire physiological function, making this body alive. It gives the energy for this body to live, to do, and to think. So *prāṇa* supplies energy. It has modifications, meaning different life functions, and the *prāṇādyāḥ* are these five vital functions, *pañca-vāyavaḥ*. They function along with organs of action beginning with speech, *vāgādi-indriya-pañcaka*, where energy is involved. The five organs of action and the five *prāṇa*s together constitute what we call *prāṇamayaḥ*.

Prāṇamaya is good enough to describe it. Why do we add *kośa* to the word? Because *ātman* is taken for the *prāṇamaya*. The person says, 'I am hungry, I am ill,' and becomes very sad, which is *manomaya*. The illness is *prāṇamaya*, and if he makes a conclusion based on that, the *prāṇamaya* becomes *prāṇamaya-kośa*. 'I am lame,' is *prāṇamaya-kośa*. With reference to that *karmendriya*, I say, 'I am lame.' If the *vāk-indrya* does not function, I say, 'I am mute.' There, the 'I' is taken

---

16 The countdown time-clock of one's longevity is *udāna*. Its last tick in terms of breath makes the *jīva* leave the body. This is the classical definition of *udāna, ud-giraṇa-kara*.

to be *prāṇamaya*. So, the five organs of action, and the five *prāṇas*, are together called *prāṇamaya-kośa*.

Manomaya-kośa

> **मनोमयः कः ?**
> **मनश्च ज्ञानेन्द्रियपञ्चकं मिलित्वा यो भवति स**
> **मनोमयः कोशः ।**
>
> *manomayaḥ kaḥ?*
> *manaśca jñānendriyapañcakaṁ militvā yo*
> *bhavati sa manomayaḥ kośaḥ.*

manomayaḥ – (the sheath which is the) modification of the mind ; *kaḥ* – what (is)?

manaḥ – the mind; *ca* – and; *jñānendriya-pañcakam* – the five organs of perception; *militvā* – together; *yaḥ bhavati* – that which is; *saḥ* – that (is); *manomayaḥ* – (which is) modification of the mind; *kośaḥ* – (and it is) a sheath.

> What is (sheath which is the) modification of the mind? The mind and the five organs of perception together is *manomaya*, (which is) the modification of the mind, (and it is) a sheath.

The *manomaya* is the five sense organs together with the mind. It includes the mind because without it the senses do not function. The mind undergoes change, as do the senses, so they are all creations, *vikāra*s, really speaking, of certain basic factors. These senses undergo changes as they bring in data of sensory objects that are many and varied. And the mind also undergoes changes relevant to the perception, *manovikāra*, so the mind is never the same. Because the mind is variable, it is *manomaya*. Emotions are included in the mind, as are desires, doubt, *saṅkalpa-vikalpa*. They are all the *manomaya*. Recollection is also included.

Why is it a *kośa*? Because it is mistaken for *ātman*. If you do not commit the mistake, you do not need to transcend the mind. If you commit the mistake, then you need to understand *ātman* – that is transcending. Understanding *ātman* as not the mind is transcending. There is no other transcending. How do you transcend anything? By understanding. Here, it is by negation, *neti*, understanding that *ātman* is not the mind, while the changing mind is *ātman*, which is the changeless reality of the mind.

Vijñānamaya-kośa

विज्ञानमयः कः ?
बुद्धिर्ज्ञानेन्द्रियपञ्चकं मिलित्वा यो भवति
स विज्ञानमयः कोशः ।

vijñānamayaḥ kaḥ?
buddhiḥ jñānendriyapañcakaṁ militvā yo bhavati sa vijñānamayaḥ kośaḥ.

vijñānamayaḥ (*kośaḥ*, the sheath which is) modification of intellect; *kaḥ* – what (is)?

buddhiḥ – the intellect; *jñāna-indriya-pañcakam* – the five organs of perception; *militvā* – together with; *yaḥ bhavati* – that which is; *saḥ* – that (is) *vijñānamayaḥ* – the modification of intellect; *kośaḥ* – (and it is) a sheath.

> What is (the sheath which is) the modification of intellect?
>
> The intellect together with the the five organs of perception is the modification of intellect, (and it is) a sheath.

The five sense organs together with the *buddhi* is *vijñānamaya* or *vijñāna-vikāra*. And it is also a *kośa*. Later, he is going to define the word '*buddhi*' as *niścayātmika-antaḥ-karaṇa-vṛttiḥ buddhiḥ*. When there is a doubt we call it the mind. When there is no doubt, and the understanding is correct, or when a doubt is resolved correctly, that is the function of the *buddhi*. When you see an object, like a pot, the mind undergoes a change. That change is called *manas*. When you see a flower, it means your mind has undergone a change in order to objectify that object; this change is called a *vṛtti*. The *vṛtti* has an object, flower, and recognising it is called the *pramāṇa-phala*. When you open your eyes and see this flower, there is a *vṛtti*, and that *vṛtti* leads to the recognition of the flower. That recognition occurs in the *buddhi*. And the conclusion that it is a rose is *niścayātmikā-vṛttiḥ*. Suppose, there is a doubt whether this is a real flower or one of those modern flowers. That doubt is *manas*.

Do you know what is modern? Having the thing without the thing! You should have hair without hair, teeth without teeth, nails without nails, sugar without sugar, milk without milk, coffee without coffee. Naturally, you doubt whether this is a real flower or one of those modern flowers. When you have such doubt, that is the mind, *manas*. You touch the petal of the flower; now you know it is not a human-made petal. There is doubt-free knowledge. The inner faculty is *buddhi*. This *buddhi*, including the subject, the *kartṛ*, with *jñānendriyas*, is the *vijñāna-maya-kośa*.

The *vijñāna* undergoes change all the time. You become a seer, hearer, thinker, and therefore, it is *vijñāna-maya*. It is never the same. And it is a *kośa* because you take it as *ātman* – I am a liker, disliker, I did this, I did not do this, and there is guilt. In 'I did this, I did not do this,' there is the conclusion that I am the *kartṛ*, the agent. You think that you are a doer, which is a mistake, and so it is a *kośa*. The doer is *ātman* but *ātman* is not the doer.

Ānandamaya-kośa

आनन्दमयः कः ?
एवमेव कारणशरीरभूताविद्यास्थमलिनसत्त्वं
प्रियादिवृत्तिसहितं सत् आनन्दमयः कोशः ।
एतत् कोशपञ्चकम् ।

ānandamayaḥ kaḥ?
evameva kāraṇa-śarīra-bhūta-avidyāstha-
malina-sattvaṁ priyādi-vṛtti-sahitaṁ
sat ānandamayaḥ kośaḥ.
etat kośa-pañcakam.

ānandamayaḥ – the *ānandamaya*; *kaḥ* – what (is)? *evam eva* – in the same manner; *kāraṇa-śarīra-bhūta-avidyāstha-malina-sattvam* – that which is abiding in *avidyā*, (in the form of) the causal body, of impure *sattva*; *priyādi-vṛtti-sahitam* – along with the thought modifications like pleasure etc.; *sat* – being; *ānandamayaḥ* – the *ānandamaya*; *kośaḥ* – (and it is) a sheath; *etat* – this (is); *kośa-pañcakam* – the five-fold sheath.

What is *ānandamaya*?

In the same manner, that which is abiding in *avidyā,* (in the form of) the causal body, of impure *sattva,* along with the thought modifications like pleasure, etc., is *ānandamaya,* (and it is) a sheath. This is the five-fold sheath.

Here too, the meaning of the suffix '*mayat*' in *ānandamaya* is the same, *ānanda-vikāra,* degrees of *ānanda.* The experience of *ānanda* is subject to change due to various degrees of inhibition. At the sight of something desirable there is a degree of *ānanda,* in owning it there is more *ānanda.* We have three words, *priya, moda, pramoda,* to express the human *ānanda* in different degrees. And the one who experiences is called a *bhoktṛ.*

The *bhoktṛ* is the most basic person, which is why *ānandamaya* is mentioned last. The basic ego with the will, but without much choice, is the *bhoktṛ.* When there is choice, and you freely identify with the will, you become *vijñānamaya.* The doer goes about doing in order to become the enjoyer, the basic person. The *kartṛ* is busy to become the *bhoktṛ.* Since *sukha* is there at that level, it is called *ānanda.* And the *bhoktṛ* is *ānandamāya* because of the experience of degrees of *sukha,* pleasure.

When you say, 'I am *sukhi* now,' this *ānandamaya* is a *kośa*. To say, 'Now I am a *sukhi*' means I was not a *sukhi* before, I was a *duḥkhi*, I was in pain. That is also a *kośa*, a mistake. Both conclusions are wrong. Even though there is some truth about yourself when you experience *sukha*, yet, it is experience whose truth is not recognised. So, you want to retain that happiness, and there is an anxiety about retaining it. It is like the sugar crystal that wants to retain its sweetness. All these are based upon self-ignorance, and like a *kośa*, sheath, the *ānandamaya* covers the self.

These are the five levels where we commit mistakes, and therefore they are *kośa*s. Now what is *ātman*?

Ātman is not any of these

When all the areas where mistakes are committed are negated, what is left is *ātman*. If it is not *ānandamaya*, *vijñānamaya*, and so on, what can it be? He says, all these qualities cannot be the *ātman* because,

मदीयं शरीरं मदीयाः प्राणाः मदीयं मनश्च मदीया
बुद्धिर्मदीयमज्ञानमिति स्वेनैव ज्ञायते तद्यथा मदीयत्वेन
ज्ञातं कटककुण्डलगृहादिकं स्वस्माद्भिन्नं तथा
पञ्चकोशादिकं मदीयत्वेन ज्ञातमात्मा न भवति ।

madīyaṁ śarīraṁ madīyāḥ prāṇāḥ madīyaṁ manaśca madīyā buddhirmadīyamajñānamiti svenaiva jñāyate tadyathā madīyatvena jñātaṁ kaṭakakuṇḍalagṛhādikaṁ svasmādbhinnaṁ tathā pañcakośādikaṁ madīyatvena jñātamātmā na bhavati.

yathā – just as; *madīyatvena* – as mine; *jñātam* – known; *kaṭaka-kuṇḍala-gṛhādikam* – bracelet, earring, house, etc.; *svasmād-bhinnam* – (are) different from oneself; *tathā* – so too; *madīyaṁ śarīram* – my body; *madīyāḥ prāṇāḥ* – my physiological functions; *madīyaṁ manaḥ ca* – and my mind; *madīyā buddhiḥ* – my intellect; *madīyam ajñānam* – my ignorance; *iti* – thus; *svena eva* – by oneself indeed; *jñāyate* – is known; *madīyatvena jñātam* – known as mine; *tad pañcakośādikam* – that which is composed of the five sheaths; *ātmā na bhavati* – is not the 'I' *ātmā.*

Just as the bracelet, earring, house, etc., known as mine, (are) different from oneself, so too that which is composed of five sheaths, different from oneself, known by oneself indeed, as 'mine' (such as) 'my body, my physiological functions, my mind, my intellect, and my ignorance' is not the I, *ātman.*

There are two types of arguments for understanding the nature of *ātman*. One is the I-argument, and the other is the I-my-argument. Both are used in the *śāstra* – *aham-idam* and *aham-mama*. *Mama*, my, includes *idam*, this, also. That is what he wants to establish, so he chooses *mama* here. Understand that *idam* is 'this' and *aham* means 'I'.

When you say, 'My house,' it is different from you. 'My house' implies that the house, the object of your sense of ownership or possession, can be referred to by the word, 'my'. Also, anything that is 'mine' can be referred to by the word, 'this'. Every 'this' is not mine but every mine is 'this'. That is the argument here.

When this is established, all he has to do is address your mistake at the level of the physical body. External to that, you do not have this problem of self-confusion. Outside, your house is there, but you do not have the confusion, 'I am the house.' Your son is there, your father is there, your mother, many others are there, but none of them is taken as 'me'. You do not commit that mistake.

We start the enquiry from wherever the confusion is. Since the confusion is at the level of the physical body, we start the enquiry there. You take the attributes of the physical body upon yourself when you say, 'I am short, I am tall, I am male, I am female, I am old, I am mortal.' All these conclusions are germane, because there is something about them that are true. What is true? That the body is tall, for instance. When you say, 'the body is tall,' you do not mean that it is tall like the mountain. You compare your tallness among the human beings, and it is tall. That is an attribute that the body has. It is all true, but 'I am those attributes' is a wrong conclusion.

It is not the sentence, 'I am tall' that I am questioning, because if you are enlightened, you can still say, 'I am tall,' and so on. Suppose I ask, "Where are you from?" You need not say, "I am not from anywhere, Swamiji, I am everywhere." If you are everywhere, why do you travel? Please understand that here again people commit mistakes. We do not change our sentences, but we need to understand. By changing a sentence you are not going to become wiser. That is where the snobbishness begins. When you say, "I am tall," you mean that with reference to the physical body you are tall. If you understand, you can still say that you are tall, and if you do not understand, then there is a mistake in the statement. That is what we are correcting.

Tallness is an attribute imposed upon *ātman*, which *ātman* does not take. Your physical body is something that is seen by you. But you say, "This is my physical body." When you say, 'My body' it becomes this body as well. And without being 'this,' it cannot be 'mine.' Without being an object of this-cognition, it cannot be mine. Anything that is understood by you as 'mine' can only be 'this' not 'I'. So, *madīyaṁ śarīram*, my body; this physcial body is mine. That is good, keep it, it is yours, but it is not you.

Madīyaṁ prāṇaḥ, my hunger, my thirst, my senses, my eyes, my ears. All these and their conditions are known to me. Then *madīyaṁ manaḥ*, my mind, my agitation, anger and so on. 'My mind is restless,' what does it mean? I am conscious of it. It is not me because I am conscious of it. Similarly, *madīyaṁ buddhiḥ*, my knowledge, my cognition, I am aware of, and again, that I am the seer, hearer, thinker, all the variations in the *ahaṅkāra* are seen by me, are known to me. Therefore that also is not 'me'. My *sukha* also has variations – *priya, moda, pramoda* – and those variations are witnessed by me, so none of them can be taken to be me. *Madīyam ajñānam*. "Do you know about yourself?" "Well, which self are you talking about?" "Brahman." "Brahman? I do not know." That is enough. It need not be explained to you; it is only to prove *madīyam ajñānam*, this is my ignorance. Therefore, ignorance is not me. All these are objects of the witness, *sākṣin*. Now, I can say, "I am *sākṣin*." What is that *sākṣin*? That also has to be pointed out.

Anything that is known as one's own, *madīyatvena jñātaṁ*, *kaṭaka*, a bracelet, *kuṇḍala* an earring, *gṛhādikaṁ*, a house and so on, is other than me. Because it is mine, and mine is not me, it is other than myself. So too, are the *pañcakośādikam*. *Pañcakośa* here is an expression for *annamaya*, *prāṇamaya*, *manomaya*, etc. All these are known as one's own, *madīyatvena jñātam* – my body, my senses. Being known, *jñātam*, they are different from myself, and therefore cannot be *ātman*. Again he confirms what was said before, that *ātman* is not any of these. If not, what is its *svarūpa*?

Ātman is saccidānandasvarūpaḥ

So far, the negation, what is not *ātman*, has been told. Now what is *atman* has to be unfolded.

आत्मा तर्हि कः ?

सच्चिदानन्दस्वरूपः ।

ātmā tarhi kaḥ ?

saccidānandasvarūpaḥ.

tarhi – then; *kaḥ* – what (is); *ātmā* – *ātman*, 'I'?
svarūpaḥ – (its) nature (is); *sat* – existence; *cit* – consciousness; *ānanda* – fullness.

Then, what is *ātman*?

(Its) nature (is) existence, consciousness, fullness.

We have seen *sat-cit-ānanda svarūpa*. These words help us recognise the nature of *ātman*. And again, *ātman* is not totally unknown to me, so these words have a special function. Every word has to be understood. I[17] have explained it; now he takes up every word by asking a question and answering it.

Sat

सत्किम् ?
कालत्रयेऽपि तिष्ठतीति सत् ।

satkim?
kāla-traye'pi tiṣṭhatīti sat.

sat – *sat*, existence; *kim* – what (is)?
kāla-traye api – in all three periods of time (past, present and future); *tiṣṭhati* – stays; *iti sat* – thus (which) is *sat*.

---

[17] Pujya Swamiji

What is *sat*, existence?

That which stays in all three periods of time (past, present, future) is *sat*.

Sat can be defined as that which cannot be negated, *abādhitaṁ sat*. Here, he defines it as *kāla-traye'pi tiṣṭhati iti sat*. This is a very adequate definition. That which is in all three periods of time. If there is any other object other than *ātman*, which exists in all three periods of time, that will also be *sat*. But the truth is, there is no other object; any object exists in time.

This *kāla-traya* we talk about is really created, *kalpita*, like different notes in a melody. Even one note, '*sa*,' is *kalpita*. If this *sa* is cut into sound bits, each one is a series of sounds. Therefore *sa* is *kalpita*. If I do the same thing for *ri*; there is no *ri*. Both these notes, like other notes, are *kalpita*. Then the combination of these notes makes a *rāga*, melody, which is further *kalpita*. Similarly, when you say time is past, present, and future, we think of the past only now, and of the future only now. The present has no length. If the present has a length of time, then there is a past and a future. Any length of time is divisible. Like even the note in the melody is divisible, time also is divisible. Therefore, what we call time, *kāla*, is really *kalpita*.

Kalpita means something that is superimposed, like a pot made of clay. Anything *kalpita* is dependent upon something which is *a-kalpita*. Like the clay becomes *a-kalpita* and the pot is *kalpita*. Now, think of time. If the past is *kalpita*, the future is *kalpita*, and a length of time in the present is also *kalpita*, because it is divisible, then what is *akalpita*? *Sat*. *Sat* alone is *akalpita*. The one who does this *kalpana*, the *kalpana-kartṛ*, is in essence *akalpitaḥ ātmā* who is the very basis of time.

There is a world that you experience and there is an order as you experience it. Now, in this comprehension of the world, two things are there as a basis – time and place, *kāla* and *deśa*. They are the basis, really speaking, for experiencing this world. When you point to an object, you are definitely pointing it in terms of its existence in time, not outside time. Your orientation towards the present tense, *vartate*, is that it exists now in time. If it exists now, then it is not going to be the same the next minute. When you look at object '*o*' at time '*t*', and then look at it again at time '*t1*', it is not '*ot*', but '*ot1*'. One element is gone, time '*t*'. The '*ot1*' is not the same as '*ot*'– the object '*o*' has changed. Therefore, when you say that it is the same object, that is another *kalpana*, which for practical purposes we accept – the change is so infinitesimally small that we are not able to comprehend it, and it does not matter much. But it does change.

How do certain things get fossilised? By change. How does it change? In time things change. From a seed a whole plant grows. Suppose, you sow a seed and set a movie camera to film the process of the seed becoming a sprout, from that a sapling, then the tree, foliage, etc. If you speed up that film you can see the whole twenty-five years of growth of the tree in one hour. It is growing; understand. Every fraction of a second there is a change, and that change is not appreciated by us because it is not appreciable. It does not mean there is no change. The object is not the same; it is always changing. In fact, you do not ever come across the same object again. This is a very disconcerting fact. You thought you had a permanent relationship with this person, but the person goes on changing. It is disconcerting to know that you do not see the same person again, and you do not see the same object again. Where is the constancy here? Constancy is only one thing. And that is *akalpita*, what is not superimposed, the truth of what is *kalpita*, that is *ātman*. It is *sat* because in the concept of time, whether it is past, present or future, there is time-consciousness. And time-consciousness is what time is. Anything you think of, or perceive, is that-consciousness, because we are talking about the world that you experience. So, object-consciousness implies time-consciousness and space-consciousness. Without time-consciousness you cannot say that the object 'is'– the 'is' that you are adding to the object is nothing but time-consciousness. The existence of any object is the existence of time, but time itself is *kalpita*. When you say, "Devadatta cooks, *pacati devadattaḥ*," what does the verb in the present tense 'cooks' mean? How long does it take? 'Cooks' indicates the present; he is cooking. Cutting the vegetables he is cooking, washing them he is cooking; all these are considered cooking. Therefore, the present is purely *kalpita*.

We need to understand the word '*kalpita*' because we need to use that. When you say, he cooks or he walks, the use of the present is *kalpita*. In fact, when you say he walks, 'walked' is also involved, because he is covering a distance. He started from point A, then walked and walked. Again, there are so many actions involved even in one step. Those actions are also past actions. What is the present action? If you look into all this it is confusing, unless you understand that it is *kalpita*. Once you say it is *kalpita*, the confusion is resolved. If you understand the significance of this word, perhaps you can live a fresh life. Nobody can say, 'I am aged,' if *kalpita* is understood. If it is one continuous present, there again, the present is a given length of time that is converted into further present. Then all that is there is **one presence.**

Cit

चित् किं ?
ज्ञान स्वरूपः ।

cit kiṁ ?
jñāna svarūpaḥ.

cit – *cit*, consciousness; *kiṁ* – what?
jñāna svarūpaḥ – of the nature of pure consciousness .

What is cit?
Of the nature of pure consciousness.

One presence. What is that presence? We call it *cit*, *jñāna-svarūpa*. Without being *cit* there is no *sat*. The reality of time is *sat* and that *sat* is *caitanya*, consciousness. *Cit* is *sat* and the *sat* is *cit*. What is *akalpita* is consciousness, and everything else is *kalpita*. Time is *kalpita*, space is *kalpita*, in time-space the pot is *kalpita*, the clay is *kalpita*, a nucleus is *kalpita*, atoms are *kalpita*, a particle is *kalpita*. The observer is also *kalpita*. And what is *akalpita*? That which is the content of the observer is *akalpita*.

What cannot exist without being something else is *kalpita*. Understand this. The desk on which you are writing is *kalpita*. It cannot exist without being the material, wood. The notebook on which you are writing cannot be without being paper, the paper cannot be without being pulp. What is paper? *Kalpita.* The pulp cannot be without being whatever its constituents are. Any constituent has its own constituents.

Let us look at it this way. Notebook-consciousness, paper-consciousness, pulp-consciousness. What is *akalpita* in all of them? Consciousness. It is present at every stage of your understanding. Notebook-consciousness, you understand, is but paper-consciousness. You understand paper as pulp-consciousness and then the pulp you understand as its-constituent-consciousness. There again, each constituent is consciousness alone. The presense of consciousness is there in all three periods of time – past, present and future. Consciousness happens to be the *sat* of every object you know.

What is the truth of the world you comprehend? The truth of the world you comprehend is the truth of your comprehension. Look at this object-consciousness here. This is a crystal for which there is a crystal-thought, crystal-comprehension. The object of the crystal-comprehension is crystal. But the truth of the crystal-comprehension is not really the crystal or even its basic constituent. That is not the truth because that also is constituent-comprehension, and again further, that-comprehension. The invariable in all these is comprehension. That comprehension is what? Comprehension minus the object. And comprehension minus the object is what? Consciousness.

The author asked what is *cit* and answered, *jñāna-svarūpa*. That *jñāna* is comprehension, the comprehension that is present in all comprehensions. A particular cognition is *jñānam*, and in every object-cognition, cognition is there. Minus the object, cognition is *cit*, *jñāna*, in the form of comprehension, which is but consciousness present in all three periods of time. That which is the *sat* of thought is *cit*. That which is *cit* is the *sat* of everything – it is *sat-cit-svarūpa*. Now, you find that timelessness is the nature of *ātman*. We have negated all but one, which we cannot negate – *atman*. Anything grasped by cognition, *pramāṇa-prāpta*, like a pot, etc., is subject to negation; it does not stay in all three periods of time. What does stay? Only *ātman*. You can understand how *trikale'pi tiṣṭhati* is a definition of *ātman*.

What is a definition? That which does not apply to another object. That alone can reveal a given object, because a definition has to distinguish the aimed object from every other object. If two objects fit the same definition, then there is no definition. That is why we have another important defining word '*ānanda*.'

Ānanda

आनन्दः कः ?
सुखस्वरूपः ।
एवं सच्चिदानन्दस्वरूपं स्वात्मानं विजानीयात् ।

ānandaḥ kaḥ ?
sukhasvarūpaḥ
evaṁ saccidānandasvarūpaṁ svātmānaṁ vijānīyāt.

ānandaḥ – wholeness; *kaḥ* – what?
sukhasvarūpaḥ – of the form of happiness; *evaṁ* – in this manner; *vijānīyāt* – may one know; *svātmānam* – one's own self; *saccidānandasvarūpam* – (to be) of the nature of existence, consciousness, wholeness.

What is *ānandaḥ*?
Of the form of happiness. In this manner may one know one's own self (to be) of the nature of existence, consciousness, wholeness.

The truth of *sukham* is wholeness, which is why *ānanda* has to be translated as 'wholeness' and not bliss. Bliss is an experiential word; it does not define. It is subject to vary in degrees. When one picks up a moment of happiness, the subject-object fusion removes any sense of deficiency and alienation. The experience is wholeness. So, *ānanda* is also a *lakṣaṇa* of the *svarūpa* like *sat* and *cit*. That is why the word '*ananta*' is also used by the *śruti* synonymously. If *sat* is in all three periods of time, *ānanda* also has to be so. The meaning of *ānanda* is 'wholeness,' 'limitlessness.' In this manner may one know the nature of one's own self as existence, consciousness, wholeness.

Understanding 'tat' in tat tvam asi

So far so good. But then, there are problems here.

"Swamiji, when you say, I am *sat-cit-ānanda*, the limitless, then am I the truth of this world, the entire world?"

"Yes."

"Does it mean there is nothing else besides me?"

"What else I can say? When I say you are the truth of everything that you comprehend, I am definitely saying there is nothing other than yourself. I do say that – there is nothing other than yourself."

"Swamiji, does it mean I am the maker of all this?"

"Yes. You are maker of all these things."

"Swamiji, then am I the maker of you?"

"Yes, you are the maker of me."

"Then how is it that I am listening to you? If I am the maker of you, where is the teacher or student? The student is the maker of everybody, of this world!"

What does it mean to you? At least, I have this comprehension that implies the existence of a brain. There is some arrangement here. There is something for me to cognise, there is an instrument to cognise, and these are all given. Simply saying, 'I am consciousness' does not address all the issues.

Yes, everything is given. Comprehending faculty, an object to comprehend and a comprehending person – all are given. Everything seems to be in an arrangement, and that arrangement does not belong to consciousness. Neither does it belong to me as an individual because I am part of the arrangement.

If this is so, who arranged this connection between me and the world that I comprehend? If there is such a person, then that person should be outside the arrangement. It can be said that there is somebody up there who made this arrangement possible.

Now, the 'up there' idea has come, because that person is not seen locally (in this *loka*). Is there a person like that? Without understanding the maker of the arrangements, merely doing some meditation and understanding yourself as consciousness does not really solve your problem. It does not solve anything. It may bring some peace, which is good. But it is not going to be permanent because the more you try to find peace, more the problems will come up. That is not going to solve the problem. If we are talking about an intelligent whole, it definitely implies one more factor.

Mere understanding of *tvam* as consciousness is not enough. We need to account for *tat*. There is an equation here. The *tat-pada* has to be analysed to understand the equation '*tat tvam asi.*' In reality there should be oneness, otherwise there is no equation. Two different things cannot be equated, and for two non-different things, no equation is possible. But then, if there is an apparent difference, even though in reality there is no difference, we require an equation. In the sentence, '*tat tvam asi,*' which is Vedanta, we have gone all the way down to see the meaning of *tvam*. Now we have to go all the way down to see *tat*. What the difference is, is of course understood, and the non-difference also has to be understood. Therefore, we need to analyse the *tat-pada*. The next section is *tat-pada-vicāra*, an enquiry into the word 'that'.

Creation

अथ चतुर्विंशतितत्त्वोत्पत्तिप्रकारं वक्ष्यामः ।

atha caturviṁśatitattvotpattiprakāraṁ vakṣyāmaḥ.

atha – now (after the discussion centred on *ātman*); *caturviṁśati-tattva-utpatti-prakāram* – the mode of origin of the twenty-four essential principles/factors (of the *jagat*); *vakṣyāmaḥ.* – we shall explain.

> Now (after the discussion centred on *ātman*), we shall explain the mode of origin of the twenty-four essential principles/factors (of the *jagat*).

Atha, now, after analysing the meaning of *tvam*, you, in the *mahā-vākya* '*tat tvam asi*,' the *tat-padhārtha* is analysed.

There seems to be a cause for everything – this physical body, this physical world – reduced here to 24, *caturviṁśati*, factors. It can be any number, but 24 is mentioned here, and that provides an adequate model for our discussion.

Utpatti is *sṛṣṭi*, creation, and *prakāra* is the mode thereof. *Caturviṁśati-tattva*, the 24 components. These 24 *tattva*s constitute, in our model of understanding, the created world. Sometimes they reduce it to five, but here 24 *tattva*s of the created world, *jagat*, are accepted. It means he is going to talk about the cause of the *jagat*, the effect, and also the cause-effect relationship. *Tat* in the sentence, '*tat tvam asi*' is the cause of the *jagat*. *Tvam asi*, you are – the sentence means you are the cause of the *jagat*. We need to find out how it is possible.

First, let us look at the immediate meaning of *tat*. The immediate meaning of *tat* is Īśvara, the *jagat-kāraṇa*, the cause of the world. And the immediate meaning of *tvam* is the individual, *jīva*. The *śāstra*, being a *pramāṇa*, makes a statement that there is a *vastu*, the reality called Brahman, defined as *satyaṁ jñānam anantam*. These three words are very important. Even if it is said to be *sat*, we have to add the equivalent of the other two words. This *satyaṁ jñānam anantaṁ brahma* is equivalent to *sat cit ānanda*. It is presenting Brahman as the cause for the *jagat*. And Brahman is presented as *satyaṁ jñānam anantam* – limitless, consciousness is. How can it be the cause for everything? How can it be the cause for anything, for that matter? It cannot. Therefore, Brahman must have something else besides being consciousness, to be the cause of the *jagat*. In a way, yes.

Brahman along with māyā is the cause of the jagat

ब्रह्माश्रया सत्त्वरजस्तमोगुणात्मिका मायास्ति ।

brahmāśrayā sattvarajastamoguṇātmikā māyāsti.

brahmāśrayā – with its being in Brahman; *sattva-rajas-tamo-guṇātmikā* – endowed with the *guṇa*s (qualities), *sattva, rajas* and *tamas; māyā asti –māyā* is.

> *Māyā* is, with its being in Brahman, endowed with three *guṇa*s (qualities) *sattva, rajas* and *tamas.*

Brahman has *śakti*, power to create, and that power is called *māyā*. Is this *māyā* independent or do we have Brahman plus *māyā*? If it is an independent power, it means there is a double reality. Then, Brahman is not the only cause at all, *māyā* is also the cause. If that is the cause, the equation, 'You are Brahman,' is not possible. *Māyā* is not a parallel reality to Brahman; it has its being in Brahman, the *āśrayā*, the basis for its existence. There is such a thing called *māyā*, which is a power, and which has its being in Brahman. Since Brahman lends its existence to this *māyā*, Brahman plus *māyā* is what? Still Brahman. Like even clay plus pot is still clay.

Brahmāśrayā māyā is there, *asti*, as the cause of this entire world, which has to account for the nature of this *jagat*. Here, the *jagat* is looked at in a three-fold way. There are things in the created world that are inert. Then there is the sentient with a power to desire, to know, and to will freely. Analysing the *jagat* implies analysis of yourself because you are included in the *jagat*. You have a world to confront and also a faculty to confront it with, which is a part of the creation. When you are trying to understand the cause of this *jagat*, which is observed to be in a three-fold form, then the cause of that should also be similarly three-fold. Therefore, that *māyā* is *sattva-rajas-tamo-guṇātmikā*.

If these are the three qualities of *māyā*, and it is not separate from Brahman, then why don't we say Brahman is *sattva*, *rajas* and *tamas*? No. Because Brahman is *satyam* depending upon which is *māyā*. It is *mithyā*. So, *mithyā-bhūta māyā* accounts for the seeming plurality of the entire *jagat*. Brahman is all-knowledge and all-power with this *māyā*. Brahman is both cause and effect because it is both *nimitta* and *upādāna kāraṇa*. How?

Brahmavit param āpnoti, not *māyā-vit*. The knower of Brahman gains the ultimate, *mokṣa*, freedom. What does it mean? It means freedom from my endless becoming – material becoming, biological becoming, physiological becoming, emotional becoming, moral becoming and spiritual becoming. Since I have to know Brahman, I have to ask, "What is Brahman?" And the *śruti* says, "Brahman is *satya.*" Does it undergo change? No. Then how does it become all? It does not 'become' all – all is Brahman; all being *mithyā*.

One thing is definite, this body is given, a set of senses are also given to me. As an individual in this world, I do not have any choice about the parentage, date of birth and childhood. That I live here on this planet for a length of time is given, and death is also given.

I encounter a world and that is also given to me. The planet earth, the systems, the sun, the planets around it, and even the satellite moon, are all given. There are a lot of things in this scheme that I do not even know of, but whatever they are, they are given. And the solar system itself is part of the galaxy, the Milky Way, which is also given. There is a black hole; given. This time-space continuum and everything in it is given. A faculty to explore and to understand how this came about, what it is all about, is also given.

When I look at myself as an individual, I find that I have no right to any kind of sole authorship. Anything that I think I author, is dependent upon a number of factors, which are given. Therefore, I cannot claim authorship of anything. Authorship is only putting all those things together, which are already given. And for that , the faculty is given, the materials are given, and the laws are given. So, I find myself in a world which is given.

When I cannot claim authorship of any given thing, should I take this given thing as something naturally occurring? There are people now, and there were people in the past too, who claimed that this is all *prakṛti*, nature. To say this is nature is not the answer, really speaking, to the question of authorship. If you say that it is all natural, not something created by an individual, then it is already known to us. It does not answer the question of authorship, and questioning about the authorship is also very natural. The human mind is capable of questioning and it questions, because it can know.

Why this search for authorship? There are a number of reasons. One basic reason is my own understanding of things. When I see something special, something that does not grow on a tree and is not produced by the earth or dropped from the heavens, naturally I question – Who is the author? Because I know there is an author. I know very well that anything like a microphone or a clock or my watch, is not naturally occurring; it does not come from the earth, and it does not get dropped from the heavens. I know that a clock is put-together. It is not natural, and it does not assemble the parts to create itself. It has to be put-together, and intelligently put-together. Whether it is car or a clock or a camera, it is put-together intelligently, to serve a given purpose; therefore, I consider it as an authored product. And this authored product is what I call a 'creation'.

I understand that there is no pot without a potter. How can I ever think of a pot without a pot-maker or a clock without its maker? A clock is a creation because it is intelligently put-together. That is what a creation is – anything intelligently put-together. That creation can be man-made, or insect-made, like a spider's web. Since this world is intelligently put-together, it is a creation. This body is intelligently put-together; it is also a creation.

However, I can trace the authorship for the clock, as I can for the web, anthill or a honeycomb. But I cannot trace the author of this body, or the world. Who put this all together? Therefore, I will definitely question who is the author.

I also know that nobody local is the author of all this. I have some 'great' logic that the author cannot be local, because the author has to be outside this world in order to create the world. Sitting here, he cannot create the world because 'here' is part of the world. So, he must be sitting there, elsewhere. The head goes up. It cannot go down because the earth stops it. It goes up and up and imagines the author in a place up, in heaven, who created the world. This statement can be questioned further. Is heaven located within space and time, or is it outside space and time? If heaven is a special place, then that special place is located only within space. And, since space has come, it means time also has come. Heaven is in space and time. Space and time are also part of this *jagat*; they are given.

Who is the author of all that is given? And this given scheme of things is intelligently put-together because there is harmony and some predictability. With its network of laws, physical laws, and varieties of laws that is so intelligently put-together, is what we call the *jagat*, *idaṁ sarvam*, all this. When we use the word '*sarvam*, all,' it includes what is known and also what is unknown. The entire *jagat* is what is known and unknown. This *jagat*, therefore, includes heaven, if it is located within space and time. So, the statement that the author in heaven created the world, will not answer the question; it will only create further questions. It is understood that God cannot sit in heaven and create this world because heaven is also part of the creation, if heaven is physical. If it is not physical, then the words of this sentence needs to be understood differently. This is where interpretation of these holy books is a necessity. If it makes sense throughout but does not seem to make sense in one place, then that place is to be looked into and interpreted differently to make sense. This is what we call *mīmāṁsā*, analysis. We have to do that analysis; it is necessary.

We make a conclusion here. Assuming that when there is an intelligent creation that is put-together, there must be an author or God who cannot be within space and time and create the world. He has to be outside of space and time. But outside space is also a spatial concept. There is no outside or inside without space; both are spatial. Therefore, God cannot sit outside space and create, because there is no such thing as outside space. He cannot be inside space either. So, where can that God be? Maybe that God is space and time.

The cause which is responsible for intelligently putting-together a product that is meant for a purpose, must be an intelligent being. This intelligent being we call *nimitta-kāraṇa* in Sanskrit. In English let us call it as efficient cause, a cause that must have the knowledge and skill to produce that particular product. Either it is skill with borrowed knowledge or knowledge with borrowed skill or inherent knowledge and skill, but definitely knowledge and skill are required. The knowledge is what makes the person *jña*, one who knows; and the skill, which is called *śakti*, makes this person the one who has the *śakti*, *śaktimān*. If he has both – the *śakti*, power, the ability, and also knowledge, *jña* – he is called *samartha*.

To produce a pot, *ghaṭa*, the pot-maker, *ghaṭa-kartṛ*, must have the knowledge and skill for that – he is therefore, *ghaṭa-jñaḥ samarthaḥ*. But if you ask him to weave, he may not have the skill, much less the knowledge. For that you require a weaver, a *paṭa-kartṛ*. So, *ghaṭa-kartā ghaṭajñaḥ*, and *paṭa-kartā paṭajñaḥ*. Each one has some skill and some knowledge, so we say that the person has limited knowledge, *alpa jñānam*, and limited *śakti*, *alpa śaktiḥ*. We have to mention both separately, because sometimes one borrows the *śakti*, and sometimes one borrows the required knowledge. A mason has the skill to lay the stone or brick, but does not have the architectural knowledge to construct a building. He has to borrow the knowledge from an architect. We see this all the time, which is why we mention these two things separately – *alpa jñānam* and *alpa śaktiḥ*. This is how we proceed; there is a method here. We give up the *ghaṭa*, *paṭa*, and convert the whole thing into a generalisation – the creator of a given thing has limited knowledge, limited power and skill – *alpasya kartā alpajñaḥ, alpaśaktimān.*

Now we look into what is given, within this given scheme called *jagat*, the world, which is also intelligently put-together. The hands that shape the pot intelligently, are themselves intelligently put-together, as is the mind. Everything 'given' is intelligently put-together, highly organised. A lot of these 'givens' are purely symbiotic and interdependent, like the flora-fauna and the human being. This very interdependence itself is an arrangement, a clean arrangement. This is how it is. When we analyse all these severally or collectively, we see that this is one huge *jñāna*. There is enormous knowledge involved, enormous skill involved. When we see this, we simply appreciate an all-knowledge being, *sarva-jñaḥ. Sarva* implies both what is known and what is unknown. Therefore, *sarvasya kartā* is *sarva-jñaḥ.*

When we talk of the whole, the knowledge must be of everything that is here – known and unknown. So, we arrive at a conscious being with all-knowledge. Does this all-knowledge being need any other help? Are there many beings sharing the job of *jagat*-creation? We have no means of knowledge except the *śruti* to tell us. And *śruti* tells us that the creator of everything is only one, *ekameva advitīyam.*[18] We take the *nimitta-kāraṇa* to be one which is vested with all-knowledge, all skill, the wherewithal to bring about this *jagat*. We can call this as efficient cause.

Any product that is intelligently put-together reveals two basic things. One, there is an intelligent being or beings called the efficient cause, *nimitta-kāraṇa*. Two, there is some material involved. We just need to understand that there should be a material that is good enough for that particular creation. Whether it is a loaf of bread or our famous pot, there should be some material without which there cannot be a creation.

If that all-knowledge being whom we call God has created this world, he must have the appropriate material. The word 'appropriate' is most appropriate here because the maker requires appropriate material for the creation of *jagat* in terms of its reality and content. It should be adequate for this world, as it is proved in a pot creation. And there is no material lying somewhere because even space is yet to come along with time.

Śruti never accepted time and space as absolutes. Space came into being, '*ākāśaḥ sambhūtaḥ,*' says the

[18] *Chāndogyopaniṣad* 6.2.1.

Taittirīyopaniṣad. Space comes into being along with other things, including time. That is amazing. Newton proposed that time and space were absolutes, meaning that they were always there, and in them creation takes place. That is classical physics. And the modern physics, with the theory of relativity, showed that everything is collapsible. The very word 'collapsible' is used by the *śāstra*; that is *laya*. Time-space being a product of creation, the Lord definitely cannot be found wanting in requirements for creating this world. That conscious intelligent being must necessarily have the material in itself. So with this knowledge, skill and material, he is *samarthaḥ, dakṣiṇaḥ*.

Now, is there a model for this? *Śruti* gives a few models, but we will look at two important ones here. One that is very often used is, 'Just as a spider creates a thread out of itself and withdraws it unto itself,'[19] unlike a weaver bird, which also builds a nest, but out of materials collected from the outside world. The *śruti* cites the spider because it does not borrow the material for its thread from anywhere outside its eight-legged body, *upādhi*. It has knowledge of how to create a web, and it also has the material in that very body.

---

[19] *yathā ūrṇanābhiḥ sṛjate gṛhṇate ca* (*Muṇḍakopaniṣad* 1.1.7)

The one who makes the web is the efficient cause, Mr. Spider. And the same spider from the standpoint of its own body, its *upādhi,* becomes the material cause, *upādāna-kāraṇa*. This example has only one purpose to serve – to show that both causes can be in one place. It does not serve any other purpose. A spider can create a web but can separate itself from it, because it has a body of its own which is independent of the web. The example cited is only thread-spinning spider.

To serve every other purpose that is necessary, the *śāstra* gives us the example of dream that gives us a great model to assimilate the *śruti*'s vision that the created *jagat* is the creator. The effect is the cause. The *śruti* does not propose two causes, but only one – He desired, 'May I be many.' Therefore, both efficient and material cause are one and the same being. The example for that is the dream, *svapna.*

A dream implies a prior state – a state wherein there was sleep. Yes, only sleep, not the waking state. One has to die to the waking reality to go to sleep. And in sleep, you do not know anything except..., there is no 'except;' all that is there is you and nothing else, neither time nor space; therefore no encounter. This is what they call *laya,* a collapsed state.

Then you dream. Where does dream come from? It is all from your knowledge, from an inherent power you are endowed with. You are the maker for this dream world. And where did you find the material for the dream world? Never outside of you, only in yourself. The creator pervades the creation, which has come out of himself, and that is brought out very well by the fact that the created object cannot be independent of its material cause. So, the whole dream is just you. What kind of you? The knowledgeable you; that is important here. Therefore, the dream-tree is the knowledgeable you, the dream-leaf is the knowledgeable you, dream-branch is the knowledgeable you, dream-trunk is the knowledgeable you, the dream-mountain is the knowledgeable you; it is all the knowledgeable you. In other words, your own knowledge is manifest in the form of the dream world.

The two causes, *nimitta-kāraṇa,* efficient cause, and the *upādāna-kāraṇa,* the material cause for this *jagat,* which includes my *sthūla-śarīra* and *sūkṣma-śarīra,* are traced in one Īśvara. So, the creation is nothing but Īśvara himself manifesting in the form of the *jagat.* If this *jagat* is the all-knowledge Īśvara, then to understand Īśvara is, therefore, to understand the *jagat* as non-separate from Īśvara.

So, the understanding of Īśvara is as one who is manifest in the form of the *jagat.* It is his knowledge that is manifest as the *jagat.* If knowledge is manifest in the form of the *jagat*, then there is nothing inert in this world. Again, you can understand this when you look into your dream. When you dream there is a dream world, which is a manifestation of your knowledge. In dream there are sentient beings and there are inert objects like mountains and so on. It is only the knowledge of the person alone that is manifest in the form of both inert and sentient *jagat*.

Here too, the knowledge of Īśvara alone is manifest as this *jagat*, which is why we do not look upon the sun as a mere inert object – it is a manifestation of Īśvara. When we worship the sun, we are not worshipping the sun, the phenomenon, but through the phenomenon we worship Īśvara. Or, every form becomes a symbol for invoking Īśvara in a particular aspect, a particular form. No form is separate from Īśvara. Since we can severally see the various forms of manifestations, we can also severally worship Īśvara as *devatā*s, deities. You can understand now what a *devatā* is. You can also understand why we do not say that there is one God. There is not one God, as I told you, there is only God.

All forms of worship are validated because of this vision. Everything is God for us. There is something special in this culture, and that is reverence. Whether people seem reverential or not, if you scratch the surface, you find in them that reverence for *pṛthivī*, the earth, reverence for air, *vāyu*, for space, *ākāśa*, and also reverence for the flora and fauna. That reverence is born of this vision of Īśvara.

So, Īśvara is the *abhinna-nimitta-upādāna-kāraṇa*, to put it technically in Sanskrit language. *Bhinna* means separate, *a-bhinna* is non-separate. *Abhinna-nimitta-upādāna-kāraṇa* is that which is both efficient and material cause; they are not separate. This is Īśvara. Therefore, Īśvara is both 'he' and 'she'. 'He' as *nimitta-kāraṇa* is just for your understanding in order to have a bonding with that Īśvara. And this bonding with Īśvara requires you looking at Īśvara as both 'he' and 'she'. In other words, as father and mother.

There is nothing that is outside Īśvara; therefore, there is nothing out of order. He is order, he is knowledge, and his knowledge is manifest in the form of this *jagat* which includes my body, mind, senses, the laws of psychology and physiology. This means that you are in order. You can say, "There is nothing wrong with my mind." Even though it seems to be a little vague, still it is part of the same order. There is a reason for everything. The day you see your mind as Īśvara, that day you have found trust in Īśvara, you have established a bonding in Īśvara. I am not giving an emotional talk here, but it is a talk with reference to looking at your emotions as Īśvara.

This presentation of Īśvara in the form of *nimitta-upādāna-kāraṇa* provides you with an opportunity to establish the bonding that started when you were a child and got disturbed, and which you have to complete now. Anything you start in innocence will be disturbed, until you get the wisdom. And, in between innocence and wisdom, which is ignorance, a lot of mistakes are committed. So, between innocence and wisdom is all the growth that is involved in this pursuit. Through prayer, etc., this bonding is what we establish. And that implies daily ritual in which you are offering flowers, you are offering food, and so on, reflecting your caring. Thus, all these rituals as well as deities gain meaning. Further, we have a whole library of esoteric literature backing up how a deity is vivified to become a real altar.

So, looking at this *jagat* we understand that there is *māyā* for Brahman. In that Brahman, which is the *āśraya* for *māyā*, the *māyā* aspect undergoes change, and is called *pariṇāmi-upādāna-kāraṇa*, a material cause that undergoes modification.

Māyā is Brahman, but Brahman is not *māyā*. It is *mithyā* depending upon Brahman for its existence, so its not a parallel reality.

Creation of the five elements

He refers to the *Taittirīya Upaniṣad* and says:

तत आकाशः सम्भूतः । आकाशाद्वायुः । वायोस्तेजः ।
तेजस आपः । अद्भ्यः पृथिवी ।

tataḥ ākāśaḥ sambhūtaḥ, ākāśādvāyuḥ,
vāyostejaḥ, tejasa āpaḥ, adbhyaḥ pṛthivī.

tataḥ – from that (Brahman with *māyā*); *ākāśaḥ* – space; *sambhūtaḥ* – is born; *ākāśāt* – from space; *vāyuḥ* – air; *vāyoḥ* – from air; *tejaḥ* – fire; *tejasaḥ* – from fire; *āpaḥ* – waters; *adbhyaḥ* – from water; *pṛthivī* – the earth.

From that (Brahman with *māyā*), space is born. From space, air (is born). From air, fire (is born). From fire, water (is born). From water, the earth (is born).

The *jagat* now is presented in a five-fold way, as *pañca-bhūta*s, five elements, which are different from the elements of physics. These *pañca-bhūta*s, the five basic elements, are the *kārya*, the product, of Brahman with *māyā*. Therefore, the product is not separate from Brahman with *māyā*, in other words, Īśvara.

From that Brahman with *māyā*, is born, *sambhūtaḥ*, *ākāśaḥ*. *Ākāśaḥ* here means space, and when we talk about space, time is included. 'Adorned with variety, spread out in time and space, which are created by *māyā*,'[20] anything born is non-separate from its material cause; therefore, *ākāśa* is Brahman.

Brahman is not mentioned again, and it is said from *ākāśa* is *vāyu*, assuming that you know *ākāśa* is Brahman. From that *ākāśa*, that is Brahman, is *vāyu*. This order has a certain meaning, which we will see later.

Then, from the *vāyu* that is Brahman, is born *agni*, fire. All these are subtle elements that undergo the process of grossification. From fire, water is born, *agnerāpaḥ*, not the water that we know but the subtle form of water. *Āpaḥ* is always plural. If you want a singular form, you have to use *jala*, *udaka*, etc. There are certain words which are always in a given number in Sanskrit, and *āpaḥ* is one of them.

From the water, earth, *adbhyaḥ pṛthivī*. Here, we must remember that *brahmāśrayā māyā* has three *guṇas*, and they will inhere in the effect because the qualities of the cause flow into the effect – *kāraṇa-guṇāḥ kāryeṣu anuvartante*. We must know that if *māyā* has three qualities, *sattva*, *rajas*, *tamas*, in an unmanifest condition, they are going to manifest in the form of *ākāśa*, *vāyu*, *agni*, *āpaḥ*, *pṛithvī*, in our model. So, each element will have these three qualities – *sattva*, *rajas* and *tamas*.

---

[20] *māyā-kalpita-deśa-kālakalanā vaicitrya-citrīkṛtam… Dakṣiṇāmūrti-stotra* 2.

From the sāttvika aspect of the five elements comes the subtle sense organs

एतेषां पञ्चतत्त्वानां मध्य आकाशस्य
सात्त्विकांशाच्छ्रोत्रेन्द्रियं सम्भूतम्।

eteṣāṁ pañca-tattvānāṁ madhya ākāśasya
sāttvikāṁśācchrotrendriyaṁ sambhūtam.

eteṣāṁ pañca-tattvānāṁ madhye – among these five elements; *ākāśasya* – of space; *sāttvikāṁśāt* – from the *sāttvika* aspect; *śrotrendriyam* – the organ of hearing (the ear); *sambhūtam* – is born.

Among these five elements, from the *sāttvika* aspect of space is born the organ of hearing (the ear).

वायोः सात्त्विकांशात्त्वगिन्द्रियं संभूतम्।

vāyoḥ sāttvikāṁśāttvagindriyaṁ sambhūtam.

vāyoḥ – of the air; *sāttvikāṁśāt* – from the *sattva* aspect; *tvak-indriyam* – the organ of touch (skin); *sambhūtam* – is born.

From the *sāttvika* aspect of air is born the organ of touch (skin).

अग्नेः सात्त्विकांशाच्चक्षुरिन्द्रियं सम्भूतम् ।

agneḥ sāttvikāṁśāccakṣurindriyaṁ sambhūtam.

agneḥ – of the fire; *sāttvikāṁśāt* – from the *sattva* aspect; *cakṣur-indriyam* – the organ of sight, (the eye); *sambhūtam* – is born

From the *sāttvika* aspect of fire is born the organ of sight (the eye).

जलस्य सात्त्विकांशाद्रसनेन्द्रियं सम्भूतम् ।

jalasya sāttvikāṁśādrasanendriyaṁ sambhūtam.

jalasya – of the water; *sāttvikāṁśāt* – from the *sattva* aspect; *rasanendriyam* – the organ of taste (the tongue); *sambhūtam* – is born.

From the *sāttvika* aspect of water is born the organ of taste (the tongue).

पृथिव्याः सात्त्विकांशाद्घ्राणेन्द्रियं सम्भूतम् ।

pṛthivyāḥ sāttvikāṁśādghrāṇendriyaṁ sambhūtam.

pṛthivyāḥ – of the earth; *sāttvikāṁśāt* – from the *sattva* aspect; *ghrāṇendriyam* – the organ of smell, (the nose); *sambhūtam* – is born.

From the *sāttvika* aspect of earth is born the organ of smell (the nose).

The sense of hearing is part of subtle body; therefore it is not the physical ear, with a pinna and lobe. It is *sattva* aspect of *sūkṣma-bhūta ākāśa*. The *sūkṣma-śarīra* reflects consciousness, so there is life. Life, *prāṇa*, and sentiency are all born of the *sūkṣma-bhuta*s. They are material, no doubt, but they are capable of reflecting consciousness. Because they are material, we have to use the word 'reflect' here.

So too is *tvak*, the sense of touch, born out of the *sāttvika* aspect of *vāyu*, the subtle element, *sūkṣma-bhūta*. From the *sāttvika* aspect of *agni*, fire, the sense organ of sight is born. From the *sāttvika* aspect of the subtle element of water is born the sense of taste. From the *sāttvika* aspect of the subtle element of *pṛthivī* is born the *ghrāṇendriya*, the sense of smell.

There is an order here, a very interesting order given by the *śruti* – *ākāśādvāyuḥ vāyoragniḥ agnerāpaḥ adbhyaḥpṛthivī*. And when the *śruti* gives an order, there should be some meaning to it. If you analyse these elements, as you know them in their gross, tangible form, you will find that space is a special element that has neither form, smell, taste, nor touch. Yet, space is an element. Being an element, it must have some distinguishing quality, and *śruti* says that it is connected to hearing, *śrotrendriya*. It is not that space has the quality of sound, but the *śrotrendriya* has a connection to space. There is a connection between the sense of hearing and *ākāśa;* the *śrotrendriya* is born of space. Thus, the subtle element of space is connected to sound.

Vāyu has not just one, but two qualities. When *vāyu* blows, you can hear it, and you can also feel it. So *vāyu* is connected to the sense of touch, *sparśendriya;* it is the object of the sense of touch. Here, we are talking about the *vāyu* outside that we experience. All these are connected because the elements outside are the grossified subtle elements. From the subtle element is born a given sense organ, which is connected to the corresponding gross element. Thus, you are connected to the external world in this way.

Next, we come to *agni*, fire, the first element that has a form. It can be seen; therefore it is more gross than *ākāśa* and *vāyu*. *Agni* is available for the senses of sound and touch, like *vāyu*, and it is also available for the sense of sight. *Vāyu* cannot be seen; it can only be inferred, but fire can be seen. That is also the reason why there is fire worship. If Bhagavān has to be given a form, this is the first form in which you can invoke him. To invoke any deity you light a lamp and say, "I invoke this *devatā* in this lamp." The lamp becomes an altar of worship. This *dīpa-pūjā* is very common in Tamilnadu and Kerala.

Agni, fire, must have its own taste, but you cannot taste it because it burns the taste buds, first. It can be touched and known as hot. *Agni* can be seen. A big conflagration will also have sound.

Water can be heard, touched and seen. It can also be tasted. You may say that water is tasteless, but that is the taste, the standard from which we determine that something is salty, bitter, sweet, etc. The standard taste is the tasteless water, *rasanendriya*. But it has no odour.

All forms of smell, even if they are found in water, are from the earth. Modern science confirms this. All aromatic molecules, the originals and their derivatives, are from the earth alone. That is why the earth is defined as *gandhavatī pṛthivī*. *Pṛthivī* has this special quality of smell in addition to everything else – sound, touch, sight and taste. All five sense organs can operate successfully with reference to the earth. When there is an earthquake there is sound. It is available for touch, for sight, and for taste. It is available for the sense of smell; therefore the grossest of the elements is earth, *pṛthivī*.

Creation and nature of the mind – antaḥ-karaṇa

The five sense organs gather five sense objects. Where do these sensory data go? By whom are they gathered? By the mind. So, the mind is born of the total *sāttvika* aspect of the five elements:

एतेषां पञ्चतत्त्वानां समष्टि-सात्त्विकांशाद्
मनोबुद्ध्यहंकारचित्तान्तःकरणानि सम्भूतानि ।

eteṣāṁ pañca-tattvānām samaṣṭi-sāttvikāṁśād manobuddhyahaṅkāracittāntaḥkaraṇāṇi sambhūtāni.

eteṣām pañca-tattvānām – of these five elements; *samaṣṭi-sāttvikāṁśāt* – from the total *sattva* aspect; *mano-buddhi-ahaṅkāra-citta-āntaḥ-karaṇāni* – mind, intellect, ego, memory, (called) the inner instruments; *sambhūtāni* – are born.

From the total *sāttvika* aspect of these five elements are born the mind, intellect, ego, memory, (called) the inner instruments.

The *samaṣṭi*, the sum of all the *sāttvika* aspects of these five elements, is responsible for the entire *antaḥ-karaṇa*, mind. That mind is defined in terms of four functions – *manas, buddhi, citta* and *ahaṅkāra*. This is the four-fold faculty of thinking that is born of the *sāttvika* aspects of all five elements.

I will illustrate this with an example. Somebody says, “Look at the rose.” Your ears bring in the word ‘rose’ and your eyes see the form rose. They see the object, and the conclusion is made that it is a rose. These are days where you can have a thing without it being there, so you have a doubt. Then you extend your hand and touch it. Once you touch it, you know it is a real rose. Every sense organ gives you a datum confirming that it is a rose. You are so sure you can eat the petals because they are edibile. Therefore, these five sense organs have told you that it is a rose. Now, where did the data from the five sense organs go? They go to one place, only then a conclusion is possible. That is why this mind has to be born from the total *sāttvika* aspect, *samaṣṭi-sāttvikāṁśa,* of these five elements. In fact, what is born is this four-fold faculty of thinking. The sense organs and the mind are together and are capable of perception because of the *sāttvika* aspect.

He tells the functions of this four-fold faculty.

सङ्कल्पविकल्पात्मकं मनः । निश्चयात्मिका बुद्धिः ।
अहङ्कर्ताहङ्कृतिः । चिन्तनकर्तृ चित्तम् ॥

saṅkalpavikalpātmakaṁ manaḥ, niścayātmikā buddhiḥ, ahaṅkartāhaṅkṛtiḥ, cintanakartṛ cittam.

saṅkalpa-vikalpātmakam – of the nature of decision followed by doubt; *manaḥ* – (is) mind; *niścayātmikā* – of the nature of resolved ascertainment; *buddhiḥ* – the intellect (is); *ahaṅkartā* – I am the doer; *ahaṅkṛtiḥ* – (this sense is) the ego; *cintanakartṛ* – thinking process in keeping with what has gone before (memory-recollection); *cittam* – (is called) *cittam.*

> Decision followed by doubt is the nature of the mind. Resolved ascertainment is the nature of the intellect. I am the doer, (this sense is) the ego. *Cittam* is the thinking process in keeping with what has gone before (memory-recollection).

What are *saṅkalpa* and *vikalpa*? This is a flower, a rose, a real rose. It is *saṅkalpa*. Then a question arises, is it a real rose? This is *vikalpa*. Yes, I think it's a real rose. *Saṅkalpa*. How can you be so sure? *Vikalpa*. I can be sure. *Saṅkalpa*. Can I be so sure? *Vikalpa*. The whole process is the mind, *manas*. The starting point is *saṅkalpa* and any doubt about that is *vikalpa*. This is what we call *saṁśyātmikā antaḥ-karaṇa-vṛttiḥ*, a process of thinking in which there is vacillation. Did I lock the door? Yes, I think I locked it – *saṅkalpa*. I don't think so – *vikalpa*, vacillation. Then you go towards the house and stop there – I think I locked the door. You walk away. I think I better check. Why do you want to check? Vacillation. After checking, you come out and wonder – did I check properly? This is another problem. The mind is not there when you are doing things; therefore they are not consciously done, and half the day is spent in this way. This is how the mind works, not only for perception and conclusions about what was done, but for emotions too. The various emotions can be brought under the mind. The *vṛtti*s that take place along with the sensory perception, and the relevant change to perceive an object, also has to take place only in the mind.

You see an object, a rose, and there is a rose-*vṛtti*, a rose-thought, and that is the mind. You recognise, 'this is a rose.' That *buddhi* is *niścayātmikā antaḥ-karaṇa-vṛttiḥ buddhiḥ*. It is the same mind but it assumes a form of decision, resolution and knowing. Deliberate enquiry is also called *buddhi*. Resolution of a perception is *buddhi*, whereas a doubt such as, 'to be or not to be,' is *manas*. Then, when you decide to suffer the slings and arrows of outrageous fortune, that is *buddhi*. In deliberate enquiry, as you are doing now, what is in operation is *buddhi*. Analysing what is going on is the operation of the *buddhi*, and taking in the data is the mind. You hear the words, and the *buddhi* processes them.

Ahaṅkartā ahaṅkṛtiḥ – the one who says, "I am the doer, this is my mind, my body, my action. This is my lot." The one who owns up things, the subject, the ego, is called the *ahaṅkṛtiḥ ahaṅkāraḥ*. And that is also a thought, a special thought. Why special? Because it owns up everything else. Other thoughts are variable, but the one who owns them up is the same. He is also a little variable with a nucleus.

There is another function, *citta*. The author defines it as *cintana-kartṛ cittam*, the one who does the *cintana*. Here, *cintana* is recollection based upon past experience. When past experience is recollected it is a different process altogether. It includes the unconscious also. Under the ego we need to bring the unconscious and the subconscious. Even intuition has to be included in this four-fold *antaḥ-karaṇa* that constitutes your thinking faculty, born of the total *sāttvikāṁśa* of these five elements.

Now, what remains to be discussed is *rajas* and *tamas*. Notice that there is an order in all this. Before that, he wants to tell us the *devatā*s responsible for these functions:

Presiding deities of the mental functions

मनसो देवता चन्द्रमाः । बुद्धेर्ब्रह्मा । अहङ्कारस्य रुद्रः ।
चित्तस्य वासुदेवः ॥

manaso devatā candramāḥ, buddherbrahmā,
ahaṅkārasya rudraḥ, cittasya vāsudevaḥ.

manasaḥ – of the mind; *devatā* – (the presiding) deity; *candramāḥ* – (is) Candra, the moon; *buddheḥ* – of the intellect; *brahmā* – (the presiding deity is) Brahmā (the creator;) *ahaṅkārasya* – of the ego; *rudraḥ* – (the presiding deity is) Rudra; *cittasya* – of *cittam*; *vāsudevaḥ* – (the presiding deity is) Vāsudeva.

> Candra, the moon, is the (presiding) deity of the mind. Of the intellect (the presiding deity is) Brahmā (the creator). Of the ego (the presiding deity) Rudra. Vāsudeva (is the presiding) deity of *cittam*.

In the *manas, buddhi, citta* and *ahaṅkāra* there are differences in terms of their functions and they are presided over by different *devatās*.

The deity for the *manas* is the Moon, not exactly this physical moon but the moon *devatā, candramas,* for which the physical moon is a symbol. In a horoscope, the moon's position is very important because the mental strength of the subject is determined from its position in the scheme of the zodiac. Bhagavān is looked uon as the deity Candra from the standpoint of the faculty called the mind.

The *devatā* of *buddhi* is Brahmāji. Sometimes it is said to be Sūrya, the sun, but here it is Brahmāji, the creator.

Among the trinity – Brahmā, Viṣṇu, Rudra – Brahmāji presides over the *buddhi* because *buddhi* is the creative faculty. Brahmāji is the deity for resolution, for proper thinking, etc. For *ahaṅkāra*, the deity is Rudra or Śiva. And for *citta*, it is Lord Viṣṇu. Vāsudeva here is Lord Viṣṇu.

Understanding this, you see that you are connected to the total. Your life is connected. You are not an isolated person. The laws connect you, so you are connected to Īśvara all the time. When you hear you are connected, when you see you are connected, when you sniff you are connected, when you taste you are connected, and when you touch you are connected. It is all one whole, and you are connected to that whole. All connections in life are within the basic connection of the individual to the total.

From the rajas aspect of the five elements comes the subtle organs of action

एतेषां पञ्चतत्त्वानां मध्य आकाशस्य
राजसांशाद्वागिन्द्रियं सम्भूतम् ।

eteṣāṁ pañca-tattvānāṁ madhye ākāśasya
rājasāṁśādvāgindriyaṁ sambhūtam.

eteṣāṁ pañca-tattvānāṁ madhye – among these five elements; *ākāśasya* – of space; *rājasāṁśāt* – from the *rajas* aspect; *vāg-indriyam* – the organ of speech; *sambhūtam* – is evolved.

> From the *rajas* aspect of space, among these five elements, the organ of speech is born.

Now, the *rajas-aṁśa* among these five elements beginning with the *rājasāṁśa* of *ākāśa* is being told. From that, the organ of speech is born. *Vāk-indriya*, the organ of speech, is an organ of action.

वायोः राजसांशात्पाणीन्द्रियं सम्भूतम् ।

vāyoḥ rājasāṁśāt pāṇīndriyaṁ sambhūtam.

vāyoḥ – of air; *rājasāṁśāt* – from the *rajas* aspect; *pāṇi-indriyam* – the (organ of action called) hand; *sambhūtam* – is born.

> From the *rajas* aspect of air the (organ of action called) hand is born.

From the *rājasa* aspect of *vāyu*, the subtle element, the hands are born, which is why Bhīma and Hanumān, the sons of Vāyu, are very strong. Vāyu is the *devatā* of *bala*, the strength in your hands and in your arms. We are still talking about the *sūkṣma-śarīra*, so remember these are the subtle *indriya*s, not the physical hands. The *sthūla* aspect is yet to come; here it is purely *sūkṣma-śarīra* as *indriya, vāgindriya,* and *pāṇīndriya*.

Further,

वह्ने राजसांशात्पादेन्द्रियं सम्भूतम् ।

vahne rājasāṁśāt pādendriyaṁ sambhūtam.

vahneḥ – of fire; *rājasāṁśāt* – from the *rajas* aspect; *pāda-indriyam* – (the organ of movement called) the feet; *sambhūtam* – is born.

From the *rajas* aspect of fire the (organ of movement called) feet is born.

जलस्य राजसांशाद् गुदेन्द्रियं सम्भूतम् ।

jalasya rājasāṁśād gudendriyaṁ sambhūtam.

jalasya – of water; *rājasāṁśāt* – from the *rajas* aspect; *guda-indriyam* – the organ of evacuation; *sambhūtam* – is born.

From the *rajas* aspect of water, the organ of evacuation is born.

All the physiological activity is included here, so from the *rajas* aspect of the subtle element, water, is born the organ of evacuation as a subtle *indriya*.

पृथिव्या राजसांशादुपस्थेन्द्रियं सम्भूतम् ।

pṛthivyā rājasāṁśādupasthendriyaṁ sambhūtam.

pṛthivyāḥ – of the earth; *rājasāṁśāt* – from the *rajas* aspect; *upastha-indriyam* – the organ of procreation; *sambhūtam* – is born.

From the *rajas* aspect of the earth the organ of procreation is born.

एतेषां समष्टिराजसांशात्पञ्चप्राणाः संभूताः ।

eteṣāṁ samaṣṭirājasāṁśātpañcaprāṇāḥ sambhūtāḥ.

eteṣām – of these (five subtle elements); *samaṣṭi-rājasāṁśāt* – from the total *rajas* aspect; *pañca-prāṇāḥ* – the five *prāṇas* (physiological functions); *sambhūtāḥ* – are born.

From the total *rajas* aspect of these (five subtle elements) are born the five *prāṇas* (physiological functions).

All these together, the total *rajas* aspect of the five elements, account for the entire physiological function, called the five-fold *prāṇa*, *pañca-prāṇas* – *prāṇa*, *āpana*, *vyāna*, *udāna*, *samāna*. They are organs of action that come from *rajas,* which is why they do not perceive.

The sense organs and the mind together perceive, as they are from the *sāttvika* aspect. Here, even though they belong to the *sūkṣma-śarīra* and keep the life going by providing energy, there is no new perception because these *pañca-prāṇa*s are *karmendriya*s, organs of action, born of *rajas*. Together they make what we call the *prāṇa-maya-kośa*, which we saw earlier. It is *prāṇa-maya*, forms of *prāṇa*, and it is a *kośa* because we confuse these with *ātman*.

Grossification of the elements

So, from Brahman with *māyā-upādhi*, *māyā-avacinna-brahmaṇaḥ*, comes the five elements that constitute the *jagat*. We saw the whole *sūkṣma prapañca*, subtle cosmos, of the five elements. Now, the whole *sthūla prapañca*, the physical cosmos, is to be covered. From the three *guṇa*s one aspect remains to account for – *tamas*. From the *tamas* aspect is born what we know as the gross *ākāśa*, the physical space, and also the four elements – *vāyu, agni, āpaḥ, pṛithvī* – 'grossified.'

What does it mean to say that they are 'grossified?' There is a process of grossification; they are not born as gross elements. It means the subtle elements undergo a process of grossification which we technically call *pañcīkaraṇa*. This is very interesting.

It means that anything can be gross or subtle. Gross matter can be converted into energy and energy is again converted into matter. This is happening all the time. What you eat is gross – in fact, groceries – and that undergoes a conversion into energy. Then again, a part of it gets grossified. Otherwise, how do you put on weight? This goes on. So, a process of grossification is involved here. Each *sūkṣma-bhūta*, subtle element, is made into a gross element in a process through which it gains an element of the other four elements. This process of *pañcīkaraṇa* is going to be told next. And with that we have *sthūla-śarira* and *sthūla prāpañca*, which are the starting points of our enquiry.

From the tamas aspect of the five elements comes the tangible world

एतेषां पञ्चतत्त्वानां तामसांशात्पञ्चीकृतपञ्चतत्त्वानि
भवन्ति ।

eteṣāṁ pañcatattvānāṁ tāmasāṁśātpañcīkṛta-pañca-tattvāni bhavanti.

eteṣāṁ pañca-tattvānām – of these five elements; *tāmasāṁśāt* – from the *tamas* aspect; *pañcīkṛta-pañca-tattvāni* – the five grossified elements; *bhavanti* – are formed.

From the *tamas* aspect of these five subtle elements, the five grossified elements are formed.

The *pañca-tattva*s are from the *tamas* aspect of these five subtle elements. What kind of *pañca-tattva*s? *Pañcīkṛta-pañca-tattvāni*. *Pañcīkṛta* means made into five; each one of them is made into five. Previously, *ākāśa*, *vāyu* and so on were subtle. But the *ākāśa* you objectify outside and which accommodates – that physical space is *pañcīkṛta-ākāśa*. In that *ākāśa* there is the presence of the other four subtle elements. Similarly, in *vāyu* there is the presence of the other four fractionally. So too, in *agni* there is the fractional presence of the other four, as there is in water and *pṛithivī*, the earth. In *sūkṣma-ākāśa*, for instance, one is divided into equal halves – one half remains and the other half is divided equally among the other four elements. All of them come and join *ākāśa*, so each of the other four elements comprise one-eighth of the whole. Yet, it is called *ākāśa* because of its predominance, being the whole half. *Vāyu*, which is the next, is going to be predominant because *vāyu* will occupy half and the other four elements will comprise only one-eighth. Similarly, fire will occupy half and the other four will each be one eighth of the whole. Thus, we have *pañcīkṛta-pañca-tattvāni*. They are called *ākāśa, vāyu,* etc., on the basis of the predominant presence of each of them. Otherwise, we would have to give each a new name, as we do to an alloy.

The process of grossification

पञ्चीकरणं कथमिति चेत्।

एतेषां पञ्चमहाभूतानां तामसांशस्वरूपमेकमेकं भूतं द्विधा विभज्यैकमेकमर्धं पृतक्तूष्णीं व्यवस्थाप्य अपरमपरमर्धं चतुर्धा विभज्य स्वार्धभिन्नेषु अर्धेषु स्वभागचतुष्टयसंयोजनं पञ्चीकरणं भवति।

pañcīkaraṇaṁ kathamiti cet

eteṣāṁ pañca-mahā-bhūtānāṁ tāmasāṁśa-svarūpam ekamekaṁ bhūtaṁ dvidhā vibhajyaikamekamardhaṁ pṛthaktūṣṇīṁ vyavasthāpya aparamaparamardhaṁ caturdhā vibhajya svārdhabhinneṣu ardheṣu svabhāgacatuṣṭayasaṁyojanaṁ pañcīkaraṇaṁ bhavati.

pañcīkaraṇam – the process of making each element five-fold; *katham* – how; *iti cet* – if it is asked;

eteṣāṁ pañca-mahā-bhūtānām – of these five (great) original elements; *tāmasa-aṁśa-svarūpam ekam ekaṁ bhūtam* – the *tamas* aspect (of) each element; *dvidhā vibhajya* – dividing into two halves; *ekam ekam ardham pṛthak tūṣṇīm vyavasthāpya* – one half (of each element) remaining distinct (without further division or combining); *aparam aparam ardhaṁ caturdhā vibhajya* – dividing the other half (of each element) four-fold; *svabhāga-catuṣṭaya-saṁyojanam* – combining of each of these quarters; *svārdha-bhinneṣu ardheṣu* – with the other half of each element (which was undivided); *pañcīkaraṇaṁ bhavati* – is (called) *pañcīkaraṇa*, grossification.

> If it is asked, how the process of making each element five-fold (takes place),
> Of these five (great) original elements, the *tamas* aspect of each element dividing into two halves, one half (of each element) remaining distinct (without further division or combining); dividing the other half (of each element) four-fold. Combining each of these quarters with the other half of each element (which was undivided), is (called) *pañcīkaraṇa*, grossification.

We need to understand an important point here. These gross elements are inert in nature. Your physical body is made up of the five gross elements. It occupies space, the gross element space. There is *vāyu* throughout the whole body. Wherever there is a blood cell there is oxygen, and that is *vāyu*. Then there is fire, temperature, and there is water giving the body shape. There is *pṛthivī*, all the tangible minerals, and elements like carbon and so on. This is the body consisting of five elements. Now, if the *sūkṣma-śarīra* is not in it, it is going to be inert. The table is inert even though it is the same Īśvara, because it is made of five *sthūla-bhūta*s, called *bhautika*s. And *bhautika* being *sthūla*, will not have a *sūkṣma* component; so it will be inert.

The gross elements are inert in nature, even though they are not separate from *caitanya*. Therefore, we can say that it is all Īśvara. We can say it poetically too – the lord sleeps in stone, stands in a tree, walks in a cow, and talks in Ram. You need to understand the spirit behind the whole vision. All these are Īśvara because nothing is away from Īśvara. When we say that something is inert it does not mean we divide things into inert and sentient. It is purely a point of view. It is the presence or absence of *sūkṣma-śarīra* that accounts for something being sentient and insentient. It is not the presence of consciousness or the absence of consciousness, nor is it the presence of Īśvara or absence of Īśvara. The *sūkṣma-śarīra* is the only factor that makes the difference. We must be very clear about this. We have to account for the inertness in the *jagat*. Why is something inert if everything is consciousness? It is the *tama*s aspect that accounts for the grossification. The purely *tamas* aspect of all five subtle elements undergoes the change to become the five gross elements. The process of grossification was already explained. These *sthūla-bhūtāni* make the entire cosmos including this earth.

Identity of Individual and Cosmos

एतेभ्यः पञ्चीकृतपञ्चमहाभूतेभ्यः स्थूलशरीरं भवति ।

etebhyaḥ pañcīkṛta-pañcamahā-bhūtebhyaḥ sthūla-śarīraṁ bhavati.

etebhyaḥ – from these; *pañcīkṛta-pañcamahā-bhūtebhyaḥ* – five elements which have undergone grossification (*pañcīkaraṇam); sthūla-śarīram* – the gross body; *bhavati* – is formed.

From these five elements which have undergone grossification (*pañcīkaraṇam),* the gross body is formed.

एवं पिण्डब्रह्माण्डयोरैक्यं सम्भूतम् ।

evaṁ piṇḍa-brahmāṇḍayoraikyaṁ sambhūtam.

evam – in this manner; *piṇḍa-brahmāṇḍayoḥ* – between the *piṇḍa*, the microcosm (individual) and *brahmāṇḍa*, the macrocosm (cosmos); *aikyam*– identity; *sambhūtam* – is born.

> In this manner, identity between microcosm (individual) and the macrocosm (cosmos) is born.

From these five grossified elements, *ākāśa, vāyu, agni*, etc., is born the *sthūla-śarīra*, the physical body. Your physical body consists of five *sthūla* elements, physical elements, and your *sūkṣma-śarīra* is also born of those same five elements in a subtle form. So, this external world and your physical body, a given individual's physical body, is nothing but these five elements. The individual physical body is called *piṇḍa*, and the total is what we call *aṇḍa*, which means *brahmāṇḍa*, the cosmos. The cosmos and the individual's *sthūla-śarīra* have certain identity, being made up of the same five elements.

While we are able to look upon the cosmos as something made up of five elements, and can accept that as a model, somehow we pull the physical body out of that physical world. So, the *śāstra* wants us to include the physical body in these five elements.

These five elements and elementals constitute both *piṇḍa* and *brahmāṇḍa;* and there is *piṇḍa-brahmāṇḍa-aikya,* oneness. There is certain identity between the two, in that, one is not independent of the other; both are nothing but the five elements. Already we have said that these elements are non-separate from Brahman, and the *sūkṣma-śarīra* is also non-separate from Brahman. All of them are born from Brahman with *māyā.* And *māyā* being *mithyā,* anything that is born of *māyā,* which has undergone some change to be this world, is non-separate from that Brahman. Therefore, all that is here is one Brahman.

Now, we are discussing this *mahā-vākya, tat tvam asi.* The *mahā-vākya* is based upon the understanding, that *tvaṁ-pada,* the word 'you' is not merely the *sthūla-śarīra* or the *sūkṣma-śarīra.* It is the *pratyagātman,* the *caitanya.* When you look into *caitanya,* consciousness, you find it is *satya,* and these two, the *sthūla* and *sūkṣma-śarīra*s, are *mithyā.* Similarly, *tat-pada* is non-separate from Īśvara, who is all, who is *saccidānandaṁ brahma.* In the *piṇḍa,* it is the same *saccidānanda-ātman,* and in the *aṇḍa* also it is the same *saccidānandāṁ brahma*. Then, how many *saccidānanda*s do we have? There is only one *saccidānandaṁ brahma,* where there is no division, and this oneness is what is revealed by the *mahā-vākya.*

The jīva

स्थूलशरीराभिमानि जीवनामकं ब्रह्मप्रतिबिम्बं भवति ।
स एव जीवः प्रकृत्या स्वस्मादीश्वरं भिन्नत्वेन जानाति ।

sthūlaśarīrābhimani jīvanāmakaṁ brahmapratibimbaṁ bhavati, sa eva jīvaḥ prakṛtyā svasmādīśvaraṁ bhinnatvena jānāti.

sthūla-śarīra-abhimāni – the one who is identified with the gross physical body; *jīva-nāmakam* – is called a *jīva*; *brahma-pratibimbam* – the reflection of Brahman; *bhavati* – is; *saḥ eva jīvaḥ* – that very *jīva*; *prakṛtyā* – by nature (without enquiry); *īśvaram* – Īśvara; *svasmāt* – from himself; *bhinnatvena* – as different; *jānāti* – knows (thinks).

The one who is identified with the gross physical body is called a *jīva*, is (but) the reflection of Brahman. That very *jīva*, by nature (without enquiry), knows (thinks) Īśvara as different from himself.

This *jīva*, I, which identifies itself with the *sthūla-śarīra*, thinks, "Up to this physical body I go, and everything else is different from me." This is the identification, *abhimāna*. The *sthūla-śarīrābhimani-ātman* takes on the qualities of the *sthūla-śarīra* as one's own.

This also includes the *sūkṣma-śarīra* because the *abhimānin*, the one who identifies, is there. So, this *sthūla-śarīra-abhimānin* who is within the confines of this body is called a *jīva*.

Brahma-pratibimbaṁ bhavati. Really speaking, this *jīva* is neither the *sthūla-śarīra* nor the *sūkṣma-śarīra*, but a conscious being. The *jīva* is a conscious being because the *antaḥ-karaṇa*, the mind, has this capacity to reflect consciousness. Therefore, there is an I-sense that is nothing but a thought. This I-sense is non-separate from consciousness; the whole mind is non-separate from consciousness. And the non-separation from consciousness with reference to a thought is called *pratibimba*, reflection. This is one way of looking at it, so the *pratibimba-vāda* is useful for us as a *prakriyā*, one of the methods of revealing the nature of *ātman*. The *pratibimba-vāda* is used by Śaṅkara. He says that any thought is not independent of consciousness, and the presence of consciousness in the thought is called *pratibimba*, a reflection. Why do we call it a reflection? Because the thought itself, being *nāma-rūpa*, being *mithyā*, has no being of its own, nor does it have consciousness as such. There is only one source of consciousness – *ātman*. The consciousness obtaining in the *antaḥ-karaṇa* is what we call the *pratibimba*. And because of this, the one who identifies with the *antaḥ-karaṇa* is called a *jīva* or *cidābhāsa*. The *jīva* is one who is conscious of the body, mind, senses, and also identifies with them. That is the problem. The one who identifies these as 'I' is called a *jīva*, and that consciousness enjoyed by the I-notion is Brahman. It is not separate.

With reference to the I-thought we say it is *cidābhāsa*, reflected consciousness, because this *jīva* has to be taken as the consistent one, even though that is also a reflection. Nothing is away from the *vastu*, but every thought that occurs in your mind is not considered 'I'. You only look at an object of thought as this-thought – this pot, this flower, this table, etc. However, there is one constant person, the *jīva*. He is the *pramātṛ*, the knower, the subject, and therefore, is nothing but *brahma-pratibimba*; in other words, the status of being a *jīva* is *mithyā*.

The word '*mithyā*' is better because *pratibimba* implies a lot of other problems. Therefore, generally, I say that this *ahaṅkāra* is purely *mithyā*. That is enough. To explain it further they will say that it is a reflection, and so on, but you have to be very careful with these words.

If it is a reflection you can ask what is the medium of reflection? Is there a reflecting medium independent of Brahman? All these questions will arise. Then, we have to say that the medium is also Brahman. If the medium is Brahman, is it *satya* or *mithyā*? It is *mithyā*. If it is *mithyā,* then what is the reflection? The *mithyā* medium is reflecting the consciousness, so the reflection is also *mithyā*. Again, we end up with *mithyā*. Therefore, *mithyā* is a very appropriate word to understand the nature of the *jīva*.

Accordingly, he points out the problem of the *jīva* here as natural, *sa eva jīvaḥ prakṛtyā svasmād īśvaraṁ bhinnatvena jānāti. Prakṛtyā* means by nature, without enquiry. Because the individual is born self-ignorant, ignorance being inherent, one has erroneous self-understanding by nature. Without *vicāra,* enquiry, without *pramāṇa,* a means of knowledge, by one's own nature, *prakṛtyā,* one concludes. What does one conclude? The *jīva* looks upon Īśvara – the creator, the sustainer and the dissolver – as someone separate from himself.

Mokṣa is possible only when you understand that the *jīva* is but Īśvara. You have to know, "I am Brahman, which is Īśvara." That is not possible if you think you are a part of Īśvara. If you say, "I am a fraction whereas Īśvara is glorious," Īśvara remains glorious, and you have to have Īśvara as your hero all your life. He is our hero no doubt, but then, if he is a permanent hero and you are only a fan, there is no *mokṣa*. You remain a fanatic *bhakta*, and you are away from that Īśvara. Why? *Prakṛtyā*, due to self-ignorance, without any enquiry.

Everyone has self-ignorance, and everyone takes on the qualities of the physical body. Why? Because the *sūkṣma-śarīra* is identified with only one body. So, you are within the confines of this body, you are an entity, an individual, transacting business with the world. The world is big, and you think, 'I am small, I am persecuted, and everything is big.' Therefore, you have to fend, defend, and offend; this is the whole stance in life, that of a ninja. But you do not give up the love for survival; you have some experience of yourself being free. In a moment of joy, in deep sleep, you have the experience of freedom, so you think that you can make it; there is a hope. That is why *apohana*, forgetting, is a grace; it keeps you going until you discover the truth. Bhagavān cannot hide himself – he is the only one who has no hiding place. All that is here is Bhagavān; he cannot hide. Only ignorance can give him a cover. There is no other way of covering Bhagavān. Ignorance covers the whole thing. And due to this naturally obtaining ignorance, one concludes that one is separate from Īśvara, *prakṛtyā svasmād bhinnatvena jānāti īśvaram.*

अविद्योपाधिः सन्नात्मा जीव इत्युच्यते ।

avidyopādhiḥ sannātmā jīva ityucyate.

ātmā – *ātmā,* the self ; *avidyā-upādhiḥ san* – being one who has the conditioning adjunct of *avidyā,* ignorance; *jīvaḥ* – *jīva,* the individual; *iti ucyate* – is called.

> The self, being one who has the conditioning adjunct of ignorance, is called *jīva,* the individual.

Avidyā, ignorance, error, is the *upādhi* because of which one is a *jīva.* The *caitanya-ātman,* which is limitless, is called a *jīva* only because of ignorance and error. Due to ignorance, one takes the physical body, mind, and senses as oneself, and that error is also called *avidyā.* Both the mistaken notion and the cause, the *āvaraṇa,* are *avidyā. Āvaraṇa* means a cover, a veil, and only because of it does *ātman* become a *jīva.*

Avidyā upādhiḥ san, being one who has *avidyā* as his *upādhi*, this *ātman* becomes the *jīva*.

Īśvara

मायोपाधिः सन्नात्मेश्वर इत्युच्यते

māyopādhiḥ sannātmeśvara ityucyate.

ātmā – ātmā 'I'; *māyopādhiḥ san* – being the one endowed with the limiting adjunct of *māyā*; *īśvaraḥ* – Īśvara, the Lord; *iti ucyate* – is called.

> *ātmā* 'I' being the one endowed with the limiting adjunct of *māyā* is called Īśvara, the Lord.

The same *ātman* with *māyā-upādhi* is Īśvara. This is a *prakriyā*. Having *māyā-upādhi*, *ātman* is called Īśvara. Īśvara is the same *ātman*. Now he drops the word 'Brahman' and uses only *ātman*, because he has already pointed that *ātman* is *saccidānanda* which is Brahman. This *saccidānanda-ātman* due to *avidyā* is called a *jīva*, and due to *māyā* is called Īśvara.

Māyā is also *mithyā*. And this *māyā-upādhi* of Īśvara continues, whether you are enlightened or not. As long as your body-mind-sense complex is there, alive, Īśvara continues. Your *sthūla-śarīra* will continue, your *sūkṣma-śarīra* will continue; it is all Īśvara. Born of five subtle and gross elements, it is all *brahmāśrayā māyā*. What can go, then? Only *avidyā*. *Avidyā* is not there in Īśvara, because Īśvara is all-knowledge, which is free from ignorance.

Now, you are looking at the *jagat*, and you want to know what this *jagat* is. *Śāstra* says it is Brahman. Brahman with the *māyā-upādhi* is this whole *jagat*, and is *sarvajña*, so it does not require a mind to know. With the very *māyā-upādhi* he is *sarvajña*, all-knowledge, and *sarva-kāraṇa*, the cause of the entire world. All that is there is Īśvara, and there is no ignorance for that Īśvara.

We can put it another way – Īśvara, with an individual *upādhi*, and Īśvara with the total, *samaṣṭi-upādhi*. With the individual *upādhi* it is called a *jīva;* with the total *upādhi* it is called Īśvara. *Jīveśvara* continues, even when ignorance is gone, but the whole understanding is different. It is understanding the individual and the total. With the total *upādhi*, which includes my body also, it is called Īśvara, and with a given individual *upādhi*, where there is a *sūkṣma-śarīra* identified with the given physical body, naturally it is called a *jīva*.

This identification will continue, because the *jīva* is born of certain *prārabdha-karma*, which is in the process of fructification through this physical body. Therefore, confinement of the *sūkṣma-śarīra* to a given physical body continues for the *prārabdha* to be exhausted. And, as will be told later, the *jīva* continues, but while living he is liberated, *jīvan muktaḥ*. Being alive, that *jīva* can still appreciate Īśvara and his glories; therefore an enlightened person will also offer his prayers in appreciation of Parameśvara, or for the sake of others. He is free enough to offer his prayers for the welfare of the country, community, and so on.

Saṁsāra is due to bheda-dṛṣṭi

एवमुपाधिभेदाज्जीवेश्वरभेददृष्टिर्यावत्पर्यन्तं तिष्ठति
तावत्पर्यन्तं जन्ममरणादिरूपसंसारो न निवर्तते ।

evamupādhibhedājjīveśvara-bheda-
dṛṣṭiryāvatparyantaṁ tiṣṭhati
tāvat paryantaṁ janma-maraṇādi-rūpa-
saṁsāro na nivartate.

evam – in this manner; *upādhi-bhedāt* – wrought by the differences in *upādhi*, limiting adjunct; *jīva-īśvara-bheda-dṛṣṭiḥ* – the perception (conclusion) of difference between the individual and the Lord; *yāvat-paryantam* – as long as; *tiṣṭhati* – remains; *tāvat-paryantam* – until such time; *janma-maraṇādi-rūpa-saṁsāraḥ* – *saṁsāra*, (a life of becoming) in the form of birth, death, etc.; *na nivartate* – does not come to an end.

> In this manner, as long as the percpetion (conclusion) of difference between the individual and the Lord, wrought by the differences in the limiting adjunct, remains, until such time, *saṁsāra,* (a life of becoming) in the form of birth, death, etc., does not come to an end.

There is a conclusion, a view that Īśvara is different from me, the *jīva*. It is due to *avidyā*. Only because of the *avidyā-upādhi,* there is this kind of contention that I am separate from Īśvara. Even though it is due to *upādhi,* I take the difference as real. There is a *bheda-dṛṣṭi* due to *avidyā*. Due to the *bheda-dṛṣṭi, saṁsāra,* a life of becoming, is there. And that *saṁsāra* is characterised as being in the form of birth, death, etc. – *janma-maraṇādi-rūpa-saṁsāra*. What is the '*ādi,* etc.,' here? It is the *sukha-duḥkha* in between. Birth itself takes place with a lot of trauma for both the mother and child. Then afterwards, life is also highly traumatic. This is called *janma-maraṇādi* – the *ādi* is *sukha-duḥkha* that include old age and illness.

How long is this kind of *saṁsāra* there? As long as this *bheda-dṛṣṭi* due to *avidyā,* ignorance, is there.

Now, in the light of this, the author of *Tattvabodha* gives us some advice about this *bheda-dṛṣṭi.*

तस्मात्कारणात् न जीवेश्वरयोर्भेदबुद्धिः स्वीकार्या

tasmātkāraṇāt na jīveśvarayorbheda-buddhiḥ svīkāryā.

tasmāt kāraṇāt – therefore for that reason; *jīva-īśvarayoḥ* – between the *jīva* (individual) and Īśvara (the Lord); *bheda-buddhiḥ* – the conclusion of difference; *na svīkāryā* – is not to be accepted.

> Therefore, for that reason, the conclusion of difference between the indiviudal and the Lord is not to be accepted.

As long as the *bheda-buddhi* is there, you have to enquire. That is what he says here. Obviously, the notion of duality being the basis of all pursuits, the view of non-difference would be the basis of only one pursuit – pursuit of knowledge. Therefore, one needs to have *śraddhā* in the *abheda* view of the *śāstra* because one is under the grip of the erroneous perception of duality of *jīva* and *jagat*.

Let us just have a little bit of fun here. One person says that there is duality. Why? Because I see you; that is good enough. 'I see you' is a perception in which 'I' is the subject and 'you' is the object. The object is not the subject, and therefore there is duality. This 'therefore' is the problem. 'I see you' is a fact that is not questioned. But it does not prove duality. You cannot use it as a cause for establishing duality. Non-duality is, in spite of the fact that there is a subject, there is an object.

In dream you see many things, but it does not mean they are different from you. Just because you see a mountain there, you cannot say that it is different from you; the dream experience denies that. This 'I see you, therefore there is duality' is contradicted in the dream. I see the mountain in the dream and still it is me. So, 'I see you' does not prove duality.

You may argue that you count many things here, not just one. You can count many things here, still there may not be duality at all. You can count a few more things, and still there is no duality at all. Here, I have – one, two, three – four pots; but all that is there is clay, one clay. Number does not prove duality. Then you may say that variety proves duality. If you know something about petro-chemicals you will understand the problem with this argument. In one place it is called gas, in another, it is oil, and the whole thing was crude once upon a time. And part of it goes onto your face as cold cream. Varieties do not prove that there are many things. In dream also you have variety, beginning with sentient and insentient. Therefore, you cannot prove duality. Only perception is there, which you do not need to prove. In fact, the perception can prove non-duality.

Every time you perceive something, there is object-consciousness, there is thought-consciousness, there is subject-consciousness – all that is there is consciousness. In consciousness alone is the object and the subject. The object goes on changing; it is variable. As a seer, hearer, and so on, the subject also can go on changing. Both subject and object exist in the same plank of consciousness, which is non-dual. In fact, perception proves non-duality. Without non-duality there cannot be perception because an object cannot be away from consciousness and still be perceived. It cannot be away from 'is'-ness, which is only consciousness. It is only due to lack of enquiry into the naturally obtaining ignorance, *avicāra-siddha-prakṛtyā*, that there is difference, *bheda*, duality. And if you really begin to question properly, with the help of the required *pramāṇa*, you end up in non-duality. Therefore, the thinking that there is difference is not to be accepted, *bheda-buddhiḥ na svīkāryā*.

An objection:

How can there be an equation of oneness between *jīva* and Īśvara?

> ननु साहङ्कारस्य किञ्चिज्ञस्य जीवस्य निरहङ्कारस्य सर्वज्ञस्येश्वरस्य तत्त्वमसीति महावाक्यात् कथमभेदबुद्धिः स्यात् उभयोर्विरुद्धधर्माक्रान्तत्वात् ।
>
> *nanu sāhaṅkārasya kiñcijñasya jīvasya nirahaṅkārasya sarvajñasyeśvarasya tattvamasīti mahā-vākyāt kathamabheda-buddhiḥ syāt ubhayorviruddha-dharma-ākrāntatvāt.*

nanu – but (in opposition to what is said); *katham* – how; *syāt* – can there be; *abheda-buddhiḥ* – the knowledge of non-differnce; *jīvasya* – (between) the *jīva*, the individual; *sāhaṅkārasya* – who has the I-notion; *kiñcijñasya* – who is of limited knowledge; *īśvarasya* – (and) of Īśvara, the Lord; *nirahaṅkārasya* –who is devoid of ego; *sarvajñasya* – of all-knowledge; *tat-tvam-asi iti mahāvākyāt* – from the sentence, (which reveals the oneness between the individual and the total) 'that thou art'; *ubhayoḥ viruddha-dharma-ākrāntatvāt* – because the two (*jīva* and Īśvara) being possessed of contradictory attributes.

> From the sentence (which reveals the oneness between the individual and the total), 'You are that,' how can there be the knowledge of non-difference between the two – *jīva* who has the I-notion, who is of limited knowledge, and Īśvara who is devoid of ego, who is all-knowledge – because the two (*jīva* and Īśvara) being possessed of contraditory qualities?

In Sanskrit commentaries of various texts, one will come across the word '*nanu*', which is meant to draw one's attention. More often than not, the word indicates that an objection is raised. It can also just draw your attention, 'look.'

Here, the objection is this. The *jīva* is *sāhaṅkāra*, has an individual ego with a biography of *sukha-duḥkha*, with an opinion about himself. The meaning of you, *tvam*, as we normally understand is *ahaṅkāra*, ego. Therefore, the 'you' in '*tat tvam asi*, you are that,' is the *ātman* with *ahaṅkāra*, that is, *sāhaṅkāra*. Not only that, being an individual, he is *kiñcitjña*, with limited knowledge. Knowledge of the individual is always limited. This is the *jīva*.

Then, Īśvara is presented as *sarvajña*, all-knowledge. And according to you, out of him everything is born, and therefore he is everything, which means that he does not have an ego. He is *nirahaṅkāra*.

In the equation '*tat tvam asi*,' we have *sāhaṅkāra*, with ego, and *nirahaṅkāra*, without ego; then *kiñcitjña*, with limited knowledge, and *sarvajña*, with all-knowledge. And I am told, "You are that Īśvara." How can I be that Īśvara? How will I ever understand the sentence, "You are that, *tat tvam asi*?" It is very difficult to understand, even though grammatically it is correct. Grammatically, a sentence may be correct, "Yesterday evening an elephant entered into my left ear. And thank God it walked through and came out of the right ear." There is no linguistic mistake; the sentences are grammatically clean. But there is no *yogyatā*, the possibility of meaningful sense. Similarly, when Īśvara who is all-knowledge is equated to me, the limited individual, it is too much.

Equation of oneness is by implied meaning – lakṣyārtha

इति चेन्न ।

स्थूलसूक्ष्मशरीराभिमानी त्वम्पदवाच्यार्थः ।

उपाधिविनिर्मुक्तं समाधिदशासम्पन्नं शुद्धं चैतन्यं त्वम्पदलक्ष्यार्थः ।

iti cenna;

sthūla-sūkṣma-śarīrābhimānī tvam-pada-vācyārthaḥ. upādhi-vinirmuktaṁ samādhi-daśā-sampannaṁ śuddhaṁ caitanyaṁ tvam-pada-lakṣyārthaḥ.

iti cet – if it is so (if that is your argument); *na* – no (there is no real difference);

sthūla-sūkṣma-śarīra-abhimānī – the one who is identified with the physical and subtle bodies; *tvam-pada-vācyārthaḥ* – (is) the immediate meaning of the word *tvam; upādhi-vinirmuktam* – the one who is free from the limiting adjuncts; *samādhi-daśā-sampannam* – the one who obtains during an experience of subject-object resolution; *śuddham caitanyam* – pure consciousness; *tvam-pada-lakṣyārthaḥ* – (is) the implied meaning of the word *tvam*, you.

If it is so (if that is your argument), no (there is no real difference). The immediate meaning of the word 'you' is the one who is identified with the physical and subtle bodies. The implied meaning of the word 'you' is pure consciousness, the one who is free from the limiting adjuncts, the one who obtains during an experience of subject-object resolution.

When this contradiction is very obvious, and in spite of it someone says, 'You are that Īśvara,' then the person who uses the sentence has, what we call, a *tātparya*. Two things are seemingly contradictory, but there is no contradiction in reality. In an equation you should expect a seeming contradiction, and the non-contradiction is to be understood. The contradiction has to be explained away so that the non-contradicting fact becomes evident. That is an equation.

The *vācyārtha*, the immediate meaning of *tat* in '*tat tvam asi*' is *jagat-kāraṇa*, Īśvara, who is all-knowledge, the cause for everything, both the material and efficient cause. Therefore, in the *vācyārtha*, there is definitely *bheda*, difference. We do not say that there is no difference. There is difference, and it is obvious. In fact, it is this difference that the *śruti* wants to resolve into a **seeming** difference.

From the standpoint of the *upādhi* alone, *ātman* becomes limited, and is found wanting. The *upādhi-dharma*, the attribute or status of the *upādhi* belongs to the *upādhi*. Its *dharma* is not the *dharma* of the *vastu*. So, the real meaning of the word 'you', *tvaṁ-pada lakṣya*, is free from the *upādhi, upādhi-vinirmukta*, because all the *upādhi*s are variable. If they are intrinsic to *ātman*, you will always be a *kiñcitjña*, a person of limited knowledge. That is not true. When you see yourself free from the *upādhi*, as in sleep, or in a moment of joy, what obtains is *śuddhaṁ caitanyam*.

This *śuddhaṁ caitanyam* is the implied meaning, *lakṣyārtha*, of the word '*tvam*'. When I say that you are sitting here, I mean the physical body because what is seated here is the physical body, *sthūla-śarīra*. If I say that you seem to be hungry, I refer to your *prāṇa*, and when I say that you seem to be restless, I mean your mind. When I say that you seem to have done this, I mean your *vijñānamaya*, your sense that you are the *kartṛ*. Suppose I say, you are the one in whose presence alone all these are known – body-consciousness, mind-consciousness, Swami-consciousness, sound-consciousness, form-consciousness, or *svarūpa*-consciousness – in every cognition you have the presence of consciousness, and that is the meaning of the word 'you'. This is *tvaṁ-pada lakṣyārtha*, the implied meaning of the word 'you', which is pure, *śuddhaṁ caitanyam*.

Pure consciousness is only an expression with reference to it being without the *upādhi, upādhi-vinirmukta.* You are understanding the *ātma-caitanya* without the *upādhi;* it is not that we are releasing it from the *upādhi*. It is exactly like understanding the crystal as a crystal. Even if you see color in it, you just remove the color cognitively and understand it as a crystal. That is called crystal clear knowledge. If you have knowledge of what a crystal is, you do not make any conscious attempt to remove the color of the crystal in order to understand the crystal. That is what I call clear knowledge.

एवं सर्वज्ञत्वादि-विशिष्ट ईश्वरः तत्पदवाच्यार्थः ।
उपाधिशून्यं शुद्धचैतन्यं तत्पदलक्ष्यार्थः ।

evaṁ sarvajñatvādi-viśiṣṭaḥ īśvaraḥ tat-pada-vācyārthaḥ
upādhi-śūnyaṁ śuddha-caitanyaṁ tat-pada-lakṣyārthaḥ.

evam – similarly; *sarvajñatvādi-viśiṣṭaḥ* – one who is endowed with all-knowledge, etc.; *īśvaraḥ* – the Lord; *tat-pada-vācyārthaḥ* – (is) the immediate meaning of the word '*tat*, that'; *upādhi-śūnyam* – free from limiting adjuncts; *śuddha-caitanyam* – (who is) pure consciousness; *tat-pada-lakṣyārthaḥ* – (is) the implied meaning of the word *tat*.

> Similarly, the immediate meaning of the word '*tat*, that' is the Lord, the one who is endowed with all knowledge, etc. The implied meaning of the word '*tat*, that' is pure consciousness, free from limiting adjuncts.

Tat-pada-lakṣya is *satyaṁ jñānam ānantaṁ brahma* and is also *tvaṁ-pada lakṣya*. How many limitless consciousness do you have? Only one limitless consciousness in which space is, time is, and everything is. That limitless consciousness, because of which all dividing factors exist, is an undivided whole.

What are the things that divide? You are sitting there and I am sitting here. What divides? Space. So, there is a spatial division. Time-wise there is division in terms of what existed before and what does not exist now. Object-wise also there is division – this is chair, not table. These are the dividing factors through which we arrive at divisions. Now here, the space itself is *sat-cit ātman*. Time is *sat-cit ātman*. And every attribute is also *sat-cit ātman*. Any substantive is *nāma-rūpa*, and all of them are one *sat-cit ātman, brahma,* which he has already proved. Nothing is outside space being born of Brahman.

Everything is born of Brahman. Being both the *nimitta* and *upādāna kāraṇa*, nothing is away from it. If that is so, where is the division? There is no division. There is only one Brahman. *Ātman* is *suddha caitanya* and Īśvara is *suddha caitanya*. It means there is no real difference. The difference is only in *upādhi*, which is *mithyā*. The *jīva-upādhi*, the entire *sūkṣma-sthūla-śarīra*, all of it, is *mithyā*. It has no existence apart from Brahman. Similarly *īśvaratva*, the status of being Īśvara, is also not independent of Brahman. The *jīveśvara* difference is there, no doubt, but the difference is *mithyā*. This non-difference is what is to be understood, and that is what releases the person from the sense of limitation, the sense of bondage.

So, the words of the *mahā-vākya*, '*tat tvam asi*,' do not contradict themselves because there is oneness. There is nothing that is apart from Brahman, and I am that Brahman, *tad brahma aham asmi*. That is the knowledge.

एवं च जीवेश्वरयोश्चैतन्यरूपेणाभेदे बाधकाभावः ।

evaṁ ca jīveśvarayoḥ caitanyarūpeṇābhede
bādhakābhāvaḥ.

evaṁ ca – and thus; *jīva-īśvarayoḥ* – between *jīva* and Īśvara (individual and total); *caitanyarūpeṇa abhede* –

there being no difference in the form of consciousness; *bādhaka-abhāvaḥ* – (there is) nothing to negate that.

> And thus, between *jīva* and Īśvara (individual and total) there being no difference in the form of consciousness, (there is) nothing to negate that.

In the reality of consciousness of *jīva* and of Īśvara, there is *abheda,* no difference whatsoever. We are not talking of a non-difference between two identical entities like two desks, both made of the same type of wood, both of the same size, shape, and so on. *Jīva* is *jīva,* Īśvara is Īśvara, is non-ditto. Then what is the oneness?

There is only one consciousness that is Brahman. From the standpoint of *vyaṣṭi-upādhi,* the *caitanya* is *jīva,* and from that of *samaṣṭi-upādhi,* the same *caitanya* is Īśvara whose cosmic order covers your mind, senses, body, the law of *karma,* and the whole world. The relationship between *caitanya* and the cosmos is one that obtains between *satyam* and *mithyā,* that is, while *mithyā* is *satyam, satyam* is always free from *mithyā.* Therefore, there is no negating factor, *bādhaka,* of this oneness. *Bādhaka* is any factor that negates a previous contention. For instance, if you mistake a rope for a snake, it has a *bādhaka.* What is the *bādhaka* here?

When you happen to recognise the rope, that *vṛtti* born of a valid *pramāṇa*, the *pramāṇa-prāpta buddhiḥ*, will negate the snake in the same place. The same object which was mistaken by you as a snake, is now seen by you as a rope. So, the rope-*vṛtti*, rope-knowledge is *bādhaka* that negates the snake error. And what is gone is called *bādhita*, the appearance of the snake.

Sometimes, what is *bādhita* will not go away from sense perception, like the sunrise. You thought that the sun rose in the eastern sky, but now you know that the sun does not rise. That conclusion is *bādhita*. The appearance of the sun in the eastern sky in the morning is not *bādhita*, because that perception is true. The perception is true and the conclusion that it rises is *bādhita*.

Similarly, the conclusion that you are of limited knowledge, limited pervasiveness, limited power, limited skill, limited time, and so on, is standing against your being Īśvara. And this conclusion is wrong. Being limited in knowledge is the quality of the *upādhi*, but due to ignorance you say, 'I am *alpajña*.' Remove that ignorance and all that is there is one consciousness, which happens to be *satya*. Where is the difference? If you say that it is due to *upādhi*, yes, it is, and the *upādhi* is *mithyā*, so the difference is also *mithyā*.

Let us understand this in a lighter vein. There was a king who was a great supporter of *vidyā*, especially *advaita-vedānta*, though he used to support all other *dvaita* traditions. He had appointed a *guru* of Vedanta who taught him daily, "*tat tvam asi*, you are Brahman, the *satya*, and everything else is *mithyā*." Then there was another teacher, a *dvaitin*, dualist. The king wanted to be impartial to all the teachers, so he also appointed this *dvaitin* who taught him from the same *upaniṣad*, '*atat tvam asi*, you are not that.' Even though that sentence does not make sense in the context, it works grammatically, so the *dvaitin* taught it that way, "*sa ātmātat tvam asi śvetaketo*, that is the *ātman*, that you are not, Śvetaketu." The king, being impartial, would listen to this. But the *advaitin* would tell him, "You are the whole, you are *ānanda*," and it was nice to hear that, so he was a little more alive to that teaching, though he did not understand all of it. And when the *dvaitin* would say, "You have to go to heaven; nothing will happen here," he would generally go to sleep.

The king's attendant, who would also attend the class, told the *dvaita* teacher, "The king listens to the *advaita guru* better than here." The *dvaita guru* was very much upset to hear this. So, this went on. One day, the king was to go to another part of the kingdom, and was passing through a forest with his entire retinue, including both these teachers. As they were walking, a wild elephant appeared. The first one who saw this elephant was the *advaita guru*. He said, "Elephant!" and ran. When he ran, everybody ran. After this episode, the king camped for the night and decided to go the next day. Then quietly at dawn the *dvaita guru* went to the king and said,

"Maharaj-ji"

"Yes."

"Did you see?"

"What?"

"Yesterday, what happened? Did you see that elephant?"

"Yes, yes, that was a wild elephant."

"No, no, did you see who was the first one to run?"

"Who?"

"Our *advaita guru*."

"Are you sure he was the first one to run?" The king did not understand the implication. "Oh, was he the first to run?"

"Yeah, he was the first one to say, 'Elephant' and run."

"Oh, that's good."

"What is good? He saw the *mithyā* elephant and ran like a shot. Why should he run? He says everything is *mithyā* and he runs from the elephant! From the *mithyā* elephant he ran."

The king was wild. "Yes, he has been telling me that everything is *mithyā*, and he ran! Call him."

The *advaita guru* came. "Maharaj-ji?"

"Did you see the elephant first?"

"Yes."

"Did you run?"

"Yes."

"Do you say that this was a *mithyā* elephant?"

"Yes."

"Then why did you run?"

"Maharaj-ji, that was a wild elephant, it could harm us, therefore I said, 'elephant' and ran."

"But that is only a *mithyā* elephant."

"Maharaj-ji, did I ever say that my running is *satya*? Who said I ran? I never ran. If elephant was *mithyā* then my running also was *mithyā*."

Ātman is *akhaṇḍa*, it is *pūrṇa*, it never runs. All running is within the *ātman*. Then someone will ask, "Swamiji if there is *advaita* why do you worship?" It is as though worship because you have as though problems. As though is all the way. There is no *bādhaka*, there is nothing that can stop the *abheda*.

You cannot prove that there is no oneness. Therefore, knowledge born of the *vākya*, the sentence, stays untouched by anything. Doubt is possible but we can remove it. Any doubt can be removed because this is the fact. In the light of the fact, all doubts can be resolved. One person asked me, "Suppose somebody comes later, updating the *upaniṣad*, telling something better?" What cannot be bettered is Brahman. Brahman is limitless – what is going to improve that? What cannot be negated is Brahman. The *upaniṣad* has the last word about you. Everybody else can say only something less, because anything else will be less than infinite. And the difference between infinite and less than infinite, is infinite! Nobody can better it, much less negate it. You are Brahman. The sentence, '*tat tvam asi,*' is non-contradictory and meaningful.

Now, there is a kind of summing up in the whole of next section.

Jīvanmukti

एवं च वेदान्तवाक्यैः सद्गुरूपदेशेन च सर्वेष्वपि भूतेषु
येषां ब्रह्मबुद्धिरुत्पन्ना ते जीवन्मुक्ता भवन्ति ।

Evaṁ ca vedānta-vākyaiḥ sadguru-upadeśena ca sarveṣvapi bhūteṣu yeṣāṁ brahmabuddhirutpannā te jīvanmuktā bhavanti.

evam ca – and, in this manner; *vedānta-vākyaiḥ* – through the sentences of Vedanta; *sadguru-upadeśena ca* – and by the teaching of a *sadguru; sarveṣu api bhūteṣu* – in all beings; *yeṣām* – those for whom; *brahma-buddhiḥ* – the knowledge of Brahman; *utpannā* – is born; *te* – they; *jīvan-muktāḥ bhavanti* – are liberated-while-living.

And, in this manner, those for whom the knowledge of Brahman in all beings is born through the sentences of Vedanta, and by the teaching of a *sadguru*, are liberated-while-living.

This knowledge is born. What knoweldge? *Brahma-buddhi*, which is *ahaṁ brahma*, I am Brahman, because that is the meaning of the sentence, '*tat tvam asi*.' That *jagat kāraṇaṁ brahma*, the cause of this entire *jagat*, is you. The contradiction is obvious, and the non-contradiction, Brahman, is what is conveyed by the *vākya*, sentence. It is to be discovered in this *mahā-vākya*, which is an equation. One is called a *jīvan-mukta*, living, he is free, in the wake of self-knowledge, knowledge of the self being free. *Sarveṣu bhūteṣu*, with reference to all beings. There is only one self that is Brahman. "May you know me as the knower of the body in all bodies, Arjuna."[21] That is the *vākya* kept in mind when the author writes here *sarveṣu bhūteṣu*. With reference to all the *kśetra*s, all the bodies, all the minds, there is only one *ātman*, myself, which is Brahman, which is *satya*. And everything 'else' becomes *mithyā*. Those who have this knowledge are called *jīvan-muktāḥ*, living they are free.

How did they get this knowledge? With the help of *vedānta-vākya*s and the teaching of the *sadguru*. The *vedānta-vākya* is not a *pramāṇa*, the means of knowledge, for establishing the existence of *ātman*. *Atman* is already *aparokṣa*, self-evident. Even when you say, "I am a *saṁsārin*," I am, *ātman*, is already self-evident. *Saṁsārin* is a conclusion, and this conclusion is wrong.

---

[21] *kṣetrajñaṁ cāpimāṁ viddhi sarva-kṣetreṣu bhārata* (*Bhagavadgītā* 13.2)

Vedānta-vākya is the means for correcting this conclusion by revealing the self as *jagat-kāraṇaṁ brahma*. Only this revelation is the subject matter of Vedanta. It does not reveal the existence of the *ātman*. Because there is *ātman*, you are able to look into Vedanta. The very *vedānta-śāstra* is due to there being a *pramātṛ*, a knower, who employs the means of knowledge, the *pramāṇa*. Without the existence of the knower, there is no pursuit of knowing, *pramāṇa-pravṛtti*.

In the operation of every *pramāṇa*, the *pramātṛ* does not use its will; it just enjoys the *phala* of the *pramāṇa*. Because the *pramātṛ* does not use the will, the *pramātṛ* does not become a *kartṛ*, a doer. Until I open my eyes to see an object, I can use my will, because opening my eyes is not *pramāṇa-pravṛtti*, it is an action; it is will based. After that, the eyes see, and in that I do not use my will. I enjoy the result of *pramāṇa*, the sight. Here, I am the *pramātṛ* who has to be understood, so what do I do? I expose myself to the teaching of *vedānta-vākya*, which is a *pramāṇa*. Being a *pramāṇa* it removes the ignorance, the error born of that ignorance, and also it removes the ego. It eliminates all these notions – I am the knower, *pramātṛ*, I am the *kartṛ*, doer, I am the *bhoktṛ*, enjoyer – because knowledge is always true to the nature of the *vastu*, the object. And, *ātman* happens to be pure *caitanya*. Therefore, when it says that you are *śuddhaṁ caitanyam*, it means you are the invariable consciousness that obtains in all variable situations.

Necessity for a Sadguru

It is enough to say that this knowledge of Brahman is due to the sentences of Vedanta, *vedānta-vākyaiḥ*. Why does he also say that it is by the teaching of a *sadguru*? The *sadguru* teaches the *sat-vastu*. *Vedānta-vākya* is a *pramāṇa*, so it is in the third case, *vedānta-vākyaiḥ*, to indicate that it is a means. Then, teaching of the *sadguru* is also in the third case, *sadguru-upadeśena*. Are two things required, *vedānta-vākya*, and *sadgurū-upadesa*? No, what is required is *vedānta-vākya* that is taught by a *sadguru*. The *guru* teaches the *vedānta-vākya*, and therefore the means is *sadguru-upadiṣṭa vākyaiḥ*, the sentences that are employed by the teacher. It means the *vedānta-vākya* is not independently enquired into; it needs to be employed.

You have to know the whole vision in order to understand the words of a given sentence. Unless you know the whole, you cannot understand the part; the part being part of the whole. And, unless you cover the topic part by part, you cannot understand the whole. You are definitely in a corner, and this you circumvent by exposing yourself to a person who is supposed to know the whole. How did he come to know? In the same way; it is a *paramparā* extending back to the *ṛṣis*. Who taught the *ṛṣis*? We do not ask that question; we go up to the *ṛṣis*, then afterwards it is Bhagavān. It is a *pramāṇa* and it works. So, the *sadguru* becomes a part of the whole thing. Why *sadguru*, why not just *guru*?

The *vedānta-vākya* will tell you the truth, and the *guru*'s *upadeśa* is, of course, the *vedānta-vākya*. But *sad-guru-upadeśa* can be something custom-made for you, that can take care of your personal needs. Your personal problems that are obstructing your understanding can also be addressed by the *sadguru*. He may say that you need to do not only *śravaṇa*, but a particular *upāsana*, meditation, or *japa*. Whatever he instructs you to do will all be connected to the primary vision. Therefore, *sad-guru-upadeśa* implies any personal *sādhana* that he may advocate for a given person, and that is the reason for the separate mention *sad-guru-upadeśena*.

More about the jīvan-mukta

How can you say whether this person is a *jīvan-mukta*? First, it is not for us to point out whether somebody is a *jīvan-mukta* or not. That is not our aim at all. Then, why mention the *jīvan-mukta*? It is only to point out the nature of this knowledge. It is a peculiar knowledge about yourself and to point out what that knowledge should be, he says who a *jīvan-mukta* is. It is for your own assimilation of the knowledge.

ननु जीवन्मुक्तः कः?
यथा देहोऽहं पुरुषोऽहं ब्राह्मणोऽहं शूद्रोऽहमस्मीति
दृढनिश्चयस्तथा नाहं ब्राह्मणो न शूद्रो न पुरुषः
किन्त्वसङ्गः सच्चिदानन्दस्वरूपः प्रकाशरूपः
सर्वान्तर्यामी चिदाकाशरुपोऽस्मि इति
दृढ-निश्चय-रूप-अपरोक्ष-ज्ञानवान् जीवन्मुक्तः।

Nanu jīvan-muktaḥ kaḥ?
yathā deho'haṁ puruṣo'haṁ brāhmaṇo'haṁ śūdro'hamasmīti dṛḍha-niścayastathā nāhaṁ brāhmaṇo na śūdro na puruṣaḥ kintvasaṅgaḥ saccidānanasvarūpaḥ prakāśarūpaḥ sarvāntaryāmī cidākāśarūpo'smīti dṛḍha-niścaya-rūpa-aparokṣa-jñānavāñ jīvanmuktaḥ.

nanu – then; *jīvan-muktaḥ* – *jīvan-mukta* (liberated-while-living); *kaḥ* – who (is)?

yathā – just as; *dehaḥ aham* – I am the body; *puruṣaḥ aham* – I am a man; *ahaṁ brāhmaṇaḥ* – I am a *brāhmaṇa*;

ahaṁ śūdraḥ – I am a *śūdra; iti* – thus; *dṛḍha-niścayaḥ* – firm conclusion (before self-knowledge); *tathā* – in the same way; *aham na brāhmaṇaḥ* – I am not a *brāhmaṇa; na śūdraḥ* – not a *śūdra; na puruṣaḥ* – not a man; *kintu*– but (on the other hand; *asaṅgaḥ* – I am unattached; *saccidānanda-svarūpaḥ* – of the nature of existence, consciousness, fullness; *prakāśa-rūpaḥ* – whose nature is effulgence; *sarvāntaryāmī* –who is (the indweller) in all beings; *cidākāśa-rūpaḥ asmi* – in the form of all-pervasive consciousness; *iti* – thus; *dṛḍha-niścaya-rūpa-aparokṣa-jñānavān* – the one who has the firm, abiding, immediate knowledge (not mediated by sensory perception); *jīvan-muktaḥ* – (is) a *jīvan-mukta* (liberated-while-living).

Then, who is a *jīvan-mukta* (liberated-while-living)?

Just as there is the firm conclusion (before self-knowledge), 'I am the body, I am a man, I am a *brāhmaṇa*, I am a *śūdra*,' so too, the one who is liberated while living has firm, abiding, immediate knowledge, (not mediated by sensory perception) that, 'I am not a *brāhmaṇa*, or a *śūdra*, or a man, but, (on the other hand) I am unattached, of the nature of existence, consciousness, fullness, whose nature is effulgence, who is (the indweller) in all beings, in the form of all-pervasive consciousness.

People have this kind of firm conclusion, *dṛḍha-niścaya*. If you ask any person, "Who are you?" he will give his name. Ask him a little more about himself, and depending upon his culture, status, etc., he is going to answer further. In India, in earlier times, one may have said, I am a *brāhmaṇa*, I am a *śūdra*, I am a *vaiśya*, I am a *kṣatriya*. At the minimum, he says, 'I am a human being, *manuṣya*; I am a mortal *martya*.' Then, 'I am male, I am female, I am old, I am young.' All these reveal one's identity; one identifies oneself with all these. The *jīvan-mukta* does not take any one of them as the nature of the self – in fact, in his understanding these do not feature in self-identity. Whatever he thought about himself before stands negated. All these can be points of view but they are not intrinsic properties of *ātman*. And the *jīvan-mukta* recognises, 'I am uninvolved with all of these.' Anything that you say you are, which is not exactly the nature of *ātman*, has to be negated by an appropriate word. *Brāhmaṇo'ham, kartā'ham, manuṣyo'ham, puruṣo'ham*, I am *brāhmaṇa*, I am doer, I am a mortal, I am male, female, and so on, are all not true.

Asaṅgo'ham negates all that. Further, *sat-svarūpo'ham*, I am the one because of whom everything has its existence.

If you say, 'I am ignorant, *ajñāni*,' he says, no, you are *prakāśa-svarūpa*, in the form of the light of consciousness. All that is there is consciousness because of which ignorance comes to light. You are witness-consciousness, *caitanya-sākṣin*, you are *prakāśa-svarūpa*, and therefore you cannot say, 'I am ignorant.' So, *prākāśa-svarūpo'ham*.

Then, if you think you are confined to this body-mind-sense complex, he says, 'You are *pratyagātman*, the inner self of everything, *sarvāntaryāmin*.' Being the inner self of everything is exactly like the clay being the inner self of the pot. Where is the clay? The inner *ātman* of the pot, that *pratyagātman*, is clay. This is *sarvāntaryāmin*. You are not someone who is locked up, confined to this body-mind-sense complex. You are *sarvāntaryāmin*.

If you say, as *sarvāntaryāmin* you are only inside, not outside, to that also he says, no, you are *cidākāśa-rūpa*, which is in the form of consciousness like space, *ākāśa*. Space is both inside and outside, and *ātman* is the truth of the very *ākāśa*, and is in the form of consciousness, *cidākāśa-rūpa*. It is all-pervasive. All inside-outside are concepts within consciousness.

Previously, he was very well convinced that he was the *kartṛ, bhoktṛ*, etc. Now all these notions are negated because they are not true. Previously, he had no doubt, *brāhmaṇo'ham*, and so on, now also he has no doubt that the opposite is true. In this he has *dṛḍha-niścaya*, firm conclusion. What we mean by *dṛḍha-niścaya* is knowledge of *ātman* that is not fraught with doubt, and which is also free from vagueness. A vague feeling will not work. Doubts may not be there, but vagueness can be a problem. With *dṛḍha-niścaya* there is no vagueness, no doubt, and, of course, error is far away; this is *dṛḍha-niścaya, aparokṣa-jñānam*. The one who has immediate knowledge, *aparokṣa-jñānavān*, is a *jīvan-mukta*. The other meaning is the knowledge that I am the self-revealing, *Aparokṣa, cidātman*, which is Brahman, which is *satya*, which is *ananta*. And that *jñāna* is *āparokṣa*, because *ātman* is already *aparokṣa*, self-revealing. Knowledge of this self-revealing *ātman* is not going to be *parokṣa*, mediate knowledge.

There is no mediate knowledge for *ātman*. This has to be understood. Those who say, "First you must gain intellectual knowledge, the theory, then you have to practice in order to experience the self," have got into the trap of theory and practice. *Ātman* is already self-evident about which you have a conclusion – that it is a *saṁsārin*. And when the *śāstra* tells, *ātman* is *satyaṁ jñānam ānantaṁ brahma*, that conclusion is negated. The knowledge is immediate, *aparokṣa*, not *parokṣa*. Brahman is not talked about as something independent of *ātman*.

The one who has this *aparokṣa-jñāna*, immediate knowledge, of *ātman* being Brahman, is a *jīvan-mukta*. Living he is liberated. He is a *jīva* because he has the body-mind-sense complex, as long as it is there. That does not disappear when he discovers, 'I am *saccidānanda*.' Why *mukta*? Because he is free in spite of the limited body-mind-sense complex. There is no bondage, therefore he is a *jīvan-mukta*, living, he is liberated.

Since this freedom is available right now, here, there is a life of spirituality. Because of this, *sannyāsa* is possible, *karma-yoga* is possible, religion gains meaning and direction – it is no longer upward or inward looking. It becomes something meaningful to help me discover who I am. Where there is a spiritual goal, *mokṣa*, to be gained in this life, then everything gets aligned to that goal. The culture of the people who have that goal is bound to be different. That is why the possibility of freedom here, while living, makes this *vaidika-dharma* something special. This *jīvan-mukti* is the end of every *jīva*. And as a human being, or an equivalent form where there is adequate free will, the *jīva* gets a chance to fulfill that, to become *mukta*. How many make use of this chance is a different thing altogether. But then, as a human being you get the chance.

> ब्रह्मैवाहमस्मीत्यपरोक्षज्ञानेन निखिलकर्मबन्ध-
> विनिर्मुक्तिः स्यात् ।
>
> *brahmaivāhamasmītyaparokṣa-jñānena*
> *nikhila-karma-bandha-vinirmuktiḥ syāt.*

brahma eva – Brahman indeed; *aham asmi* – I am; *iti* – thus; *aparokṣa-jñānena* – by the immediate knowledge; *nikhila-karma-bandha-vinirmuktaḥ* – totally freed from all bonds of *karma*; *syāt* – one would be.

> Thus, by the immediate knowledge, 'I am indeed *Brahman*,' one would be totally freed from all bonds of *karma*.

Really speaking, this *jīvan-mukta*, because of his immediate knowledge, 'I am Brahman,' would be totally freed from ignorance. As a consequence, he is also freed from anything that was born of that ignorance. The first thing born of *ajñāna* is *kartṛtva*, doer-ship, and when there is doer-ship, there is also enjoyer-ship. You become the *karma-phala-bhoktṛ*, the reaper of the fruits of action. There are different types of pleasant situations, which are all *puṇya*. And there are a lot of difficult, unpleasant situations, from a mosquito bite onwards, which are *pāpa*. These different types of *puṇya* and *pāpa* are the results of actions. Therefore, in the *karma* model, we say that the person is completely free from the bondage of all *karma*, *nikhila-karma-bandha-vinirmukta*. Even without the *karma* model we can say that this individual is free from ignorance, and therefore, from doer-ship and enjoyer-ship. There is no guilt because the doer-ship is not there, and no hurt because the enjoyer-ship is not there either. No guilt, no hurt. This *jīvan-mukta*, knowing he is Brahman, who is neither a doer nor an enjoyer, is free from guilt and hurt. *Ātman* is free, he is free; he is *pūrṇa*. This is the immediate result.

Then, from the standpoint of *karma*, if the *jīva* has survived death, it means he has always been around; therefore, has gathered any number of *karma*s. Not only *karma*s in this lifetime but also those that were gathered in the *jīva*'s journey. New *karma*s gathered in this life and old *karma*s standing in his account, all constitute his *karma*, *nikhila-karma*, which the author of *Tattvabodha* is going to talk about. This *jīvan-mukta* is freed from the bondage of all types of *karma*. It means that *karma* binds. There is bondage of *karma*; being a *kartṛ*, he is bound by *karma*. And the basic bondage is born of ignorance, creating the notion, 'I am a *jīva, kartṛ, bhoktṛ*.' So *karma* has limitation, and the sense of limitation starts the problem.

You can only solve the basic problem that, 'I am the *jīva, kartṛ, bhoktṛ*.' And everything born of that confusion is also resolved. This is why he says, *karma-bandha-vinirmukta*, completely freed from the bonds of *karma*. Without doing anything to neutralise or remove all the *karma*s, he is freed from them. It is something like a dreamer who performs varieties of actions, good and bad, in the dream and then wakes up. The dreamer is recognised as a projection on the part of the waker, and is therefore falsified. This is what we call *karma-bandha-vinirmukti*.

We have to say it because *karma-phala* is considered *ṛta*, real; it is bound to manifest in time. If there is *karma*, there will be a *karma-phala*. But *karma-phala* you cannot avoid; that is what the *śāstra* says here. You can neutralise it by doing other *karma*, but you cannot avoid *karma-phala*. When you perform another *karma* to neutralise the result of an old *karma*, that is not avoidance, but taking action against a wrong action.

Karma is never anulled; in fact, what cannot be annulled is *karma*. If that is so, how can you avoid the results of all the *karma*s that you have collected so far? How can you neutralise all of them? How can there be *mokṣa* from *karma*?

Really, there is no attempt to eliminate them, we only examine its reality. It is after all centred on the *kartṛ*, the doer. On enquiry the doer-ship imputed to the self is falsified in the wake of knowledge, 'I am Brahman.' So he is completely freed from the bondage of all *karma*s, *nikhila-karma-bandha-vinirmuktaḥ*. *Nikhila* means without any left over.

Are there different types of *karma*?

Three types of karma

āgāmi, sañcita and prārabdha

*Karma*s are many and varied. That is the reason why experiences are not the same, they are always different. *Karma* is called *viśvato mukhaḥ*, facing all around; it has eyes everywhere. It has to take into account varieties of things like time, place, parentage, personal world, contemporary society, flora, fauna, and so on. Therefore, *karma*s that take all of these into account, are many and varied, *nānāvidhāni karmāṇi*. These *karma* combinations and how they express themselves are amazing. Suppose, someone has to eat and eat and eat, the whole day. What kind of body should one have? This human physical body will not do if one has that type of *karma* for eating; the whole body must be a stomach, and the mouth must be small. The *śarīra*, body, of a pig will be perfect. The whole day it can go on eating and still be ready to eat. This is all planned by *karma*. It is a complex network of combinations – you can get entirely different and unexpected types of results, yet, it is in keeping with the all encompassing law of *karma*.

These many and varied *karma*s can be grouped from the standpoint of the order of fructification as shown below.

कर्माणि कति विधानि सन्तीति चेत् ।
आगामिसञ्चितप्रारब्धभेदेन त्रिविधानि सन्ति ।

karmāṇi kati vidhāni santīti cet;
āgāmi-sañcita-prārabdha-bhedena
trividhāni santi.

karmāṇi – *karma*s; *kati vidhāni* – of how many kinds; *santi* – are; *iti cet* – if asked;
āgāmi-sañcita-prārabdha-bhedena – with differences as *āgāmi*, *sañcita* and *prārabdha*; *trividhāni* – three types; *santi* – are.

If asked, 'How many kinds of *karma* are there?'
They are of three types with differences as
āgāmi, sañcita and *prārabdha.*

Here, he is not talking about the varieties of *karmas* that call for varieties of bodies and experiences, but from the standpoint of *karmas* when they fructify. There are *karmas* that you can gather in this life called *āgāmi*. Then there are *karmas* standing in your account which are unmanifest, called *sañcita*. And there are *karmas* that are manifest now, in this life, called *prārabdha*. He himself explains what they are.

आगामि कर्म किम् ?
ज्ञानोत्पत्त्यनन्तरं ज्ञानिदेहकृतं पुण्यपापरूपं कर्म
यदस्ति तदागामीत्यभिधीयते ।

āgāmi-karma kim?
jñānotpattyanantaraṁ jñāni-deha-kṛtaṁ puṇya-pāpa-rūpaṁ karma yadasti tad āgāmītyabhidhīyate.

āgāmi-karma – āgāmi-karma; kim – what (is)? *jñāna-utpatti-anantaram* – after the dawn of knowledge; *jñāni-deha-kṛtam* – performed by the body of the wise man; *puṇya-pāpa-rūpaṁ karma* – *karma* in the form of (the result of action) *puṇya* and *pāpa; yad asti* – which is; *tat* – that; *āgāmi iti* – as *āgāmi* (that which fructifies in the future); *abhidhīyate* – is called.

What is *āgāmi-karma*?

Karma, in the form of (the result of action) *puṇya* and *pāpa*, performed by the body of the wise man (the self), after the dawn of knowledge, is called *āgāmi-karma*.

सञ्चितं कर्म किम् ?
अनन्तकोटिजन्मनां बीजभूतं सद् यत् कर्मजातं पूर्वार्जितं तिष्ठति तत् सञ्चितं ज्ञेयम् ।

sañcitaṁ karma kim?
ananta-koṭi-janmanāṁ bīja-bhūtaṁ sad yat karmajātaṁ pūrvārjitaṁ tiṣṭhati tat sañcitaṁ jñeyam.

sañcita-karma – *sañcita-karma* (accumulated result of action); *kim* – what (is)?
ananta-koṭi-janmanām – in countless crores[22] of births; *karma-jātaṁ pūrvārjitam* – the accumulated load of *karma* that was gathered before; *bīja-bhūtam* – in a seed form; *yat* – which; *tiṣṭhati* – stands (exists); *tat* – that; *sañcitam* – *sañcita* (accumulated result of action); *jñeyam* – is to be known.

What is *sañcita karma* (accumulated result of action)?

[22] one crore is ten million.

The accumulated load of *karma* that was gathered before in countless crores of births, which stands (exists) in a seed form, is to be known as *sañcita*.

प्रारब्धं कर्म किमिति चेत्।
इदं शरीरमुत्पाद्येह लोक एवं सुखदुःखादिप्रदं यत्कर्म तत्प्रारब्धम्। भोगेन नष्टं भवति। प्रारब्धकर्मणां भोगादेव क्षय इति।

prārabdhaṁ karma kimiti cet;
idaṁ śarīram utpādya iha loka evaṁ sukha-duḥkhādi-pradaṁ yat karma tatprārabdham, bhogena naṣṭaṁ bhavati, prārabdhakarmaṇāṁ bhogādeva kṣayaḥ iti.

prārabdhaṁ karma – *prārabdha-karma*; *kim* – what (is); *iti cet* – if asked;

yat karma – that *karma* (which); *idaṁ śarīram utpādya* – having created this physical body; *iha loke* – in this world; *evam* – in this manner (of parentage, limitations of body etc.); *sukha-duḥkhādi-pradam* – which gives comfort, pain, etc.; *tat prārabdham* – that (is) *prārabdha*; *bhogena* – by going through experiences; *naṣṭaṁ bhavati* – gets destroyed; *prārabdha-karmaṇāṁ kṣayaḥ bhogāt eva iti* – thus (it is said), 'only by going through experiences does the exhausion of *prārabdha-karma* take place.'

If asked, what is *prārabdha-karma*?

That *karma* (which) having created this body in this world in this manner (of parentage, limitations of body etc.), which gives comfort, pain, etc., is *prārabdha*; it gets destroyed by going through the experiences; thus, (it is said) 'only by going through experiences does the exhausion of *prārabdha-karma* take place.'

Sañcita-karma

He first talks about *āgāmi-karma*, but we will discuss what is *sañcita-karma*. *Sañcita* means collected, accumulated. It is the whole host of *karma* that was gathered before, and in an unmanifest form, like a seed, which can fructify in countless crores of *janma*s.

Sañcita-karma is *anādi*, without beginning. Suppose, in one cycle of creation – one cycle being billions and billions of years – you got a human body, either on this planet or elsewhere. Every star is a sun and every sun can have a system of planets, and also life, so elsewhere you may get an equivalent to a human body. It means you gather new *karma*, *puṇya* and *pāpa*.

And if, in one cycle of creation, *kalpa*, you get only one such birth, even then you will have *karma*s for countless, *ananta*, births. Then again, the cycles are also *ananta*. Therefore, this *sañcita-karma* is the cause for countless births later, standing in your account, waiting for fructification.

Prārabdha-karma

Prārabdha means *prāk ārabdham*, it is already begun. It is the *karma* that you are reaping now. With a particular parentage, on a particular day, at a particular place, you were born. Then, you underwent certain education in childhood, and now you are here; this is *prārabdha-karma*. It is getting unfolded moment to moment, every day. First, it wakes you up in the morning, and from then on, it is all today's *karma* getting exhausted. Tomorrow's *karma* is going to be different, and therefore you have varieties of *karma* waiting for unfoldment in this life.

Having created this body, in this world itself, the *prārabdha-karma* gives you *sukha* and *duḥkha*, situations that are pleasant and unpleasant. In fact, *karma* cannot give you happiness or sorrow, but it can give you pleasant and unpleasant situations; that is *prārabdha*. And this *prārabdha* gets exhausted only through experience.

Āgāmi-karma

While *sañcita-karma* is like fixed deposit, not available for any transaction, the *prārabdha-karma* is like the matured deposit, available for use. It has brought about this body and while it is getting unfolded, there can be new *karma*. One can do some benevolent action, which is like investing and making a profit. As with money expenditure, credit and debit are possible here, because you still have the will which originally got you these *karma*s. It will continue to exist even now, therefore you can gather new *karma*s in the process of exhausting the *prārabdha-karma*. These new *karma*s are called *āgāmi*. So, *āgāmi-karma* is understood as the *karma* that is gathered in this life.

Three-fold karma for a jīvan-mukta

For a *jīvan-mukta,* the *āgāmi-karma* will be a little different. A *jīvan-mukta* is liberated from doer-ship. That being so, the *sañcita-karma* is gone because all that was standing in the account of the *jīva* is falsified. All the *sañcita karma* is gone. Anything gathered here, up to the point of knowing *brahma ahaṁ asmi,* is gone. *Puṇya* and *pāpa* are also gone because there is no one to claim it. So, the whole account is finished.

Will there be a new account for a *jīvan-mukta*? New results of *karma* cannot come to him. The law of *karma* will give *karma-phala*, necessarily, but it will look for an appropriate recipient. If this *jñānī*, the *jīvan-mukta*, has done some *puṇya-karma* like teaching, then the result of that *puṇya-karma* will go to whoever worships that *jñānī*. If there is any *pāpa-karma* like inadvertently stepping on an insect, which according to the law of *karma* is *hiṁsā* and creates *pāpa*, it will not touch him. Where will that *pāpa* go? There is always somebody who is going to say something against that *jñānī*, and he will get the *pāpa*. This is what is said here. Someone will get the *pāpa* and someone will get the *puṇya*, so the *jñānī* is free. And because of *prārabdha-karma*, he continues to have this body. It is *īśvara-sṛṣṭi*.

Īśvara's law is empirically real, so it will not just go away with the knowledge of its reality, unlike the rope-snake. The moment you see *satya*, the reality, of the snake, the snake disappears. But when you see the *satya* of sunrise, the perception of the rising sun would continue – because it is *īśvara-sṛṣṭi*, empirically true. The *pratīti*, experience, will continue to be there, even though it is not real. There is the difference between *jīva-sṛṣṭi*, rope-snake, and *īśvara-sṛṣṭi*, the sunrise.

The rising sun is in Īśvara's creation, so it follows its laws, that is, it has an empiricality. The *prārabdha-karma* belongs to this order of reality.

When a *jīvan-mukta* understands, 'I am *saccidānanda-ātman,*' what goes away is ignorance and the ignorance-born notions that I am a doer and an enjoyer. But then, there is a doer with reference to an action. The body continues to exist, the mind remains, the senses continue, the whole *śarīra* the *kārya-karaṇa-sanghāta,* the body-mind-sense complex, continues to exist. It is so because this complex was given to the *jīva* to exhaust the *prārabdha-karma,* so it will continue to appear – like even the sun. Thank God. Otherwise, the moment the *jīva* recognises, 'I am *saccidānanda-ātman,*' he is gone. He said *brahmāham,* and even before he said *asmi,* he was gone. Because *asmi* is not necessary, *brahmāham* is enough, and he is gone. Then there will be no *guru,* no *śiṣya,* and no *mokṣa* either. Imagine Descartes sitting in a restaurant, having his morning breakfast. And the waitress asked, "Sir, can I serve you more coffee?" Descartes said, "I do not think so," and disappeared, because his philosophy was, 'I think, therefore I am!' Is this *jīvan-mukta* also gone in a jiffy? If that is what happens, how is anyone going to become a *jīvan-mukta*? Thank God, he does not disappear.

Your physical body is *īśvara-sṛṣṭi*. That is why it behaves in the manner it should – it is subject to old age, disease, and death. It is a *śarīra* that has certain longevity, and within its span certain experiences to be gone through; until you exhaust the fructifying *karma*, it will continue. Sometimes, before the exhaustion of the *karma*, the body can disappear, as in homicide or suicide. But normally, when the exhaustion of *karma* takes place, the body will naturally fall. That is law. It is like an arrow that has been released. It has certain maximum distance it can travel. It will not stop traveling until it hits an object or loses its momentum. You have no control over the momentum gathered after it is released from the bow. Until you release it you have control, but not after that. And, this body has already come from the bow of Bhagavān. He is the *karma-phala-dātṛ*, the one who has released the arrow according to the law of *karma*. The law is the bow, and the one who wields the law is Bhagavān. He is the archer, and the *jīva* with a *śarīra* is the arrow. It is released once it is born in a given form, from conception onwards. This will keep going as long as the momentum of *karma* lasts, which he has set. Whether it is meant for a hundred years, fifty years, or whatever, each one is set to last.

The human body has certain maximum distance of one hundred and twenty years with reference to our speed of light. It is relative. A body of a celestial, a *deva,* also has a span of one hundred years, but it is an entirely different frame of time. And Brahmāji's time is entirely different, again. If Brahmāji goes to sleep, there will be a collapse of the whole *jagat*. We cannot even imagine all these different series of time. But it is accepted that this human body on this earth has a span of one hundred and twenty years. Bhagavān set the arrow in motion, and it will travel.

In the process of traveling, you understood, 'I am Brahman.' You do not disappear, you still keep going. Knowing you are Brahman does not make the physical body disappear. Only the notion, I am a doer, enjoyer and so on, will go, and whatever is naturally there as part of *īśvara-sṛṣṭi,* will not go. For seeing there should be a seer, for hearing there should be a hearer. So, the subject-object situation will be there, but that is not opposed to Brahman because both are Brahman. From the standpoint of the world it is Īśvara. This is what we call *īśvara-prāpti, īśvara-darśana* and *mokṣa*.

To sum up, among these three types of *karma,* the *prārabdha* gives this *śarīra,* the enquirer's *śarīra,* the one who is studying *Tattvabodha,* in this world itself, which gets exhausted in time through various experiences. *Āgāmi-karma* is generally the *karma* that is acquired in this life by anyone, which is carried over to *sañcita*. This three-fold *karma* with reference to a *jñānī* is presented here.

सञ्चितं कर्म ब्रह्मैवाहमस्मीति निश्चयज्ञानेन नश्यति ।

sañcitaṁ karma brahmaivāhamasmīti niścaya jñānena naśyati.

sañcitaṁ karma – the *sañcita-karma* (accumulated results of actions); *brahma eva aham asmi* – I am indeed Brahman; *iti niścaya-jñānena* – thus by this definite knowledge; *naśyati* – is destroyed.

The *sañcita-karma* (accumulated results of actions) is destroyed by this definite knowledge, I am indeed Brahman.

The definite knowledge is, '*brahmaivāhamasmi*, I am indeed that Brahhman, which is *akartṛ*, which performs no action.' By this well-ascertained knowledge, free from doubts and vaguness, the *sañcita-karma* is destroyed. The person who was responsible for all the *karma*s, and in whose account this *sañcita-karma* was standing, is falisified. In falsifying the doer-ship, everything centred on the doer is falsified. There is no question of real destruction, but it is all gone by knowledge of what is.

आगामिकर्मापि ज्ञानेन नश्यति । किञ्चागामिकर्मणां नलिनीदलगतजलवज्ज्ञानिनां सम्बन्धो नास्ति ।

āgāmikarmāpi jñānena naśyati, kiñca āgāmikarmaṇāṁ nalinī-dala-gata-jalavajjñāninām sambandho nāsti.

āgāmi-karma api – the *āgāmi-karma* also; *jñānena* – by knowledge; *naśyati* – perishes; *kiñca* – further; *nalinī-dala-gata-jalavat* – just like the water on a lotus leaf; *āgāmi-karmaṇāṁ sambandhaḥ* – the connection with *āgāmi-karma*; *jñāninām* – for the wise men; *na asti* – is not there.

The *āgāmi-karma* is also destroyed by knowledge. Further, just like the water on the lotus leaf, the wise men have no connection with *āgāmi-karma*.

किञ्च ये ज्ञानिनं स्तुवन्ति भजन्त्यर्चयन्ति तान्प्रति ज्ञानिकृतमागामिपुण्यं गच्छति ।

kiñca ye jñāninaṁ stuvanti bhajantyarcayanti tān prati jñānikṛtamāgāmipuṇyaṁ gacchati.

kiñca – further; *ye* – those who; *jñāninam* – wise man; *stuvanti*– praise; *bhajanti* – serve; *arcayanti* – worship; *tān prati* – to them; *jñāni-kṛtam āgāmi puṇyam* – *āgāmi puṇya* (good results) done by the wise man; *gacchati* – goes.

Further, those who praise, serve, and worship the wise man, to them goes the *āgāmi puṇya* (good results) done by the wise man.

ये ज्ञानिनं निन्दन्ति द्विषन्ति दुःखप्रदानं कुर्वन्ति तान्प्रति ज्ञानिकृतं सर्वमागामि क्रियमाणं यदवाच्यं कर्म पापात्मकं तद्गच्छति ।

ye jñāninaṁ nindanti dviṣanti duḥkha-pradānaṁ kurvanti tānprati jñāni-kṛtaṁ sarvamāgāmi kriyamāṇaṁ yadavācyaṁ karma pāpātmakaṁ tadgacchati.

ye – those who; *jñāninaṁ nindanti* – abuse the wise man (verbally); *dviṣanti duḥkha-pradānaṁ kurvanti* – dislike, give discomfort; *tān prati* – to them; *jñāni-kṛtam* – done by the wise man; *sarvam āgāmi* – the entire *āgāmi*; *kriyamāṇam* – (that is) the *karma* being done; *yat avācyaṁ karma* – that which cannot be described; *pāpātmakam* – (and which) is of the nature of *pāpa*; *tat gacchati* – that goes.

> To those who abuse (verbally), dislike, give discomfort, to the wise man, goes the entire *āgāmi,* (that is) the *karma* being done by the *jñānī*, which cannot be described (and which) is of the nature of *pāpa*.

As we have seen, the *āgāmi karma* of a *jñānī* is also destroyed for him, as there is no doer to claim it. Both *puṇya-karma* and *pāpa-karma* are destroyed for him by the knowledge, 'I am *akartṛ*, not the doer,' because he has no connection with them. There is *sambandha* only between the doer and the *karma-phala*, the result of the action. The doer becomes the enjoyer of the *karma-phala*, the result of *karma* that he has done. But the *jñānī* does not have this *adṛṣṭa-karma-phala* of *puṇya* and *pāpa*. *Dṛṣṭa-phala*, the immediate, manifest result, will be there for him, but not the unmanifest *adṛṣṭa-phala*, which fructifies later. Why? *Kartṛtva-abhāvāt*, doership being not there. Because of the same knowledge which was responsible for destroying the *sañcita-karma*, new *karma* cannot come to him.

The *jñānī* has a body-mind-sense complex, with which he seems to be doing *karma*. However, there is no connection, *sambandha*, with that *karma*, like even the drops of water standing on a lotus leaf. It is amazing to see this lotus leaf holding water without getting wet. It remains untouched, *asaṅga*. So too, the *jñānī* has no *sambandha*, connection, with any form of *karma* even while doing, much less afterwards.

A *jñānī* may teach, and also do various things. So, what happens to the *puṇya* and *pāpa* generated by those *karmas*? The day-to-day *puṇya* of the *atmajña* is taken away by the people who worship him, who praise him. Therefore, the *jñānī* does not get it, somebody else gets it. Similarly, there are also those who censure, dislike the wise man, using abusive words, and even do some actions that will cause affliction to him. The *āgāmi-karma* done by a *jñānī*, because of *prārabdha*, which may attract *pāpa*, and which is not even to be talked about, goes to such people.

The question here is, will a *jñānī* perform a *pāpa-karma*? That is possible because indirectly, unknowingly, he may share responsiblity for a *pāpa-karma* done by someone else. If he is eating food given to him by somebody who has earned that food through *pāpa-karma*, indirectly he is participating in that *pāpa*. This is our *śāstra*. That is why it says that you should eat in the house of somebody who follows *dharma*.

Some *pāpa-karmas* may accrue due to certain *karmas* of a *jñānī* but they do not touch him. They go to whoever censures or abuses him. Therefore, *jñānī*'s *āgāmi-karma* has nothing to do with him save the immediate result, *dṛṣṭa-phalam*.

The one who knows ātman crosses sorrow

तथा च आत्मवित्संसारं तीर्त्वा ब्रह्मानन्दमिहैव प्राप्नोति ।

tathā ca ātmavit saṁsāraṁ tīrtvā
brahmānandam ihaiva prāpnoti.

tathā ca – and thus; *ātmavit* – the knower of *ātmā*; *saṁsāraṁ tīrtvā* – crossing the *saṁsāra*; *brahmānandam* – Brahman that is fullness; *iha eva* – here itself (while living); *prāpnoti* – gains (by knowledge).

And thus, the knower of *ātmā*, crossing *saṁsāra*, gains (by knowledge) Brahman that is fullness here itself (while living).

The *ātmavit*, the one who knows *ātman*, crosses sorrow, *śokam tarati*. The one who knows *ātman* is free from sorrow centred on 'I'. Therefore, the author says here, *ātmavit*, the knower of *ātman*, crosses the ocean of *saṁsāra*, which was once real, by knowledge, here itself; he gains *ānanda* which is Brahman. That *brahmānanda*, which is *mokṣa*, he gains right here, in this world, in this life, within this body. After death there is only travel, not freedom. If one dies, one travels; if one knows the self being *aja*, one does not die, so there is no travel. Death is only for the born – *ātmā* is not born, it is *aja*.

The dead are called the departed because there is no death, there is only departure. The departed person always travels. When one departs from this place, one is dead to all in this place; people will say that the person is gone. But one goes to another place, where people will say that one has arrived; one is reborn there. In our culture, the word 'departed' is widely used because there is travel after leaving a given body. We are not doing rituals for the dead people, but for the departed souls. This is an expression that reveals our attitude towards our ancestors.

The one who discovers, I am *ajāta*, unborn, is neither born nor subject to death, which is departure.

The *śruti* is cited here.

तरति शोकमात्मविदिति श्रुतेः ।

tarati śokamātmaviditi śruteḥ.

iti śruteḥ – (this is so) because of the *śruti* (statement) being there; *ātmavit* – the knower of *ātmā; śokam* – sorrow; *tarati* – crosses.

(This is so) because of the *śruti* (statement) being there: 'the knower of *ātmā* crosses sorrow.'

Tarati śokamātmavit,[23] is the *śruti* that is referred to here. Because the *śruti* says that knower of *ātman* crosses sorrow, there is *puruṣārtha*. Otherwise, why should you know the *ātman*? People will ask you, "Will you get a new job by knowing *ātman*? Will there be an increase in your income by being an *ātmavit*?" You cannot even include it in your curriculum vitae. "Then, what do I get out of it?" Freedom from sorrow. The truth is, there is freedom from the mistake that 'I am subject to sorrow.' So, seeing, 'I am not subject to sorrow,' makes you *ātmavit*. You are not subject to sorrow because *ātman* is not subject to sorrow. It is not just a thought that you go on hypnotising yourself with, 'I am not subject to sorrow, I am not subject to sorrow, I am not subject to sorrow.' It is knowledge, cognitive knowledge, that *ātman* is not subject to sorrow. Seeing that very clearly makes one cross sorrow.

तनुं त्यजतु वा काश्यां श्वपचस्य गृहेऽथवा ज्ञान-
सम्प्राप्तिसमये मुक्तोऽसौ विगताशय इति स्मृतेश्च ।

---

[24] *Chāndogyopaniṣad* 7.1.3

tanuṁ tyajatu vā kāśyāṁ śvapacasya gṛhe athavā jñānasamprāptisamaye mukto'sau vigatāśayaḥ iti smṛteśca.

iti smṛteḥ ca – (this is so) also because of the *smṛti* (statement); *tanum tyajatu* – let him abandon (cast off) the body; *kāśyāṁ vā* – in Kāśī; *athavā* – or else; *śvapacasya gṛhe* – in the house of a dog-eater; *vigatāśayaḥ* – (and is) one whom all abodes have left (he has no special preference for a place); *asau* – he; *jñāna-samprāpti-samaye* – at the time of gaining knowledge; *muktaḥ* – is liberated.

> (This is so) also because of the *smṛti* (statement): "Let him give up the body at Kāśī or in the house of a dog-eater, (and is) one whom all abodes have left (he has no special preference for a place), is liberated (even) at the time of gaining knowledge."

There is a belief that if one dies in Kāśī, one will go to heaven, *svarga*. So, lot of people go to Kāśī and wait for death to happen. In fact, some charities have established houses for old people who go there to wait for death because of this belief. Kāśī is called *mokṣapuri*; it is a symbol of *mokṣa*.

The *smṛti* says, 'let this wise man give up his body, either in Kāśī, or in the house of a dog-eater, at the time of gaining knowledge, he is already free.' He is liberated not because of a special place of death; that is a relative liberation, *āpekṣika-mukti*, which is not what is talked about here. Because he is already liberated, where he dies does not matter. He is *vigatāśaya*, all places, all abodes, *āśaya*, have completely gone, *vigata*, from him. He is *aghehānanda*, no longer subject to any place because every place is he, all heavens are he. Therefore, there is no question of his going to some place or coming back.

इति तत्त्वबोधप्रकरणं समाप्तम् ॥

iti tattvabodha-prakaraṇaṁ samāptam.

iti – thus; *tattva-bodha-prakaraṇam* – the *prakaraṇa* called *Tattvabodha* (discriminative knowledge of truth); *samāptam* – is completed.

Thus, the *prakaraṇa* called *Tattvabodha* (discriminative knowledge of truth) is completed.

So, this *prakaraṇa*, book, talks about the subject matter unfolded in *vedānta-śāstra*, the various terms and *prakriyās*, methods, that are used for showing the *tattva,* reality. *Samāpta* is a very beautiful word whose meaning is not 'end' or 'over' or 'finished,' but 'completed,' 'accomplished.'

Oṁ tat sat

Books by Swami Dayananda Saraswati

Public Talk Series :

1. Living Intelligently
2. Successful Living
3. Need for Cognitive Change
4. Discovering Love
5. The Value of Values
6. Vedic View and Way of Life

Upaniṣad Series :

7. Muṇḍakopaniṣad
8. Kenopaniṣad

Prakaraṇa Series :

9. Tattvabodhaḥ

Text Translation Series :

10. Śrīmad Bhagavad Gītā
    (Text with roman transliteration and English translation)
11. Śrī Rudram
    (Text in Sanskrit with transliteration, word-to-word and verse meaning along with an elaborate commentary in English)

Stotra Series :

12. Dīpārādhanā
13. Prayer Guide
    (With explanations of several Mantras, Stotras, Kirtans and Religious Festivals)

Moments with Oneself Series :

14. Freedom from Helplessness
15. Living versus Getting On
16. Insights
17. Action and Reaction
18. Fundamental Problem
19. Problem is You, Solution is You
20. Purpose of Prayer
21. Vedanta 24x7
22. Freedom
23. Crisis Management
24. Surrender and Freedom
25. The Need for Personal Reorganisation
26. Freedom in Relationship
27. Stress-free Living
28. Om Namo Bhagavate Vāsudevāya
29. Yoga of Objectivity
30. Īśvara in One's Life

Bhagavad Gītā

31. Bhagavad Gītā Home Study Course
    (Hardbound - 9 Volumes)

Meditation Series :

32. Morning Meditation Prayers
33. What is Meditation?

Essays :

34. Do all Religions have the same goal?
35. Conversion is Violence
36. Gurupūrṇimā
37. Dānam
38. Japa
39. Can We?
40. Moments with Krishna
41. Teaching Tradition of Advaita Vedanta
42. Compositions of Swami Dayananda Saraswati

Exploring Vedanta Series : (*vākyavicāra*)

43. śraddhā bhakti dhyāna yogād avaihi ātmānaṁ ced vijānīyāt

Books translated in other languages and in English based on Swami Dayananda Saraswati's Original Exposition

Tamil

44. Veeduthorum Gitopadesam (9 Volumes)
    (Bhagavad Gītā Home Study Course)
45. Dānam

Kannada

46. Mane maneyalli Adhyayana (7 Volumes)
(Bhagavad Gītā Home Study Course)
47. Vedanta Pravesike

Malayalam

48. Muṇḍakopaniṣad

Telugu

49. Kenopaniṣad

Hindi

50. Ghar baithe Gītā Vivechan (Vol 1)
(Bhagavad Gītā Home Study Course)
51. Antardṛṣṭi (Insights)
52. Vedanta 24X7
53. Kriya aur Pratikriya (Action and Reaction)

Marathi

54. Gruhe Gītā Adhyayan (Vol 1 available)
(Bhagavad Gītā Home Study Course)

English

55. The Jungian Myth and Advaita Vedanta
56. The Vedantic Self and the Jungian Psyche
57. Salutations to Rudra
58. Without a Second

Biography (Hardbound Deluxe)

59. Swami Dayananda Saraswati Contributions & Writings (Smt. Sheela Balaji)

Biography (Hardbound Regular)

60. Swami Dayananda Saraswati Contributions & Writings (Smt. Sheela Balaji)

Also available at :

ARSHA VIDYA RESEARCH AND PUBLICATION TRUST
32 / 4 Sir Desika Road
Mylapore Chennai 600 004
Telefax : 044 - 2499 7131
Email : avrandpt@gmail.com
Website : www.avrpt.com

ARSHA VIDYA GURUKULAM
Anaikatti P.O.
Coimbatore 641 108
Ph : 0422 - 2657001
Fax : 0422 - 2657002
Email : office@arshavidya.in
Website : www.arshavidya.in

ARSHA VIDYA GURUKULAM
P.O.Box 1059. Pennsylvania
PA 18353, USA
Ph : 001-570-992-2339
Email : avp@epix.net
Website : www.arshavidya.org

SWAMI DAYANANDA ASHRAM
Purani Jhadi, P.B.No. 30
Rishikesh, Uttaranchal 249 201
Telefax : 0135 - 2430769
Email : ashrambookstore@yahoo.com
Website : www.dayananda.org

Other leading Book Stores:

Chennai:	**044**
Motilal Banarsidass	2498 2315
Giri Trading	2495 1966
Higginbothams	2851 3519

Pustak Bharati	2461 1345
Theosophical	
Publishing House	2446 6613 / 2491 1338
The Odessey	43910300
Bengaluru:	**080**
Gangarams	2558 1617 / 2558 1618
Sapna Book House	4011 4455 / 4045 5999
Strand Bookstall	2558 2222, 2558 0000
Vedanta Book House	2650 7590
Coimbatore:	**0422**
Guru Smruti	9486773793
Giri Trading	2541523
New Delhi:	**011**
Motilal Banarsidass	2385 8335 / 2385 1985
Trivandrum:	**0471**
Prabhus Bookhouse	2478397 / 2473496
Kozhikode:	**0495**
Ganga Bookhouse	6521262

Mumbai:	**022**
Chetana Bookhouse	2285 1243 / 2285 3412
Strand Bookstall	2266 1994 / 2266 1719/ 2261 4613
Giri Trading	2414 3140
Bardoli (Surat):	**0622**
Dr. Anil Patwardhan (BGHS course - Marathi)	220283 0-9377715684
Mysore :	
Swamini Varadananda (BGHS course - Kannada)	0-9242890144 0-8762464014